Included or Excluded?

Should all children be included in the same schools? Or should some be 'excluded', or at least offered separate provision so that their needs may be more successfully met elsewhere? 'Excluded' is an emotive term. In the context of education, what does it mean?

In 2005 the Philosophy of Education Society of Great Britain published a pamphlet by Baroness Warnock in which she expressed serious concerns about the effects of her report on special education, published almost thirty years earlier. Not least of these was the suffering of some SEN children in mainstream schools, who had nowhere else to go since the closure of special schools in their area. Baroness Warnock's concerns raised a storm with the press and with many educationalists and disability groups.

Included or Excluded? provides a considered response to that over-heated debate. It is a forum in which conflicting arguments may be heard and reflected on, independently of media hysteria. It does not pretend that the inclusion debate is solely an intellectual one. Some of the chapters are by teachers or parents of children with special needs, or by people who have such needs themselves. Some are by educationalists, psychologists, lawyers, philosophers.

The lives of children are at stake, and this book is for anyone who cares about young people and the society we are creating for their future.

Ruth Cigman is lecturer in philosophy at Birbeck Faculty of Continuing Education, University of London, UK.

Baroness Warnock, peer and lead author of *The Warnock Report* (1978) that radically shaped UK education policy.

Included or Excluded?
The challenge of the mainstream for some SEN children

Edited by

Ruth Cigman

Routledge
Taylor & Francis Group

LONDON AND NEW YORK

First published 2007 by Routledge
2 Park Square, Milton Park, Abingdon, Oxon OX14 4RN

Simultaneously published in the USA and Canada
by Routledge
270 Madison Ave, New York, NY 10016

Transferred to Digital Printing 2008

*Routledge is an imprint of the Taylor & Francis Group, an informa
business*

Typeset in Galliard by RefineCatch Limited, Bungay, Suffolk
Printed and bound in Great Britain by
TJI Digital, Padstow, Cornwall

British Library Cataloguing in Publication Data
A catalogue record for this book is available from the British Library

Library of Congress Cataloging in Publication Data
A catalog record for this book has been requested

ISBN10: 0–415–40119–4 (hbk)
ISBN10: 0–415–40118–6 (pbk)
ISBN10: 0–203–96606–6 (ebk)

ISBN13: 978–0–415–40119–7 (hbk)
ISBN13: 978–0–415–40118–0 (pbk)
ISBN13: 978–0–203–96606–8 (ebk)

Contents

PART 2
Philosophical and practical perspectives on
inclusive education

Contributors

Mel Ainscow is Professor of Education and co-director of the Centre for Equity in Education at the University of Manchester. Formerly a head teacher, local education authority inspector and lecturer at the University of Cambridge, his work explores connections between inclusion, teacher development and school improvement.

Marion Bennathan was formerly Principal Educational Psychologist of Bristol. With Marjorie Boxall, the creator of nurture groups, she led the setting-up of the Nurture Group Network. She was a founder and first Director of Young Minds, and for many years Chair of the Social, Emotional and Behavioural Difficulties Association.

William Colley has taught at many schools, and was head teacher at the New School in Perthshire, a co-educational boarding school for children with special needs.

Paul Cooper is a Chartered Psychologist and Director of the School of Education at the University of Leicester. He has researched and published widely in the area of Social, Emotional and Behavioural Difficulties, is Editor of the journal *Emotional and Behavioural Difficulties* (Routledge). In 2001 he was winner of the TES/NASEN Academic Book Award for *Positive Alternatives to Exclusion* (Routledge), which he co-wrote with Mary Jane Drummond, Susan Hart, Jane Lovey and Colleen McLaughlin.

Alan Dyson is Professor of Education and co-director of the Centre for Equity in Education at Manchester University. He was formerly Professor of Special Needs Education and Director of the Special Needs Research Centre at the University of Newcastle upon Tyne. His research examines the relationship between social and educational inclusion and he is currently leading the national evaluation of full service schools. Email: d.a.dyson@manchester.ac.uk

William Evans is former Chair of the Special Educational Needs Disability Tribunal.

Peter Farrell is co-director of the Educational Support and Inclusion Research and Teaching group and Research Dean in the Faculty of Education at the University of Manchester.

Frances Gallannaugh is Research Associate in the School of Education at the University of Manchester.

Graeme Hutcheson is Lecturer in Quantitative Research at the University of Manchester.

Joy Jarvis is Principal Lecturer in Education at the University of Hertfordshire. She is also a teacher of deaf children and runs courses for professionals in this field. She has taught in a range of educational contexts, and has published many books and articles about special education, inclusion and hearing impairment. Email: j.jarvis@herts.ac.uk

Wendy Lawson is a psychologist with an autistic spectrum disorder and parent of a son with an autistic spectrum disorder. She is working towards her Ph.D. in Psychology with Deakin University, Victoria, Australia, and her research explores the concept of 'different ability' ('diffability') in the world of neurodiversity. She has published several books on autism and the autistic spectrum.

Geoff Lindsay is Director of CEDAR (Centre for Educational Development, Appraisal and Research) and of the Psychology and Special Needs Research Unit at the University of Warwick. His main research interests are in special needs and inclusive education, educational psychology, and ethical issues in professional practice. Email: Geoff.Lindsay@warwick.ac.uk

Colin Low CBE is Chairman of the Royal National Institute of the Blind, President of the European Blind Union and Visiting Professor at City University. He is a well-known campaigner for disability rights and has written extensively on disability issues. He was recently appointed to the House of Lords as a non-party political peer.

Ingrid Lunt teaches at the University of Oxford where she is Director of Graduate Studies in the Department of Educational Studies. Her research interests include special and inclusive education, and professional educational psychology particularly at an international level. Email: ingrid.lunt@edstud.ox.ac.uk

Charlotte Moore is a full-time writer and mother of three boys, two of whom are autistic. She has published three novels and a highly acclaimed book about autistic family life called *George and Sam*, published by Penguin. For two years she wrote the 'Mind the Gap' column in *The Guardian* and she has written extensively on autism in the national press.

Dinah Murray is a tutor for Birmingham University's distance learning course in autism, and has published widely about autism both in Britain and abroad.

Brahm Norwich works at the School of Education and Lifelong Learning at the University of Exeter. His research interests include policy and practice in special needs and inclusive education and psychological aspects of education. He has published widely in these fields. Email: b.norwich@ex.ac.uk

Filiz Polat is Lecturer in Education (Special and Inclusive Education) at the University of Bristol, and M.Ed. pathway Co-ordinator for Special and Inclusive Education.

Dame Dela Smith is executive director of the Darlington Education Village and was formerly head teacher of Beaumont Hill School, which is now incorporated in the village.

Will Spurgeon is former head teacher of Marshfields School in Peterborough. He now works for the National Strategies Team as Regional School Improvement Partner Coordinator for London North.

Lorella Terzi recently completed a Ph.D. in the philosophy of education at the Institute of Education, University of London, and is now senior lecturer at Roehampton University. Her interests are in political philosophy, with specific reference to issues of disability and disadvantage, and to theories of social justice in education. Email: L.Terzi@Roehampton.ac.uk

Lorna Wing is a psychiatrist. She had an autistic daughter and was a co-founder of the National Autistic Society in 1962 with other parents of autistic children. She is the author of many books and papers on autism and, in 1981, published a seminal paper on Asperger's Syndrome. Email: Elliot.House@nas.org.uk

Foreword

Baroness Warnock

I am delighted to introduce this timely contribution to the debate on provision for children with special educational needs. It is timely in that, at the time of writing, the Commons All-Party Select Committee on Education and Skills is examining the subject, and will shortly be publishing its findings. These will no doubt fuel further debate. Moreover, the Conservative Party is formulating its own policy on the subject, and should benefit from the different arguments put forward in this book.

In June 2005 the Philosophy of Education Society of Great Britain published a pamphlet written by myself, in which I urged government to set up a committee of inquiry to consider the case for radical reform of the framework of provision that had been in place since the Education Act of 1981. This framework, I argued, was failing some children disastrously. The need for a review centred on two issues. The first was the policy of issuing statements for some but not all children who had been identified as having special needs. The second was the commitment to including in mainstream schools all those children whose parents wanted it, and many whose parents did not, regardless of the nature of their needs. The habit of using the expression 'special educational need' as though it described a uniform category that could be treated in a uniform way was blinding policy-makers and local authorities to important differences between children, and what precisely they needed in order for learning to be possible.

The launch of the pamphlet on 29 June 2005 was disfigured by the tactics of the British Council for Disabled People, who tend to speak somewhat intemperately about special schools, and who regard inclusion in mainstream schools as something to which disabled children are entitled as of right. And it has to be said that the Special Educational Needs and Disability Act 2001 lends colour to this contention. For, if a school either refuses to admit a child or, having admitted him, subsequently excludes him, that school may have committed a criminal offence under this act. However, the position is far from clear. And, far more important than the legal niceties is the undoubted fact that all children, whatever their disabilities, have a right to be educated. My contention was and is that there are some children who simply fail to get that education in a mainstream school, and no adaptation of the school can turn it into an environment in which such children can learn.

The matter of statements and that of inclusion are connected, though some-what loosely. All children in special schools have statements, but not all children with statements are in special schools. Those people who would like to see special schools abolished usually argue for retaining statements, presumably for those children who are most severely disabled and who would need one-to-one teaching or continuous support even if they attended a mainstream school. However, there are no clear criteria determining who is and who is not to be issued with a statement, and local authorities show great variation in the number of statements they produce. The heart of the matter is, of course, funding. Local authorities have a statutory duty to provide what is deemed in the statement to be needed by the child, whereas, though they may be morally committed to making provision for other children identified as having special needs, if they fail to do so they are not legally liable. This leads to endless disagreements between local authorities and parents, who understandably want statements for their disabled children in order to be sure that they will get at least some extra support. Many of these embattled parents believe that the mainstream school will never provide enough support, and seek a statement so that their child may attend a special school. But since in many areas special schools have been closed, this would involve the local education authority in the expense of sending him to a school in another area, or to a fee-paying school, and this above all they want to avoid.

Since the publication of my pamphlet I have had literally hundreds of letters from parents in this position, many of them terrified of the battles ahead, with tribunals and all the anxiety and exhaustion that they bring. Most of the letters are from parents of children with moderate learning difficulties: Asperger's Syndrome, Attention Deficit and Hyperactivity Disorder (ADHD), social, emotional and behavioural difficulties (SEBD), or some combination of these. It seems that children with very severe learning difficulties are generally well looked after, their needs met either in well-equipped and highly professional special schools, with expert teachers, or in units attached to mainstream schools (often less well equipped). Similarly pupils with physical disabilities and those who are deaf, blind or deaf/blind will automatically get a statement of need and, depending on resources available, either go to a special school or a special unit or get proper additional support in the mainstream. The children who really suffer from the present system are those whose disabilities are not obvious or visible, particularly those at the moderate end of the autistic spectrum, who may also suffer from moderate learning difficulties (though many Asperger's children are highly, if idiosyncratically, intelligent), not to mention communication and/or behavioural difficulties.

Governments over the years have much to answer for here. For not only have they encouraged us to think of special schools as places only for the most profoundly intellectually disabled (those who used to be deemed ineducable, but who are now fortunately recognised as needing education up to the very limit of their abilities), but there is the unspoken corollary that all of those with lesser disabilities can be accommodated in the mainstream with a few hours a week of support. This is far from true, especially by the time the child reaches secondary school. For a child of ten with Asperger's, the transition from primary to second-ary school may be traumatic, even catastrophic. Such a child may no longer even pretend to keep up, feeling defeated by the inevitable demands of the school environment: the bustle and clamour, the pushing and shoving, the rushing from one classroom to another, the need for top speed whatever the activity, the teachers who are different every hour of the day, and many of whom are in the school only temporarily. Some of these horrors can be mitigated for such children if they have a personal assistant, but it is unlikely that any school can provide the level of assistance they need, all day and every day. Moreover, excessive reliance on assistants can present its own problems, not least feelings of dependence and inferiority.

The tragic result for some children with autistic difficulties is trauma and even regression. I am convinced that for such children, and for those with ADHD and other behavioural problems, what is needed is a mixture of care and small-class teaching in the environment of a small school. Without such an environment, education will be impossible: they will constantly be too anxious and miserable to learn. They may begin to refuse school; they may become self-destructive or suicidal; they may be induced to stay at school only by antidepressant drugs. For such children 'inclusion' is a nightmare. If they are to flourish and benefit from education, they need the relatively protected environment of a small or smallish special school. It is really not enough to say that the mainstream schools must so change as to accommodate them. However tolerant and supportive the policies, and however understanding the members of staff, there are limits to what real-istically can be achieved in mainstream schools, given the diversity of children's needs and the finite available resources. It should be acknowledged, moreover, that not all teachers are particularly understanding; they are likely to be rushed off their feet and determined that the class as a whole must get on, score well in tests, climb the league tables. We need to stop thinking that special schools are either prisons from which children must be rescued at all costs, or wicked self-indulgent places in which the pupils will never learn the harsh realities of life. A special school may be the only place where a fragile child will learn anything at all.

In October 2005 the government published a White Paper under the catchy title 'Higher Standards, Better Schools for All: More Choice for Parents and Pupils'. True to the title, the great emphasis is on parental choice. The parents of children with special needs must laugh when they read it. For the majority of them there is no choice. They cannot choose to have a statement for their child; that is for the local authority to decide. And therefore they cannot choose what school their child will go to. They must take a place in any mainstream school willing to accept a difficult pupil, and one unlikely to enhance the competitive status of the school. This will most probably be the school with the lowest stand-ards, which parents with bright and successful children are unlikely to put at the top of their list.

There is deep confusion in the White Paper, moreover, about admissions policy. Schools are expected, by and large, to become independent of local authorities, and thus free, presumably, to decide on their own admissions. At the same time there will be a code of practice obliging them to admit students in bands of ability. No one seems to know whether they can be directed to take a proportion of children with special needs or not. The report of the All-Party Commons Select Committee on the White Paper, published in January 2006, was highly critical of this confusion.

The White Paper speaks coyly about 'pupils who have fallen behind' (paragraphs 4.12–4.16), for whom extra resources are to be supplied; as a subgroup of these pupils there are those with special needs who are to receive 'tailored support' (paragraph 4.17). (One cannot but think of pre-1911 corsetry.) Between them these pupils make up the group that are now referred to in Scotland as meriting Additional Learning Support, the term SEN having been abolished. But in Scotland the local authority has a statutory obligation to supply Additional Learning Support to all who need it. In England and Wales that duty applies only to those with statements. We do not know, any more than we ever did, who merits a statement; I presume that it is not all those who have 'fallen behind', but only those with special needs and, presumably, not all of these.

It is paragraphs 4.19 and 4.20 that are, in my view, the most important and novel in this part of the White Paper. In reading these paragraphs it is necessary to keep one's wits about one, because of the intensely confusing terminology. But they strongly suggest a crack in the programme of inclusion that may not be welcome to the full-blown anti-segregation lobby. First, in paragraph 4.19, the Trailblazer schools are mentioned, of which there are at present 12. These schools are otherwise known as specialist special schools. Each concentrates on a particular disability or group of disabilities, cognitive, behavioural, autistic and so on. They not only educate children with these disabilities, but also send out teachers to neighbouring mainstream schools to 'share their expertise', doubtless with the mainstream teachers and classroom assistants. It is proposed that the number of these schools will go up to 50 within the next two years.

But in addition there are already 30 special schools of a different kind, known as specialist non-mainstream schools. These are all former special schools that sought permission to take on a particular specialism, as all mainstream schools may, and, provided they can raise some initial capital, they will then receive extra government money to enhance their buildings and other facilities relevant to their specialism. So they can become, let us say, a school specializing in IT or in music or in sport, but because they are special schools at heart, no one can attend unless he has a statement. And again, because historically they are special schools, they are all small, with probably no more than 400 or so pupils, and with a very favourable staff/pupil ratio, and plenty of 'tailored support'. It is proposed that there should be 50 more such schools by 2008, and special schools will be encouraged to apply for this status. This cannot but seem like an acknowledgement that special schools are no longer to be considered the last resort for the profoundly disabled.

I would like to propose that the statement of need should be tied to special schools, so that if a parent wanted a statement for her child she would in effect be asking that he go to a special school. This would signal that special schools were no longer officially beyond the pale. However, mainstream schools that admitted children with special needs would still have an obligation to provide support for them, according to the terms of the Disability Discrimination Act. Some might decide to apply for specialist status, specialising in special needs and perhaps also in sport or IT. (Clearly something will have to be done about this terminology.)

At present, government seems to be spending money on new school buildings. There might be a chance here for new specialist special schools to co-locate with mainstream schools, which would increase the ability of mainstream schools to look after children with, say, health difficulties such as asthma or epilepsy or cystic fibrosis, as well as enabling the two schools to cooperate socially. All these possibilities need to be discussed. But decisions must be taken on the basis of evidence. What is needed is well-funded and well-publicised research, perhaps funded in part by charities. Such research, on how children with different disabilities flourish or fail to flourish in different settings, should be carried out, I would suggest, as much by teachers on secondment as by academics. At present there is a vast quantity of anecdote but, for most people, little else. And anecdote is not enough. I believe this collection of essays will help to clear up the issues, clarify the arguments, and perhaps even suggest some solutions.

Editorial introduction[1]

Background to this book

In the summer of 2005, the news broke: Mary Warnock had done a U-turn on special education. I had worked with her on the pamphlet in which this was allegedly announced, and I was surprised. U-turn? What were they talking about? Was Mary Warnock arguing that all children with special needs should be segregated from other children, as they were in the 1960s and 1970s? Not at all, but this was politics. News of the U-turn was a response to a phrase that Warnock had used in her pamphlet, which had been subjected to the sound bite treatment.

The phrase in question was 'disastrous legacy'. Warnock was talking about her own 1978 report, known as the *Report of the Committee of Inquiry into the Education of Handicapped Children and Young People* (Department of Education and Science, 1978). This report banished the concept of 'ineducability' and replaced the policy of segregated schooling for so-called handicapped children with a policy of integration. The passage in which the phrase appears is this:

> I now want to move on to what is possibly the most disastrous legacy of the 1978 report, the concept of inclusion (formerly known as integration). Like an inheritance that grows and becomes more productive from one generation to another, this concept has gained a remarkable foothold in our society.
>
> (Warnock, 2005, p. 22)

What was 'disastrous' was not the policy of integration, as implemented during the years following the report. Nor, if one reads on, was it inclusion in all its forms, for Warnock makes it clear in the pamphlet that she supports inclusion in at least one commonly accepted sense of that word. She quotes the National Association of Head Teachers approvingly:

> Inclusion is a process that maximises the entitlement of all pupils to a broad, relevant and stimulating curriculum, which is delivered in the environment that will have the greatest impact on their learning. All schools, whether special or mainstream, should reflect a culture in which the institution adapts

to meet the needs of its pupils and is provided with the resources for this to happen.

(ibid., p. 41)

Warnock supports inclusion in this sense, and she would no doubt agree with this statement by Jim Sinclair, an autistic man (Sinclair, 1998):

> I do not know of any advocate from within the disability community who believes that inclusion should not be an available option. Disability advocates believe that disabled people should be *able* to go anywhere and do anything in mainstream society. . . . However there are concerns within the disability community that inclusion is not always the best option for every person with every disability, and that involuntary inclusion is as problematic as involuntary segregation.

This is an argument about choice, and it has implications about special schools that tally with the NAHT definition of inclusion above. Inclusion, according to that definition, is a 'process' rather than an environment. It is not about which roofs children have over their heads, or who else is under that roof. It is about educating children 'in the environment that will have the greatest impact on their learning'. 'Learning' should be broadly construed; the NAHT definition goes on to say that an inclusive schooling is 'the one in which [children] can be most fully included in the life of their school community and which gives them a sense both of belonging and achieving' (cited in Warnock, 2005, p. 41). If a disabled child does not feel included in a mainstream community, she or her parents should be free to choose an environment in which she is more likely to feel included. In many cases, this will be a special school, the closure of which will mean 'involuntary inclusion' for many children.

The argument sounds simple and straightforwardly liberal; people should have a choice, especially perhaps if they have difficulties or disabilities that make their lives harder than most. However, the response to Warnock's pamphlet was anything but simple. The U-turn accusation was literally meant, with large numbers of disabled people attributing to Warnock a desire to 'exclude them', that is, revert to segregated education. Other accusations were thrown at her during the weeks and months following the pamphlet's publication. Baroness Warnock had a 'monstrous ego'; she 'seems to think she is always right'. In fact the last two sentences of the pamphlet could hardly have been more humble. Warnock acknowledged that she was expressing a personal conviction, and called for 'hard evidence' to support her views because 'one person's conviction is not enough' (ibid., p. 55). How, one might ask, did people get it so wrong? What was going on?

There was another sound bite that the media latched on to. 'At the heart of our thinking about education,' Warnock had written, 'there is confusion of which children are the casualties' (ibid., p. 14). I believe that she was right about this. Special education is in a state of crisis, with the government having closed many special schools and being accused from two directions of closing too many and not closing enough; with parents pleading publicly against the closure of the special schools that they see as lifelines for their children; with disabled people accusing Warnock of wanting to exclude them, when her avowed aim was precisely the opposite. There is instability in our present education system which cannot be good for children, and indeed some of the contributors to the book (including Wing, Moore, Jarvis, Murray and Lawson) describe its ill effects. At the launch of Warnock's pamphlet, people were denying what no one was asserting: that disabled children and children with difficulties should be *forced* to go to special schools.

All this is the background to, and inspiration for, the present book. No doubt people will never be in perfect agreement about what counts as an optimal or a just educational system, but it is inexcusable for the inclusion debate to remain as it is, mired in confusion. The book will achieve something if it helps people to deny no more than what others are asserting. Perhaps, as Baroness Warnock says in her foreword, it may even go further and suggest some solutions.

Included or excluded: a false dichotomy?

The book contains chapters by some of Mary Warnock's critics, as well as chapters that support and elaborate her views. On the whole the supporters are represented in Part 1, but this is not true without qualification. Some of the contributors to Part 2 – for example, Murray and Lawson, Cooper, and Bennathan – share Warnock's reservations about sending all children to mainstream schools, which is the basic issue of Part 1. I have placed them in Part 2 because they also address the question 'how can inclusive education be improved?', which is the basic theme of Part 2. The bipartite division of the book thus represents positions that are compatible rather than exclusive.

It is commonly believed that one is either for or against inclusion. The question 'included or excluded?' suggests that inclusion is an either/or matter, and by choosing this as the title of the book I hope to convey both how the issue is typically perceived, and that it is wrongly perceived this way. In fact the book is based on an important premise: that in at least one significant sense of the word, we are *all* in favour of inclusion. As Brahm Norwich (Chapter 8) says: 'It is rare to find arguments against inclusion, as it is rare to find arguments against democracy. Where disagreement lies is in the extent and nature of inclusion.' We disagree about how schools should be arranged so that children can be most effectively included. Some believe that this goal can be achieved only if all children attend the same schools; others (with Warnock) passionately deny this. The disagreement is practical, but it is also conceptual, and it relates in part to the troublesome little word 'all'. I shall say more about this below.

We need to ask 'included in what?', 'excluded from what?' and indeed 'excluded by whom?' No one (I am assuming) wants children to 'feel excluded' by virtue of the schools that they attend. Some are concerned about their feeling excluded *from* mainstream schools; others are concerned about their feeling excluded *within* mainstream schools and *by* other children. The latter is the ground for Warnock-like reservations about inclusion for all at the same schools, and it leads to disagreement between those who say that exclusion within schools (i.e. stigmatisation and bullying) can be eliminated given time and a will to succeed, and those (like Low in Chapter 1) who see this view as ideological and unassailable (and therefore empirically suspect).

The concept of inclusion has implications about how schools can develop and improve so that all children can become engaged in the process of learning. It involves a vision of how education could be, and a principle about being open to new ideas. This vision is the theme of Part 2. It is here that we read about projects like nurture groups for emotionally deprived children (Chapter 17) and ideas stores for autistic children (Chapter 15). It is here that issues of fairness are discussed, since it is not acceptable to distribute resources in such a way that some children feel included at the expense of others (see Chapters 9 and 10). Also represented in Part 2 (particularly in Chapters 8, 9 and 10) are discussions of the crucial concepts of sameness and difference, and (in Chapter 11) of the role and function of statements of special educational need.

It is inevitably a simplification to 'count' positions on the inclusion debate, but I want to argue nonetheless that there are at least three. Representatives of one of these positions declined my invitation to contribute a chapter, so I need to begin by explaining (to the best of my capacity) what they are saying. The position that is not represented in this book is the radical inclusion argument, presented by the Centre for Studies on Inclusive Education (CSIE) and Parents for Inclusion, among others. Parents for Inclusion runs a campaign which it calls the 2020 Campaign, the aim of which is to see all special schools closed by 2020, and indeed as soon as possible. The significant word here is 'all'. The argument is not that some special schools should be closed because they are not cost-effective or because they are failing. Rather:

> The 2020 Campaign is based on the experience of disabled adults who went to special education schools and colleges. They experienced abuse, isolation and failure that emotionally scarred thousands for life. End this shameful exclusion that ruins lives.
>
> (Parents for Inclusion, 2004)

This is a radical position, and I would also call it universalist because it is concerned with all special schools. Such schools mean 'shameful exclusion that ruins lives', and it is no surprise that those who think this way want to see them closed without delay. What is interesting about this position is that it is universalist in aspiration but not in meaning. It aspires towards a society in which all children attend mainstream schools, but it is based on an understanding of what special schools mean which is conspicuously unshared.

Consider an alternative understanding of what special schools mean. In Chapter 6 of this book William Colley, head teacher of a special school, conveys what his school means to him and some of his pupils, not with a definition but with a potent metaphor:

> I had, as a final-year student at university, cycled alone from London to Marrakesh at the height of summer and with the Saharan heat spilling down through North Africa and into southern Spain. On crossing the straits of Gibraltar, I found myself in an alien land in which every gesture and expression that had served me in France and Spain suddenly had no resonance. I was mobbed by youths, spat at by vendors and chased by those who tried to sell me huge watermelons by the roadside as I cycled past.

This experience, he suggests, was akin to that of many of his pupils when they attended mainstream schools. To Colley and his pupils, special schools mean a kind of refuge from an 'alien land'. This is not to say that they are seen as day-care centres rather than educational establishments. Rather, they are environments in which education becomes possible, where formerly it was all but impossible.

The radical position naturally provokes an antagonistic response from those who attribute a different meaning to the key term 'special school', and whose lives and fortunes are threatened by these universalist aspirations. It is my contention that Warnock, Colley and the other contributors to Part 1 of this book, are essentially, and understandably, responding to this universalist position. They see it as actually or potentially catastrophic for some children, and they are engaging in what one might call an 'all–some debate'. The radical inclusionists want to close *all* special schools and put *all* children in the mainstream. Warnock and others respond that *some* children will suffer terribly in such schools, and make a case for moderation.

The position that is represented in Part 2 is distinct from both the radical/ universalist and moderate positions in terms of its basic rationale. It is not about 'all' versus 'some'; it is about inclusion as opposed to integration. In particular, it is about advancing historically in our thinking about special education, which was originally shaped by the philosophy of segregation, was replaced by the philosophy of integration, and has been gradually introducing and refining the philosophy of inclusion. This philosophy is based on a simple idea: that schools should adapt to the diverse needs of children. It is about changing the assumptions around which schools were formerly built, particularly the assumption (implicit in the philosophy of integration) that schools cater predominantly for 'normal' children. The philosophy of inclusion has little use for the normal/ abnormal distinction. It conceptualises children as different from each other in all sorts of ways, and addresses these differences as a matter of priority.

This philosophy was expounded in an influential document, the 1994 UNESCO Salamanca Statement (discussed by Lindsay in Chapter 2), which helped to shift the focus of special education from integration to inclusion. Integration does not challenge the normal/abnormal distinction; it merely seeks to accommodate those who are considered 'abnormal' (or as having 'special' as opposed to 'ordinary' needs) in mainstream schools by providing them with extra support as required. The Salamanca Statement went much further. It addressed the issue of difference in a central way, and presented inclusive schools – schools which welcome everyone, remove barriers to learning, combat discriminatory attitudes, and so on – as the basis for a just society.

Much of the Salamanca Statement is uncontentious. It expresses a humane ideology about the equal right of every individual to education, dignity, self-respect. These are fundamental ethical principles with which few disagree, as Brahm Norwich (quoted earlier) observes. Disagreement arises, in part, because of confusion about the relationship between the philosophy of inclusion and what I have called the all–some debate. The Salamanca Statement is equivocal on this. Much of the language in which it is couched is universalist; it talks about the rights of *every* child, and about providing an 'effective education for all'. However, it does not promote the closure of all special schools, but says:

> It is worth noting that . . . the education of children in special schools or in special classes within ordinary schools, should be the exception and be recommended only in rare cases where children with special educational needs cannot be catered for in ordinary classes.
>
> (UNESCO, 1994, B a.)

It also says that inclusive schools provide an effective education for the *majority* of children, which is the position I have called moderate as opposed to radical or universalist.

What has happened, I suggest, is this. Salamanca expresses an inspirational vision of a just and equal society, which is the basis of the philosophy of inclusion. However, the means by which this vision is to be realised are equivocated about in the document, and this allowed radical inclusionists to emphasise its universalist implications while other inclusionists moderate these or refuse to take them seriously. In a way it is understandable that one would want to universalise the inclusive vision. How can one have justice and equality for some but not all? How can one be moderate about a value like justice?

However, the vision is one thing and the means by which it is realised is another. The idea of including everyone in the same schools may sound like the best way to achieve justice, but on closer inspection things can seem more complicated. In particular – and this is what concerns Mary Warnock and the other moderates – some children may simply fail to get a reasonable education if they are in the same schools as the majority of children. They may be miserable; their needs may be overlooked. In this sense they may be discriminated against if placed in mainstream schools.

The universalist response is that, if some children are discriminated against, this means that the schools are not inclusive enough; they have not adequately adapted to children's diverse needs. This implies that all mainstream schools can adapt successfully to the needs of all children, which is a curious claim, part empirical, part ideological. In Part 1, the contributors say why they think that, as an empirical claim, it is false. Some children's difficulties are such (they argue) that the mainstream will never be a positive experience for them.

Another point is worth noting. The Salamanca Statement talks about the right of every child to an education; it does not say that every child has a right to an *inclusive* education. Yet this is how the radical inclusionists have interpreted it, giving rise to a debate about whether sending a child to a special school means denying her right to an inclusive education. This misinterprets the Statement, and it is also confusing about the concept of a right. Having a right to do something is not normally associated with the absence of a right not to do that thing. The argument that special schools should close because all children have a right to a mainstream education is rather like saying, for example: not only do I have a right to park in Judd Street, but I *must* do so. In this way the human rights argument for inclusion conflates the ideas of having a right and having a duty. (Colin Low discusses this issue in Chapter 1.)

Where does this leave us? I have argued that there is a universalist or radical position which is countered by a moderate position, and that there is a further position that promotes inclusion as opposed to integration. The latter I call simply the inclusion position, or the philosophy of inclusion. This is the idea that there should be (as Low says in Chapter 1) a *presumption* in favour of mainstream education for all, as opposed to an *assertion* that the mainstream is right for every child. Presumptions may be unjustified in particular cases, and this position is represented in Part 2 by contributors who variously explore legal, economic, ethical, educational, social and conceptual questions relating to this philosophy.

I said that the two parts of this book represent different questions, and in this sense are independent. It should be noted, however, that their independence is not total, for the philosophy of inclusion does generally presuppose the existence of communities of children to which the majority, if not all, belong. Insofar as special schools are completely independent of mainstream schools, it is certainly true that children will lack opportunities to interact with each other across barriers of difference. Depriving them of these opportunities means allowing the barriers to remain in place, whereas the goal of inclusion is to break them down. Inclusive schools must therefore include children of mixed abilities, not only academically but in the sense of mixed difficulties, physical, sensory, behavioural and so on. In Chapter 14, Dela Smith describes her 'visions for a village' in which this goal is realised; children with a variety of needs are accommodated under different roofs or the same roofs, flexibly, on a single site and within a single community. Many will see this as a promising model for how to proceed.

Although Smith claims that all children may be accommodated at her village, I want to distinguish her position from that of the radical inclusionists, who wish to ensure that what they call segregated education ceases to be an option. To have a vision of universal inclusion – to *offer* to include everyone – is different from aiming to structure society in such a way that choice becomes impossible. It is the latter aspiration, I believe, that prompted Warnock to describe inclusion (Warnock, 2005, p. 22) as 'an inheritance that grows and becomes more productive from one generation to another'. The attempt to banish special schools from the educational agenda polarises the debate between those who want 'inclusion for all' and those who want 'exclusion for some'.

Of course, this terminology is misleading because 'exclusion for some' is not what the moderate inclusionists say they want; it is how the radical inclusionists provocatively describe the position to which they are opposed. What the moderate inclusionists want is to prevent some children from feeling excluded in the mainstream, and being unable to learn properly as a consequence. They turn the radical inclusionist argument on its head by suggesting that feeling excluded in the mainstream can ruin, or blight, lives (see Moore, Murray and Lawson, and Wing in this book).

From the moderate perspective, the idea of including all children in the mainstream is hardly credible. What about the child who is brain-damaged and asleep most of the time? What about the 14-year-old in nappies, whose mental age is two? What about the child who is so autistic that she does nothing all day but rock? At the very least, the moderates would argue, we should keep an open mind about such children. If it turns out that the most inclusive or 'village-like' environment has nothing to offer them (indeed could harm them), we have a duty to acknowledge this. The sting in the tail of the radical argument is the promotion of universal special school closure, so that such a discovery would be impossible to respond to.

The moderate position draws our attention to something that, in my view, all inclusionists need to address. This is the question: what kinds of difficulties might be unsatisfactorily met in mainstream schools? To put this more philosophically: what counts as an educationally significant difference, such that children who have such differences are likely to be significantly disadvantaged when placed in inclusive mainstream schools? To address this question is not to deny that other issues are at stake. Economic considerations demand (as Lunt argues in Chapter 11) a principle of minimal identification of difference, and considerations of justice demand (as Lunt and Evans argue) a principle of transparency and clarity for allocating resources. Such considerations are compatible with the possibility that some (possibly extremely rare) differences are hard or impossible to accommodate in even the most inclusive mainstream environments. We need to conceptualise this possibility so that we can address it empirically. It is this conceptualisation that I now want to explore.

Who is different and who is the same?

This brings us to the central theoretical tension in special education, known as the 'dilemma of difference'. Several contributors to this book (notably Norwich, Terzi, Evans and Lunt) address it in helpful ways, and Mary Warnock referred to it in her 2005 pamphlet as a major source of confusion. Briefly the dilemma is this. We either treat all children as essentially the same, which means treating them as fairly as possible but with the risk of neglecting individual differences, or we treat them differently, with the consequence that some are better off than they would otherwise have been, but there is a risk of being unfair by devoting more resources or expertise to some than others.

Alan Dyson (2001) describes this as follows:

> [There is] a series of dilemmas for education professionals and policy-makers. Put simply, the more their educational responses emphasise what learners have in common, the more they tend to overlook what separates them; the more they emphasise what separates them and distinguishes each individual learner, the more they tend to overlook what learners have in common. It is, of course, special education that has tended to face these dilemmas in their most acute form. . . . Dealing, as it does, with those students who are most obviously 'different' from the majority, it is the part of the education system which more than any other has had to reconcile the dual perspectives of commonality and difference.

It is my belief that the tendency to emphasise sameness at the expense of difference, or vice versa, has to be overcome. *Both* require due recognition, and this is not an optional requirement but an essential one, for anything else will bring discrimination by the back door. The emphasis on sameness risks (as the moderate inclusionists believe) neglecting the vital interests of a minority and in effect discriminating against them. The emphasis on difference may mean defending the vital interests of a minority at the expense of others who receive less than their due and less than, in some cases, they need (see the chapters by Lunt and Evans). There may be a case for parents to defend the interests of a minority (their own children) in this way, but this is not something that policy-makers can reasonably accept. Policy-makers must conceptualise both sameness and difference, and do this in a reasonably balanced way.

So who is 'different' from the rest? Or, as I put it above, what counts as an educationally significant difference? The answer to this question, since the Warnock report of 1978, has basically been framed in terms of special educational needs (SEN). There are children with special needs and children with ordinary needs. There is an educationally significant difference between these, to which policy-makers must have regard. When it was first introduced, such thinking represented an advance on the idea that some children are 'normal' and others have handicaps or 'deficits'. The SEN concept alerted people to the fact that there is a *spectrum* of needs, and people with 'special' needs are not a 'race apart'. However, the concept of SEN brought its own problems. What are needs? Some are obvious, others are less so, and in many cases they come to light (or even come into existence) by virtue of being claimed. This means that parents who know how to play the system may contribute to an inflationary situation in which increasing numbers of children are identified as having special needs. (In fact the numbers of children identified with SEN have been growing over the past few years.) This can bring injustice: two children whose needs are identical may receive different allocations from the pie of scarce resources. Further, as Lunt points out in Chapter 11, the present system provides schools with a perverse incentive to identify more rather than fewer children with special needs, in order to get a larger portion of the pie. These are consequences of the poor conceptualisation of 'difference' in terms of special needs, and it is an issue with which several contributors to this book try to come to grips.

The conceptualisation of difference must work on economic, legal and ethical levels, and a framework of thought known as the capability approach (developed by Amartya Sen and Martha Nussbaum) is identified by Terzi and Evans in this book as a promising candidate for this. Applying the framework to special education, Terzi begins by introducing a distinction between an impairment and a disability. An impairment is an 'individual feature, such as the lack of a limb or the loss of a function'; a disability is 'a functional limitation or an inability to perform some significant functionings, which in an educational context can mean a barrier to learning'. What are significant functionings? They are the '*real* freedoms people have to promote and achieve their own well-being'. They are 'the "beings" and "doings" that individuals have reason to value. Walking, reading, being well-nourished, being educated, having self-respect and acting in a political capacity are all examples of functionings.' Finally, these functionings exist in the 'space of capability', and it is within this space that we get an answer to the basic egalitarian question 'equality of what?' When one asks whether two people are being treated equally well or whether one is being discriminated against, the question should not be along the lines of 'what kinds of goods have they received?' It should be 'to what extent are their significant functionings being promoted? Are they being enabled to be and do what they want to be and do?'

The task of identifying those children for whom mainstream schools are possibly unsuitable may be explored by reference to this framework. The question should not be whether a child has an impairment; it should be whether her impairments are likely to be disabling in an inclusive mainstream environment. To what extent, it should be asked, can a mainstream environment be adapted so that particular impairments are not disabling? Are there some impairments which are almost inevitably disabling in mainstream environments?

I suggested earlier that some impairments may fit this description. It is hard to see how a teenager in nappies could benefit from a mainstream environment, however creatively it is adapted. This is not to deny that there could be fruitful interaction between such a child and her peers, or that there is educational potential in such interaction on both sides. It is to say that the business of learning to 'be and do what one wants to be and do' may not be promoted for this teenager by such interactions on a daily basis.

There is another group of children for whom the benefits of mainstream education are widely viewed with scepticism. These are autistic children. It seemed reasonable to devote several chapters to them in this book (Chapters 3, 4 and 15) because of the important role they play in the moderate position. Autistic children have been in the news a lot recently in precisely this connection, and Warnock referred to them several times in her 2005 pamphlet. At a glance, most autistic children look much the same as other children. Their 'differences' are not necessarily obvious. Yet Charlotte Moore, who has two autistic sons, says in Chapter 4 that 'of all the conditions that go under the heading of "special needs", autism is the one most accurately described as "differently abled" '. She writes:

> Above all, autists never do anything simply because that's the social norm. They learn very little in a group. Many people believe that if an autistic child attends a mainstream school the 'normality' will rub off on him, and his autistic behaviours will decrease. This is wishful thinking. A core feature of autism is the lack of imitative behaviour, or rather, there's an inability to learn through imitation. Neurotypical children have an innate curiosity about the way other people do things; in autists, this instinct has gone awry. Autists may imitate an action or a gesture in the same way that they may echo a phrase, but they fail to grasp the meaning underlying that action. Being with non-autistic children doesn't normalise the autists' behaviour; if anything, it accentuates the difference. Self-stimulatory autistic habits (humming, rocking, hand flapping, even self-harming) increase at times of stress, and if the child is in an environment he doesn't understand, stress levels will be high.

There is also the matter of bullying. Moore quotes passages from the writings of autistic people which confirm what she has experienced with her own children, that 'for a pupil with an autistic spectrum disorder in a mainstream school, being bullied will become a fact of life'. The radical or universalist response will be 'bullying can and in properly inclusive schools will be stopped'. Moore would call this wishful thinking.

Moderate inclusionists like Mary Warnock are concerned that *feeling different* for long periods at school is a disabling experience. They suspect that children with particular impairments will inevitably feel this way in mainstream schools, and I believe their point is that this is not only painful; it undermines the *real* freedoms discussed above. (It also undermines the 'confidence to fail' that these freedoms presuppose. See Cigman, 2006, and Chapter 6 of this book.) Seen thus, the argument that mainstream schools can adapt to all children is from this perspective ideological rather than empirical, and the testimony of many children, parents and teachers suggests that they are wrong.

Consider, for example, the following passage, from the unpublished diary of a young autistic man called Charlie Keeble:

> I went to a secondary mainstream school, and when I first started I was shy and dumbfounded so I didn't speak much at all. I just distanced myself and withered away into my own personal thoughts. I kept myself to myself by retreating into my own world of daydreams. It was hard for me to try and see life in the way the other children did. I just couldn't understand them. It was like I saw the world differently to them. Even when I talked to them I found that they hardly seemed to understand the words I was using. I suppose this was because I was using my own idiosyncratic forms of dialogue like a wordsmith who hadn't properly studied a thesaurus. For the most part I preferred to use words that were meaningful to me and avoided speaking in slang and

other popular ways of talking. . . . I didn't blend in to all the latest trends and found myself constantly buried in my own special interests. For example, I absorbed myself in reading scientific non-fiction and was particularly interested in space and rockets. . . . I preferred to keep myself in isolation. All the other children would tease me about the way I engrossed myself into my hobbies. . . . Moving into my teens was more hellish than ever. . . . I didn't want a mobile phone or an email address for example. My special interests were my only lifestyle. I didn't see any need to join in with the others. . . . I was hardly speaking to anyone during my early years at school and when I did speak I would just clumsily mimic and repeat everything that I enjoyed from various sources . . . I was often the victim of bullying and on one occasion one kid slashed the back of my hand with an art and craft knife. To make matters worse, all the other students saw this as a playground spectacle and just wanted to gawp at me and look at the cut. If only that cut could have revealed something about me to them, so that they could begin to understand why I was different.

It is against the background of testimony like this that we need to think seriously about the concept of difference in special education. The reason for emphasising sameness at the expense of difference is a good one: it is that talk of difference can be stigmatising and disrespectful. It reminds us of the philosophy of segregation, and there is no doubt that many people suffered from this. The moderate argument is that we do not protect people from such suffering by abandoning talk of difference altogether; rather, we promote another kind of suffering that comes with the denial of difference.

Consider the issue of labels. Radical inclusionists dislike what they call labels, that is, terms like 'autistic', 'ADHD', 'deaf', whatever. They see these as disrespectful, and some will at most talk about people with autism and so on, so that the person is acknowledged before his or her impairment. However, Jim Sinclair (1998), whom I quoted at the start, says:

> I am not a 'person with autism'. I am an autistic person. . . . Saying 'person with autism' suggests that autism is something bad – so bad that it isn't even consistent with being a person. Nobody objects to using adjectives to refer to characteristics of a person that are considered positive or neutral.

Once again, the radical argument is turned on its head. Sinclair is not alone among autistic people in saying that he prefers the straightforward use of the word 'autistic' to the various substitutes that some see as more respectful. One looks for a substitute for a word only if one is embarrassed about using it because one sees it as negative or shameful.

The concept of difference needs both to shed its shameful connotations and to be retained so that people can use it to affirm who they are and what kinds of impairments they struggle with. There is an autistic pride movement that says exactly this and, like Sinclair, demands the right not to be involuntarily included in mainstream schools. Interestingly, there tends to be a clash of views between people who have different kinds of impairments. The 2020 Campaign (many of whose members have physical impairments) objects to indicators of difference, like special schools and labels. Many autistic people, on the other hand, welcome such indicators, and the same is true for many deaf people (see Chapter 6). In a sense this is a simple clash of views, but it is also something more serious, for those who dislike indicators of difference have universalist aspirations that threaten those who do not share their views.

Social and communication impairments (particularly autism and deafness) are intrinsically more disabling in mainstream environments than physical impairments. Physical adjustments can be made, and have been made, in a great many schools, so that children in wheelchairs (for example) are simply part of the scene. Children will quickly ignore a wheelchair if the person in it can hold a friendly conversation or share an interesting task. Much harder to deal with is the child who cannot communicate or form relationships in the familiar ways, and this child, as Moore says, is highly vulnerable to bullying.

We need to find out which differences are likely to be disabling in mainstream schools, however inclusively such schools are oriented. That there are such differences should not be denied; our task should be to find practically applicable and acceptable criteria for identifying them, and address the role that they should play in a fair education system.

Conclusion

So is the concept of inclusion a 'disastrous legacy' of the 1978 report? Only, I have argued, insofar as it is universalised in terms of all children attending the same schools. When Warnock described the concept of inclusion as 'an inheritance that grows and become more productive from one generation to another', she was (I believe) talking about the tendency of the radical inclusionists to shift from talking about 'the majority' (as in the Salamanca Statement) to talking about 'all'. This shift is hardly credible when one thinks about certain children, and it involves a distortion of meaning. All children are said to have a 'right' to an inclusive education in a sense that (unusually) denies them a right not to avail themselves of this right. And special schools are said to *mean* 'exclusion' in a sense that denies what they mean to many people.

We may represent the disagreement about special schools like this:

Radical inclusionists	Moderate inclusionists
Special schools mean:	*For some children, special schools mean:*
Segregation	Integration
Being excluded	Being included
Feeling excluded	Feeling included (feeling that one belongs)

Being denied a choice	Being allowed a choice
Being humiliated by a label	Being helped by a label
Neglect of human rights	Respect for human rights
Being ashamed of who/what one is	Being proud of who/what one is

My argument is that those who wish to see special schools closed do not make their case by reiterating their objections to special schools in the terms set out here. They need to acknowledge that some people like special schools, in a rather profound sense of the word 'like'. If the argument for special school closure is to gain ground, it must, I believe, meet the following conditions:

1   It must acknowledge *that* and *why* some people see themselves as 'different' and like special schools.
2   It must do so using the language in which people typically express this feeling, in order to minimise misunderstanding.
3   It must argue convincingly that, despite the fact that some people like special schools, there is a strong case for their closure.

I have expressed scepticism about whether the radical inclusionists can meet this challenge, but I could be wrong. Whatever the outcome, I hope that readers of this book will feel inspired to think more philosophically about education. As Jarvis and others suggest, the basic issue is not about location; it is about values and also about vision. We need to look ahead on behalf of future generations as wisely as possible, and this means being attentive to, and learning from, the viewpoints of others. Our aim, in short, should be to focus our collective, long-term vision.

Ruth Cigman

Note

1   This book is a response to Mary Warnock's 2005 publication, *Special Educational Needs: A New Look*, London: Philosophy of Education Society of Great Britain. Through the book 'Warnock, 2005' refers to this publication.

References

Cigman, R. (2001), 'Self-esteem and the confidence to fail', *Journal of Philosophy of Education*, vol. 35 (4), 561–76.
Dyson, A. (2001), 'Special needs in the twenty-first century: where we've been and where we're going', *British Journal of Special Education*, vol. 28 (1), 24–9
Keeble, C. (2006), unpublished journal, private collection
Parents for Inclusion (2004), http://inclusion.uwe.ac.uk/csie/2020%20Press%-20Release%20Nov%2004%20.pdf, accessed 9 August 2006
Sinclair, J. (1998), http://web.syr.edu/~jisincla/
UNESCO (1994), *The UNESCO Salamanca Statement and Framework for Action on Special Needs Education*, Paris: UNESCO
Warnock, M. (2005), *Special Educational Needs: A New Look*, London: Philosophy of Education Society of Great Britain

Acknowledgements

All but one of the essays in this collection were written especially for the book. I would like to thank the contributors who provided its bricks and mortar, responding quickly and cogently to Mary Warnock's 2005 pamphlet and enduring my often niggling suggestions.

Warm thanks too to Mary Warnock herself, for her continuing inspiration and support.

I would like to thank Paul Standish, editor of the *Journal of Philosophy of Education*, for permission to re-print (with amendments) Lorella Terzi's essay.

I am grateful to many others for their help and support. Not least are my colleagues at the Philosophy of Education Society of Great Britain, especially John and Patricia White, Christopher Winch and Judith Suissa. I would also like to thank Caroline Pound, James Mariner and Charlie Keeble, as well as my very helpful editors at Routledge, and Sarah Brolly and Colin Morgan of Swales & Willis. Above all, special thanks must go to my mainstays, Michael and Adam.

Part 1

Moderate inclusion and the case for special schools

1 A defence of moderate inclusion and the end of ideology

Colin Low

Introduction

Throughout most of its history, the field of special education has been bedevilled by dogma. For a long time this asserted that disabled children could thrive only in special schools. For the last twenty-five years, however, in the wake of the Warnock report, the field has been blessedly free from such dogma. A settlement was arrived at based on a mixed economy of provision that acknowledged a decisive shift towards inclusion, with progressive re-engineering of the system to support inclusion as the goal, but with a place reserved for specialist provision for those whose needs cannot be met in the mainstream, either now or in the future. However, this consensus is now being challenged by those who believe in what 'full inclusion' or, as the Centre for Studies on Inclusive Education (CSIE) has put it, 'the right to education in a single, inclusive system of education which is adapt- able to the best interests of each and every child' and from which 'the possibility of choosing segregation should be entirely removed' (CSIE, 2004). This is the position that is currently being strenuously advocated at the United Nations, in the negotiations intended to lead to the development of a UN convention on the rights of disabled people by organisations such as CSIE and Disability Equality in Education.

Some time ago, I distinguished between what I called 'hard' and 'soft' inclusiv- ists. These terms broadly correspond to the positions of those who believe in educational inclusion for all children without exception and the post-Warnock settlement based on a mixed economy of provision, respectively (Low, 1997). But neither of these labels seems particularly complimentary, and in this chapter I shall distinguish between 'full' inclusion (this is the universalist or radical position discussed in the introduction) and 'moderate' inclusion. In this chapter, I present the case for the moderate inclusion perspective, with particular emphasis on issues relating to visual impairment. I suggest that it is time to confirm the post- Warnock settlement, and banish ideology and dogma from the field of special education once and for all.

The case for inclusion

The Centre for the Study of Inclusive Education (CSIE, undated) has set out ten reasons for inclusion. It is not possible to go into each of these in detail here. In any case I shall wish to disagree with some of them later on. But essentially they boil down to a threefold proposition: 'Inclusive education is a human right, it's good education and it makes good social sense.'

A human right?

The human rights and social arguments are closely aligned. 'There are no legitimate reasons to separate children for their education', it is said. 'All children have the right to learn together.'

But why? It is not self-evident that it is wrong to provide a separate regime for children with particular difficulties so that attention can be focused appropriately and as required. Two reasons are given for denying them such a regime:

1   Children should not be devalued or discriminated against by being excluded or sent away because of their disability; and
2   Children belong together – with advantages and benefits for everyone. All children need an education that will help them develop relationships and prepare them for life in the mainstream. Segregation teaches children to be fearful, ignorant and breeds prejudice. Only inclusion has the potential to reduce fear and to build friendship, respect and understanding.

In other words, separate special education is seen as devaluing and discriminatory, and inclusion promotes the mutually accepting social relationships which are so important for full participation in society.

If we get rid of emotionally loaded expressions like 'excluded' and 'sent away', is it necessarily discriminatory to make special arrangements for some, except in a purely neutral or technical sense? Some might hold that it is more like positive discrimination. So it begins to seem as if the social component of the argument is the more important.

The National Federation of the Blind and the Association of Blind and Partially Sighted Teachers and Students prefigured essentially the same arguments in the 1980s and the early 1990s:

> It is generally agreed that handicapped people should take their place as fully integrated members of the unhandicapped community if at all possible. Quite apart from its inherent value, the education of handicapped children in intimate association with their unhandicapped peers is fundamental to the achievement of this end.
>
> (JEC report, 1981)

> Separate socialisation restricts the full development of disabled and non-disabled people alike, and the education system . . . can do much to remove

the barriers of ignorance, prejudice, intolerance and misunderstanding that ultimately lead to discrimination and a refusal to accept disabled people as full members of the community.

(Low, 1992)

Two specific advantages of integration, as inclusion was then called, are cited:

1   It teaches disabled children to grow up as members of a non-disabled world, and not a self-enclosed disabled world in the most practical way – by living in it. This is the world in which they will have to operate for the rest of their lives, so they might as well get used to it right from the start.
2   It fosters in the non-disabled an appreciation of disability as a wholly normal incident of natural and totally human variation instead of something alien to be at best uneasy about and at worst to reject.

It should be acknowledged straight away that differentiation, or treating people differently, can have a distinct downside and that inclusion can do much to help 'normalise' disability. The claims of inclusion should therefore be preferred unless they are outweighed by a need for targeted help from a specialised regime in a particular case. This is the basis of the right to inclusion I wholly accept. It is compatible, however, with the right to choose not to avail oneself of this right in favour of more specialised provision.

What kind of a right is the right to be included? There are three reasons for thinking that it is a qualified rather than an absolute one:

1   The JEC asserts that inclusion has an 'inherent value', but what is this? The closest the advocates of full inclusion come to substantiating it is when they speak of separate special education as being discriminatory. But as we have seen, the worst thing about this appears to be its undesirable social consequences – the fact that it leads to separate socialisation, which restricts disabled people's full development as human beings, and has other undesirable consequences in terms of people's attitudes, which in turn reinforce the spiral of discrimination. Thus it can be seen that the value of inclusion in combating discrimination is largely instrumental. This must mean that it is not absolute. If the right exists in virtue of its instrumental purpose and the purpose cannot be realised, there cannot be a right. There is some recognition of this when people speak of disabled people taking their place as fully integrated members of the community 'if at all possible'.
2   The right to inclusion is not the same as other human rights like the right to life or the right to be free from torture. These are about ends, or at least more about ends than the right to inclusion, which is more about means to valued ends. There can be a right to education, but a right as to where it takes place is much more doubtful.
3   The right to inclusion cannot be absolute when, as is the case, some people want it and some do not.

It is important to remember that it is a right we are talking of, which people are free to avail themselves of or not as they see fit, and not a duty, which is what the advocates of full inclusion might be thought to be creating when they argue for a system from which 'the possibility of choosing segregation should be entirely removed'. I shall say something about the relationship between choice and provision in a later section of this chapter. For now it is simply necessary to observe that, while those in favour of moderate inclusion tend to see a role for parental choice in decisions about the placement of children with special educational needs, those in favour of full inclusion do not. Even so, it is probably true to say that the latter envisage a situation in which the mainstream education system is made so attractive that parents of children with special needs will spontaneously wish to choose it. Only the most hard line are likely to favour compulsion. But the possibility of choice could be designed out. That is the direction in which CSIE would seem to be pointing. However, to the extent that it is not, there must remain scope for people to waive their right to inclusion and for the right thus to be a qualified one.

If the right to inclusion is a qualified right, how then should we characterise it? Since 1975 I have consistently argued for

> a presumption in favour of integration based on handicapped people's common humanity with unhandicapped people and their membership of the same communities. On this basis integration should be defended as a value to be pursued unless there are very good reasons to the contrary, and not just if all other things are equal or it can demonstrate a clear balance of advantage.
>
> (Low, 1975)

In the 1990s I wrote that 'the principle of integration rests essentially on the belief, succinctly distilled by the Warnock Committee, in the sentiment that, so far as is humanly possible, handicapped people should enjoy the opportunities for self-fulfilment enjoyed by other people'. The qualification 'so far as is humanly possible' is important. Some people have been won over to the principle of integration, but still hold it in a rather watered-down form: integration is all right if all other things are equal. We should try to do better than that and hold on to 'so far as is humanly possible' (Low, 1992, 1995), meaning that every effort should be made to meet the needs of all children in the mainstream without removing other options in case we should fail. This is a strong and precisely delineated statement of the moderate inclusion position, and it is the position I still hold today.

Good education

Three points can be distinguished here:

(1) Many commentators have referred to the low expectations fostered by special schools and to their consequent unstimulating character, and CSIE maintains that 'research shows children do better academically and socially in inclusive settings' (CSIE, undated). Furthermore, Disability Equality in Education (2005),

citing Department for Education and Skills (2004), claims that research has shown that effective inclusion improves achievement for all pupils/students.

If we acquit Disability Equality in Education of the charge of tautologous thinking, evident elsewhere, and accept that effective inclusion and improving achievement for all pupils/students are not the same thing, there are still good reasons for treating bald assertions such as these with caution. For a start the 2004 DfES research report found no correlation between pupil achievement and inclusion, though there was some evidence in relation to socialisation. It is true that this could have more to do with the validity of national tests than with inclusive practice, but it still does not justify the claim which is made. More generally, the considerable body of research which now exists on inclusion hardly justifies such sweeping conclusions. Not only do the findings differ from one study to another, but particular studies, like the DfES report indeed, can point to different conclusions, depending on which aspect of inclusion they are looking at.

(2) CSIE maintains that, 'Given commitment and support, inclusive education is a more efficient use of educational resources' (CSIE, undated). This is questionable. They are probably referring to the inefficiency involved in the duplication of mainstream and specialist systems, particularly in the duplication of subject teaching.

> Economically, it is far more efficient to target resources towards a single inclusive education system from the outset than to develop a dual system of separate education for disabled and non-disabled persons and then have to work towards bringing about inclusive education.
>
> (CSIE, 2004)

But against this can be urged the greater efficiency inherent in the better targeting of specialist resources towards pupils with special needs, made possible by the existence of at least some special schools. Such resources are inevitably much more dispersed and thinly spread throughout a wholly mainstream system. The case for inclusion probably rests much more securely on its social value than considerations of economic efficiency.

(3) CSIE also asserts: 'There is no teaching or care in a segregated school which cannot take place in an ordinary school' (CSIE, undated). That may be so, but the existence of individual examples of inclusion is not the same thing as the generality of schools being geared up to cater for the full range of disabilities. This raises the question of the kind of inclusion being sought. As against the mixed economy advocated by the proponents of moderate inclusion, those in favour of full inclusion aspire to the ideal of a 'restructured and appropriately resourced and supported mainstream education system that aims to meet the needs of the full diversity of children in their local areas' (CSIE, 2004). In other words, their ideal is 'a single, inclusive system of education which is adaptable to the best interests of each and every child' and from which 'the possibility of choosing segregation should be entirely removed'. The system of education being referred to here is probably the education system of the country as a whole. The philosophy of full

inclusion is more defensible in relation to the education system as a whole (the macro education system) than it is in relation to the individual school (the micro education system) but, as we shall see, that does not prevent its being advocated in relation to the individual school as well.

These two positions will presently be examined in turn. For now I simply wish to observe that the full inclusion perspective also has a strongly generic thrust. This is the reason why CSIE and others have opposed the efforts of organisations representing blind, deaf and deaf/blind children at the United Nations to retain the option of specialist provision for children with those disabilities. 'Giving persons with certain disabilities a right to receive education in their own "groups" . . . would undermine the right to inclusive education' (CSIE, 2004). In order to do this, they have had to subordinate value of self-determination to the value of inclusion.

Total inclusion at the level of the school – the micro education system – and models of disability

The advocates of full inclusion adopt a radical critique of traditional 'individualised' or 'deficit' models of special education, which see the individual child as the proper focus of remedial efforts. They see the problem rather as one of classroom organisation and teaching being sufficiently specialised and differentiated to meet the needs of all children with disabilities, no matter how profound, multiple or complex. Even more radically, they may see the problem as residing in the school as a whole – in its culture, structure and organisation – or in the content of the curriculum and how it is taught, which they see as dysfunctional for all children, not just those with special needs. They focus attention on improving the learning experience for all children in such a way that those traditionally conceived of as having special needs will be benefited. The benefits will be indirect rather than direct, and involve whole-school approaches, or what the criminologist Nigel Walker (1969) called 'unfocused' measures when talking of crime reduction. In the field of criminology, an 'unfocused' measure might be the more human design of housing estates, as opposed to the 'focused' measure of punishing offenders (Ainscow, 1993). This 'unfocused' approach is evident in the following statement by Disability Equality in Education: 'At present, statements remain as a safeguard for parents and pupils until all schools have the expertise, with the backing of the LEA, to restructure teaching and learning to meet the needs of all pupils/students' (Disability Equality in Education, 2005).

This imports into the educational arena the perspectives of those who espouse the 'social' as distinct from the 'medical' model of disability. In this regard, Disability Equality in Education (2005) says:

> We believe that the problem is not in the child and their impairment, but in the social and attitudinal barriers in the education system. This 'social model' draws on the thinking of disabled people and underpins all inclusive education.

Now, thinking based on an outdated 'medical model' is being used to argue for the establishment of many new special schools.

But, if anything, full-blown social models are even less plausible in the educational arena than elsewhere. If education is about anything, it is about influencing and indeed changing the individual child. One may do this by modifying the social environments in which the child is placed, but one cannot eliminate the individual dimension altogether. We shall certainly see this when we come to talk of visual impairment. One might argue for the salience of the social dimension when considering the response to be made to children with, say, physical, emotional and behavioural difficulties, but the child with sensory or learning difficulties has specific impairments that need to be addressed individually.

Doubt has been cast on the viability of the social model perspective in relation to special education on the ground that it is both utopian and elitist (Low, 1997):

> Can one seriously imagine society undertaking all the transformations that would be required to accommodate all the special needs of all those groups which have them? Might these not come into conflict from time to time? . . . Is this not an unattainable ideal? Does the notion of 'special needs' have any meaning left at this point? . . . It is hardly to be expected that anyone's special needs will be adequately addressed by non-specialists charged with the task of meeting everyone's special needs simultaneously. . . . Disabled people do have certain needs which it is right to think of as special. A system which attempts to meet everyone's needs together meets nobody's. Indeed the notion of special needs and fully inclusive provision is a contradiction in terms.

In other words, the prospect of the general education system being geared up in terms of staff, expertise and facilities to cater for every kind of disability as an integral part of its provision is something of a utopian ideal. However, when faced with examples of children failing in the mainstream and having to be rescued by special schools, the proponents of full inclusion are apt to turn this to their advantage and insist that the experience of mainstream was not an example of genuine inclusion at all. As Disability Equality in Education (2005) says: 'Baroness Warnock is talking about the problems of poor integration. This is not inclusion, which means changing the school so all children can flourish.' Of course it may not be good inclusion. Inclusion may fail because it is inadequately resourced or badly implemented, and the instinct of inclusionists to call for the mainstream system to be improved, rather than for more special schools to be opened, may be a legitimate one up to a point. But we should not be fooled into thinking that examples of poor inclusion are not examples of inclusion at all. The argument that any case of failed inclusion is not a case of true inclusion fatally fails Popper's falsifiability test and puts inclusion beyond empirical evaluation, because it assumes its own conclusion and thus becomes true by definition. If the only kind of inclusion is successful inclusion, it becomes impossible to point to any instances where inclusion does not succeed. This flies in the face of common sense.

As for elitism, many disabled people are obviously able to cope in a mainstream environment, but others are clearly not. The feasibility of full inclusion is usually urged by those in the first category or those with no disability at all. It does not seem right to sacrifice the interests of those who need a more supportive environment to the prescriptions of those who can do without one. In the same vein, CSIE (undated) claims that disabled people who describe themselves as 'special school survivors' are demanding an end to segregation. In my experience, some are and some are not.

Total inclusion at the level of the school – the macro education system – planning and choice

As I have said, the full inclusionist's ideal of a restructured and appropriately resourced and supported mainstream education system that aims to meet the needs of the full diversity of children in their local areas is more credible at the level of the education system as a whole, the macro education system, than it is at the level of the individual school, the micro education system. But we should be clear exactly what is being contended here. As will be recalled, the organisation Disability Equality in Education harbours the vision of all schools being restructured to meet the needs of all pupils and students. A modified version of this vision would see the mainstream system as a whole planned so that it catered for the full range of needs, but there might be some specialisation between schools, regarding the needs that are catered for. One imagines this would be second best for the most radical inclusionists, whose vision is of the inclusive school catering for the full diversity of children in a microcosm of the good society.

The vision of the moderate inclusionist differs in that it envisages the system as a whole incorporating an element of special school provision. On what basis should this be available? The usual answer is that it should be available to be accessed by the exercise of parental choice. Against this there are those who say that the crucial question is what is the most appropriate provision, mainstream or special, and that parental choice may not always be the best or the only guide to this. Their vision is of a continuum of provision, planned and resourced to match the diversity of need with diversity of provision. But how is this matching to be achieved? Presumably it involves weighing the values of inclusion and the most effective education of the individual child against one another. But who is to operate this beneficial calculus?

There are two levels at which this question needs to be considered – the level of the system as a whole and the level of the individual placement. At the level of the system as a whole, the moderate inclusionist will want to see mainstream schools resourced and progressively developed to provide inclusive provision for the maximum number of those with special needs who can benefit from it, and specialist provision optimally located for those who need to take advantage of it. This makes sense as a principle on which to base a rational public policy. But it may need to yield some ground to more adventitious considerations at the level of the individual placement decision. For a start, even those applying the 'appropriate provision' test may be forced to opt pragmatically, at least in the short term, for special provision, in preference to mainstream, in the face of the patchy nature and quality of existing mainstream provision. More generally, a continuum implies a measure of choice at the level of the individual placement. The continuum is not so neatly arranged into appropriate and inappropriate provision matched to need as to make placement decisions automatic and uncontentious. That is too schematic an approach. Things are messier than that in practice and individual placement decisions are a matter of negotiation as to what is appropriate and inappropriate between resource-constrained professionals and parents wanting the best for their child. That enables, or perhaps requires, parents to exercise a measure of parental choice. The patchy nature of inclusive mainstream provision and the comparative absence of planning may also suggest the retention of a number of special schools that might have disappeared in the moderate inclusionist's perfectly planned system which favoured the proper resourcing of mainstream schools.

In the remainder of this chapter I shall illustrate the foregoing argument by reference to the moderate inclusionist position set out by RNIB, with respect to the education of children with a visual impairment, in its evidence to the Education and Skills Select Committee's recent inquiry into special educational needs.

RNIB's policy position on the education of blind and partially sighted pupils

RNIB believes that every pupil with a visual impairment is entitled to high-quality education with equal access to appropriate specialist provision no matter where he/she lives within the UK. This requires a range of specialist resources and support arrangements which match the range and distribution of educational needs among the whole population of visually impaired children, including those with additional needs and/or disabilities. For most visually impaired children the appropriate placement is a mainstream school with specialist support. The provision must be of sufficient standard to enable the visually impaired child to access the full range of educational opportunities available to fully sighted children, as well as providing for the particular needs arising from the visual impairment. While well resourced and properly supported mainstream placements should be the usual form of provision, a special school placement continues to be the most effective way of meeting need for some children, in particular those who have severe and complex disabilities in addition to visual impairment. Wherever children are being educated, it is essential that schools as well as support services take full responsibility for ensuring that the child's needs relating to visual impairment are properly addressed. Inclusion is as much about the ethos and social life of schools as it is about access to the taught curriculum. It is essential, therefore, to provide the range of educational and social opportunities that enable children to participate on an equal basis with their peers in order to become fully included members of the community.

Fundamental to achieving these objectives is the full involvement of parents and children in decisions about their educational provision.

Provision for blind and partially sighted pupils in mainstream schools

As previously stated, children with a visual impairment have specific difficulties that require specialised help and specific kinds of assistance, such as instruction in Braille and mobility skills, the provision of materials in accessible formats and a high degree of specialist teaching support. They are not best served by a generic approach to meeting the needs of pupils with special educational needs. Even in special schools, blind and partially sighted children may not receive adequate specialist support to meet their visual impairment needs. Of more immediate importance, RNIB has significant concerns about provision for pupils with a visual impairment in mainstream schools, which ought to give one pause about the early implementation of a policy of full inclusion. A major concern is the huge variation across the country in educational provision for blind and partially sighted pupils. There is variation between local education authorities in terms of type of educational placement available, and standards of educational support provided.

A particular risk for low-incidence disabilities such as visual impairment is that the drive towards greater delegation of SEN funds from central LEA control will lead to fragmentation of central visual impairment services, with consequent loss of expertise and specialist advice and support for schools, and capacity for strategic planning and monitoring of provision. Despite the publication of the national *Quality Standards for Education Support Services for Children and Young People with Visual Impairment* (DfES, 2002), there is no consistent standard of specialist support across LEAs, which suggests that the standards are not being implemented. Some support services are well organised, have a sufficient number of additionally qualified staff with an appropriate range of skills to meet the needs of all the pupils, and are committed to meeting the quality standards. However, there are also services that, for a variety of reasons, are failing to meet the quality standards and, as these are not mandatory, there is no pressure on local authorities to improve their provision for blind and partially sighted pupils if they do not wish to. Despite the Special Educational Needs and Disability Act (2001), which makes discrimination on the basis of disability illegal in education, RNIB continues to hear of schools that are unwelcoming towards blind and partially sighted pupils. Rather than taking ownership of these pupils, such schools regard them as the responsibility of the specialist support services. While many LEAs are committed to promoting inclusive practice in all their mainstream schools, in others this does not appear to be a priority. A well-staffed and flexible central support service is essential for supporting schools that are new to meeting the needs of blind and partially sighted pupils, thereby enhancing their capacity to become truly inclusive for such pupils.

Many pupils with a visual impairment are supported by teaching assistants who have received little or no training, in either the general or specialist aspects of their role. The teaching of Braille is suffering, and there is research evidence that blind and partially sighted pupils often do not receive written materials in accessible formats at the same time as their sighted peers. Indeed, even in core curriculum areas at GCSE level, textbooks are frequently unavailable in a form in which pupils can use them. The most frequent outcome is that adult support becomes necessary to compensate for the lack of accessible materials, thus lessening the pupil's opportunities to acquire the skills of independent learning and creating a barrier to interaction with peers.

Across the country provision of mobility education is extremely patchy, with no one agency taking responsibility for providing or funding it. The result is that many pupils are denied their full entitlement to mobility education, and, for many of those who do receive it, it is provided by mobility officers whose own training was in rehabilitation for adults rather than mobility for children.

Conclusion

This chapter has argued for a strong presumption in favour of inclusion. The education system as a whole should be planned and developed to provide inclusive provision for the maximum number of those with special needs who can benefit from it. This is a principle that it is harder to implement at the level of the individual school. However, like any rational public policy, it cannot afford to be pursued blindly, irrespective of circumstances and evidence pointing in a different direction. This may have to do with the needs of individual children and the state of the mainstream education system. Generic and 'social model' approaches are unlikely to be sufficiently sensitive to the specific needs of individual children with particular disabilities. At the level of the individual placement decision, account must be taken of the fact that special school placement may be the most effective way of meeting the needs of a particular child, especially if he has severe and complex disabilities, and especially while the mainstream continues to exhibit so many deficiencies. This means that at the level of the education system as a whole, sufficient specialist provision needs to be available for those who need it. The system must cater for the diversity of need by providing a diversity of provision, and individual placement decisions must be determined on the facts of each individual case. Monolithic prescriptions will not do, and nor will mechanical or ideological rules of thumb. It would therefore seem sensible to confirm the post-Warnock settlement based on a mixed economy of provision, at least until the transformation of the mainstream education system for meeting special educational needs is complete or there is a radical change in the needs themselves.

Acknowledgements

I am indebted to the following colleagues at RNIB whose work has contributed significantly to the preparation of this chapter: Elizabeth Clery and Sue Keil for material on visual impairment; Olga Miller for the evaluation of research evidence; and Eamonn Fetton and Terry Moody whose critical comments helped me to refine considerably the ideas contained in the chapter. However, I alone bear responsibility for the ideas as they have finally emerged.

References

Ainscow, Mel (1993), *Towards Effective Schools for All: Policy Options for Special Educational Needs in the 1990s*, London: David Fulton

Centre for Studies on Inclusive Education (2004), *Article 17 and Inclusive Education in the New UN Disability Convention*, Bristol: CSIE

Centre for Studies on Inclusive Education (undated), *Ten Reasons for Inclusion*, http://inclusion.uwe.ac.uk/csie/10rsns.htm

Department for Education and Skills (2002), *Quality Standards for Education Support Services for Children and Young People with Visual Impairment*, Nottinghamshire: Department for Education and Skills, LEA/0138/2002

Department for Education and Skills (2004), *Inclusion and Pupil Achievement*, Research Report RR578, http://www.dfes.gov.uk

Disability Equality in Education (2005), 'In Defence of Inclusion: Warnock Challenges the Rights of Disabled Children to Inclusion', *Times Educational Supplement* (8 July 2005)

Low, C. (1975), 'Some Principles of Integration', memorandum to the Working Party on the Integration of the Disabled under the chairmanship of the Rt. Hon. Earl of Snowdon, personal communication

Low, C. (1992), 'Resourcing the Education Service to Meet the Needs of Students with Disabilities', presentation to Special Educational Needs Joint Initiative for Training (SENJIT) governor training course, 18 March 1992

Low, C. (1995), 'Sense and Nonsense Relocated', in Micheline Mason (1995), *Provision for Special Educational Needs from the Perspectives of Service Users: Policy Options for Special Educational Needs in the 1990s*, London: NASEN, 9–14

Low, C. (1997), 'Is Inclusivism Possible?', *European Journal of Special Needs Education*, vol. 12 (1), 71–9

National Federation of the Blind of the UK, Association of Blind and Partially Sighted Teachers and Students (1981), 'Joint Education Committee Report on the Development of Integrated Education for the Visually Handicapped in the Inner London Area', private collection

Walker, N. (1969), *Sentencing in a Rational Society*, London: Allen Lane, Chapter 4

2 Rights, efficacy and inclusive education

Geoff Lindsay

In this chapter I shall consider the need for participants in the inclusive education debate to address both children's rights and issues of efficacy. I shall argue that it is not sufficient to develop inclusion based on a rights perspective independent of empirical evidence. The term 'inclusion' is of course open to different interpretations, but in this chapter I shall address the view held by many that a properly inclusive education system would see all children educated in the same schools. This is sometimes known as the full inclusion model or radical position, and I shall be arguing that it neglects the important dimension of efficacy.

Rights

The Salamanca Statement (UNESCO, 1994) was proclaimed by delegates representing 92 governments and 25 international organisations in June 1994 for the World Conference on Special Needs Education. Paragraph 2 is the key statement of belief and comprises five clauses. The first argues that every child has a fundamental right to education; the second asserts each child's uniqueness; and the third argues that the education system be designed to take into account the diversity of children's characteristics and needs.

The fourth clause develops the third, and states that children with SEN must have access to regular schools which should accommodate them within a child-centred pedagogy capable of meeting their needs. Finally, clause five provides a rationale for regular schools:

> Regular schools with this inclusive orientation are the most effective measures of combating discriminatory attitudes, creating welcoming communities, building an inclusive society and achieving education for all; moreover, they provide an effective education to the majority of children and improve the efficiency and ultimately the cost-effectiveness of the entire education system.

The Salamanca Statement, therefore, contains an explicit statement concerning children's rights to education and level of learning, and goes on to argue that regular schools are the most effective form of school organisation, at least for the 'majority of children'.

The designation of each child as having *unique* characteristics, while true in a sense, is also a rather vacuous statement. By definition individual children, by virtue of being individual, cannot have all their characteristics in common. This statement also ignores the large degree to which salient factors are shared (cf. Norwich, 1996). The requirement for 'regular' schools is not uncontentious. First, 'regular' may refer to an absolute definition (not provided in the statement) or be interpreted relative to the system in place in any country. But consider size; nature of amenities; secular or religious; levels of achievement, etc. Does regular mean 'non-special'? If so, consider special schools that partner mainstream schools; and those with designated special provision which range from segregated units to highly inclusive class-based provision (e.g. Lindsay *et al.*, 2002). Second, this rationale is a statement of asserted empirical fact: regular schools *are* the most effective. Is this the case? If not, then the argument in favour of 'regular' schools is brought into question. Third, if they are effective only for the majority, what are the implications for the minority?

Hence the Salamanca Statement is based on an assertion of children's rights, moral imperatives for action that do not directly relate to the rights proclaimed, and empirical assertion. Also implicit is a tension between application of the proposed system for all children, and recognition that it may not be effective for all.

Within the UK the development of policy towards inclusion is not a recent phenomenon (cf. the Wood Committee of 1928). The 1945 Regulations recognised that the majority of children requiring 'special educational treatment' would be in mainstream schools. The Warnock report (Department of Education and Science, 1978) argued for integration based on evidence accumulated from progressive practice during the 1970s. For example, a number of educational psychologists (e.g. the Sheffield Psychological Service) challenged the system of special school placements (Loxley, 1978). As a result almost no child was referred to what were then called ESN (M) schools (for the 'educationally subnormal') for almost a year. Other psychological services were also adopting different approaches to support children and schools, as part of the 'reconstructing educational psychology' movement (Gillham, 1978).

These initiatives were driven by one question: were the rights and educational opportunities of children with SEN being promoted or harmed by special schools? This concern was fuelled by evidence, unsystematic and anecdotal as much of that was, that children leaving special schools were not in an advantageous position. Also, the Warnock report noted that only 22 per cent of teachers in special schools had special qualifications for the job (DES, 1978, para 12.24). A third concern at that time was the numbers of children from the Caribbean who had been inappropriately placed in ESN (M) schools, a finding confirmed by a systematic study of Sheffield ESN (M) schools. These initiatives in the 1970s and 1980s accelerated the development of inclusion.

The Labour government has accelerated the policy of inclusion through various initiatives (cf. Department for Education and Skills, 2001). A child who has SEN and a statement *must* be educated in a mainstream school unless this would be incompatible with (a) the wishes of the parents or (b) the provision of efficient education of other children. However, a third caveat which has, since Warnock, referred to the protection of the interests of the child concerned, has been removed, the implication being that this is no longer an issue. Hence the promotion of inclusion is more advanced, although some might argue that this development of a policy of inclusion is still insufficiently strong.

However, others argue that social justice and the right to inclusion are not so straightforward and that social justice, for example, is not a unitary or universally shared concept (Christenson and Dorn, 1997). Furthermore, differing views on social justice may underlie the apparent contradictions in implementation of policies. The development of communitarian principles may promote common values, with negative impact on people with disabilities. However, a common argument compares battles to promote inclusion to those challenging racist discrimination and segregation policies.

This approach is often referred to as the 'social model' (compared with the 'medical model'), and has been in the ascendancy. It was a necessary development from the worst aspects of previous practice which was condition-related, categorical and deterministic to a very large degree. However, there is a need to analyse these models more critically. The so-called medical model in fact has at least two quite different elements. The first concerns the medical profession rather than educationists effectively running the system, as the key decision-makers of need and of necessary intervention and provision. Medical practitioners are seen by some as promoting mystification relative to their role as 'the expert', especially when the rights of parents are very limited and they are less likely to challenge the opinions and decisions of these professionals. The second element is the focus on 'within-child' factors, stressing the impairment and underplaying, even ignoring, the impact of environmental factors.

However, the social model has been superseded. Wedell (1978) proposed the concept of compensatory interaction to represent these two major influences of within-child and environmental factors, later supplemented by a third dimension of time (Lindsay, 1995). Children's functioning, and hence their needs, are conceptualised as an interaction between their inherent characteristics and the supports, and barriers, of the environment; these elements and their interaction may change over time. The difficulty with the social model is that it plays down or actively ignores both the within-child factors and the issue of interaction. In its 'hardest' form it is proposed that the only salient factor to consider is the external world which disables the individual. As Low (2001) argued, drawing on a statement by Oliver that disability is wholly and exclusively social: 'In a kind of reductionism, "not *only* the individual" has become mistranslated as "only social", and "the individual is not everything" has become "the social in everything".' Low's critical review of the social model carefully and persuasively indicates its logical and practical inadequacies, while stressing the importance of recognising the social dimension.

Others have also offered critical perspectives on arguments based on rights, including Mithaug (1998), who argues that: 'By now it should be apparent that the inclusive society as conceived by policymakers of the 1960s and 1970s is not going to happen. There have been too many policy failures and unexpected negative consequences in the last decade' (p. 5). The reason for these failures is that inclusion is only one of several competing values which might be embraced. Mithaug identifies freedom and equality as others. Further, there is an important distinction between negative freedom, or freedom *from* (obstacles, interference, coercion, etc.), and positive freedom, or freedom *to* (determine the kind of life one wants to live, etc.) Regarding the first, we might say that all children are equal; no child should be forced, for example, to accept an education that she (or her parents) deems seriously unsuitable. Regarding the second, it might be said that children are 'unequal', that is, some children need greater protection and support than others if they are to exercise their positive freedom.

These different conceptualisations of disability, rights and required action lead to different policies, which must in turn interact with the policies for general education. Hence the post-1988 emphasis on standards, increasing freedom of choice and diversity (Lindsay, 2003a) set a backdrop for the development of SEN policy. It is clear that these same concerns are central to government thinking on SEN. However, what is less clear is the relationship between these factors and evidence.

Research evidence

Researching 'inclusion' is problematic. The primary difficulty is that it is not a simple, unambiguous concept and so operationalising inclusion as a variable is a necessary step in the research process. Evaluation of inclusion becomes increasingly difficult as complexity increases. There have been a number of studies which have reviewed the evaluation of inclusion – see Lindsay (2003b) for a summary. Overall, these overviews and meta-analyses fail to provide clear evidence for the benefit of inclusion. For example, the review of meta-analyses by Baker *et al.* (1994) evaluated the effectiveness of inclusive education in a number of studies using the effect size statistic. This allows comparisons of two types of intervention even if each uses a different set of measures (e.g. different reading tests). A positive effect size indicates that the intervention under consideration (inclusion in this case) shows a greater effect (improvement in academic attainment, for example) than another intervention or control (non-inclusive education in this case). Following Cohen (1988), an effect size of 0.2 is described as small, one of 0.5 as medium, and one of 0.8 as large. Across the three meta-analyses and two types of outcome, academic and social, Baker *et al.* found positive but small effect sizes for inclusive education, although in one analysis the effect size for academic achievement at 0.44 could be described as medium (see Table 2.1). At best, the support for inclusion is weak. It is not at the level implied in the Salamanca Statement.

However, given that the policy development for more than 75 years has been towards increasing inclusion, we might ask whether evaluating inclusion is appropriate at all. A more profitable route may be that of examining the effectiveness of

Table 2.1 Effects of inclusive placements: three meta-analytic studies

	Carlberg and Kavale	Wang and Baker	Baker
Year published	1980	1985–6	1994
Time period	Pre-1980	1975–84	1983–92
No. of studies	50	11	13
Academic effect size	0.15	0.44	0.08
Social effect size	0.11	0.11	0.28

(from Baker, Wang and Walberg, 1994)

particular aspects of inclusion. I shall discuss a small number of studies in order to give a flavour of this approach.

Mills *et al.* (1998) report the differential effectiveness of three approaches with varying degrees of inclusion: special school, integrated resource and mainstream. They found evidence of the greatest benefit to the children's development was provided by an 'integrated' resource rather than special school or mainstream, so challenging the full inclusion model. The integrated resource allowed the benefits of mainstream together with specialist expertise available on site. A similar finding is provided by Marston (1996), who also compared three models: inclusion only, 'pull-out' only, and a combined service for children with mild disabilities, reporting significantly higher increases in reading for the combined service over the two alternative approaches. Vaughn and Klingner (1998) found that, generally, students preferred to receive assistance in a resource room rather than in the regular class: they reported being better able to concentrate and learn, though they also cited social benefits of the general education setting. Investigation of individual schools as case studies has also produced important evidence. As an example, the study of six schools by Dyson and Millward (2000) provides a rich description and analysis of inclusion, revealing the variety, tensions and conflicts to which I have previously alluded. However, no data on child outcomes are presented.

What these studies provide is evidence of a number of different elements relevant to inclusion. They are essentially concerned with implementation and so help us with questions of *how* rather than *why*. Frederickson and Cline (2001) have summarised the evidence from a number of studies which they consider indicative of factors relevant to successful inclusion. These include, perhaps not unexpectedly, the quality of the programme, which of course needs to be operationalised, and the extent to which the general education system accommodates the academic and social needs of a diverse range of young people with disabilities and SEN. However, there is a danger of policy-makers and practitioners copying early school effectiveness work, where research findings of *correlations* between factors were interpreted as if school effectiveness were *caused by* factors such as strong leadership, attractive environments and displays, etc. In fact the relationships are more complex with some factors needing to operate in tandem. For example, a strong leader may be a necessary but not sufficient requirement: even the most effective heads have limited room for action if they do not have competent staff.

Further evidence is provided by the Lipsky and Gartner (1998) report on the National Study of Inclusive Education which reviewed about 1000 school districts and identified seven factors as playing a role in successful inclusion:

- visionary leadership
- collaboration
- refocused use of assessment
- support for staff and students
- funding
- effective parental involvement
- use of effective programme models and classroom practices.

Inspection of this list reinforces my earlier caution. These are general factors which require further, detailed explanation. For example, collaboration is relevant at levels from national policy down to classroom practice (Law *et al.*, 2000). Support includes teaching assistants, for which there is an accumulating evidence base (Riggs and Mueller, 2001), and non-educational support, for example speech and language therapists. However, the means by which these different professionals collaborate varies, and the increasingly popular approach of consultation is not unproblematic in terms of its implementation (Law *et al.*, 2002; Lindsay *et al.*, 2005).

Conclusions

Inclusion is now a central plank of educational policy, and hence discussion of 'whether' to promote inclusion is less useful than the interpretation and implementation of inclusion in practice. I have argued that a simple focus on rights is unjustified. While it has proven politically useful in the past, we must now examine the evidence; it is not enough to assert that inclusion is always best. We need to ensure that there is a dual approach focusing on both the rights of children and the effectiveness of their education; to develop beyond concerns about inputs and settings and focus also on experiences and outcomes, attempting to identify causal relationships. We need research to inform policy and practice, but it must be research which is rigorous. In addition to descriptive case studies of examples of 'good practice', useful though these can be, we need careful analysis that examines the question of whether 'good' practice is an appropriate descriptor. In methodological terms, we also need more highly developed, substantial studies using quasi-experimental approaches to examine the strengths and relative impacts of a range of factors, together with qualitative examination of the experiences of key participants. This is not a question of rights versus efficacy. Rather, rigorous, substantial research projects demonstrating effectiveness will show whether our concern with children's rights goes beyond abstraction or ideology into the sphere of their daily lives. We need not only to have their rights in mind, but to enquire whether, and to what extent, we are meeting them effectively in practice.

References

Baker, E. T., M. C. Wang and Walberg, H. J. (1994), 'The effects of inclusion on learning', *Educational Leadership*, 52(4), 33–5

Christenson, C. A. and S. Dorn (1997), 'Competing notions of social justice in special education reform', *Journal of Special Education*, 31(2), 181–98

Cohen, J. (1988), *Statistical Power Analysis for the Behavioural Sciences* (2nd edn), Mahwah, NJ: Erlbaum

Department for Education and Skills (2001), *Inclusive Schooling: Children with Special Educational Needs*, Nottingham: DfES

Department of Education and Science (1978), *Special Educational Needs (The Warnock Report)*, London: HMSO

Dyson, A. and A. Millward (2000), *Schools and Special Needs*, London: Paul Chapman

Frederickson, N. and T. Cline (2001), *Special Educational Needs, Inclusion and Diversity*, Buckingham: Open University Press

Gillham, W. (1978), *Reconstructing Educational Psychology*, London: Croom Helm

Law, J., G. Lindsay, N. Peacey, M. Gascoigne, N. Soloff, J. Radford, and S. Band, with L. Fitzgerald (2000), *Provision for Children with Speech and Language Needs in England and Wales: Facilitating Communication between Education and Health Services*, London: DfEE

Law, J., G. Lindsay, N. Peacey, M. Gascoigne, N. Soloff, J. Radford, and S. Band (2002), 'Consultation as a model for providing speech and language therapy in schools: a panacea or one step too far?' *Child Language Teaching and Therapy*, 18(2), 145–63

Lindsay, G. (1995), 'Early identification of special educational needs', in I. Lunt., B. Norwich and V. Varma (eds), *Psychology and Education for Special Needs: Recent Developments and Future Directions*, London: Arena, Ashgate Publishing

Lindsay, G. (2003a), 'Implementing the revised Code of Practice: ethics and values', in D. Galloway (ed.), *Children with Special Educational Needs: A Response to the New Code of Practice*, Occasional Papers of the Association for Child Psychology and Psychiatry, 20, 47–55

Lindsay, G. (2003b), 'Inclusive education: a critical perspective', *British Journal of Special Education*, 30, 3–12

Lindsay, G., J. E. Dockrell, C. Mackie, and C. Letchford (2005), 'Specialist provision for children with specific speech and language difficulties', *Journal of Research in Special Educational Needs*, 5(3), 88–96

Lipsky, D. K. and A. Gartner (1998), 'Factors for successful inclusion: learning from the past, looking forward to the future', in S. J. Vitello and D. E. Mithaug (eds), *Inclusive Schooling: National and International Perspectives*, Mahwah, NJ: Erlbaum

Low, C. (2001), 'Have disability rights gone too far?' City Insights Lecture, 3 April 2001, London, City University (obtainable from the author)

Loxley, D. (1978), 'Community psychology', in W. Gillham (ed.), *Reconstructing Educational Psychology*, London: Croom Helm

Marston, D. (1996), 'A comparison of inclusion only, pull-out only and combined service models for students with mild disabilities', *Journal of Special Education*, 30(2), 121–32

Mills, P. E., K. N. Cole, J. R. Jenkins, and P. S. Dale (1998), 'Effects of differing levels of inclusion on preschoolers with disabilities', *Exceptional Children*, 65, 79–90

Mithaug, D. E. (1998), 'The alternative to ideological inclusion', in S. J. Vitello and D. E. Mithaug (eds), *Inclusive Schooling: National and International Perspectives*, Mahwah, NJ and London: Erlbaum

Norwich, B. (1996), 'Special needs education or education for all: connective specialisation and ideological impurity', *British Journal of Special Education*, 23(3), 100–4

Riggs, C. G. and P. H. Mueller (2001), 'Employment and utilization of para-educators in inclusive settings', *Journal of Special Education*, 35(1), 51–62

UNESCO (1994), *The UNESCO Salamanca Statement and Framework for Action on Special Needs Education*, Paris: UNESCO

Vaughn, S. and Klingner, J. K. (1998), 'Students' perceptions of inclusion and resource room settings', *Journal of Special Education*, 32(2), 79–88

Wedell, K. (1978), 'Early identification and compensatory interaction', paper presented at the NATO International Conference on Learning Disorders, Ottawa

3 Children with autistic spectrum disorders

Lorna Wing

In *Special Educational Needs: A New Look,* Mary Warnock (2005) describes and discusses with refreshing honesty and clarity the muddled policies concerning this issue and the unfortunate consequences for the children concerned. She points out the weaknesses in the idealised concept of inclusion in mainstream education for all children regardless of any disability they might have. She makes special reference to the problems and needs of children with disorders in the autistic spectrum.

Mary Warnock points out how important it is to recognise the many different patterns of disability that can lead to different kinds of special educational needs. As she notes, autistic disorders differ from other childhood conditions insofar as they involve a most unusual way of experiencing the social world and an unusual pattern of development. Because the underlying psychological impairments that characterise autistic disorders can be manifested in so many different ways, in different environments and at different ages, the educational needs of children with these conditions are probably the least well understood of all the types of disability. In this chapter I shall explore and develop Mary Warnock's idea that children with autistic spectrum disorders have quite distinctive needs that in many cases are difficult or impossible to meet in mainstream environments. In order to do this, I shall outline the evolution of ideas concerning the nature of autistic spectrum disorders, the complex pattern of skills and disabilities found in these conditions, and how these affect educational and social needs of the children concerned.

Evolution of the concept of the autistic spectrum

The child psychiatrist Leo Kanner was the first person to describe in young children a particular pattern of behaviour he called 'early infantile autism' (Kanner, 1943). He chose this name (from the Greek 'auto', meaning 'self') because he had observed how cut off from other people these children were from their infancy onwards. Together with his colleague Leon Eisenberg, he laid down strict criteria for diagnosing early infantile autism, emphasising above all the aloofness and indifference to others and elaborate repetitive routines (Kanner and Eisenberg, 1956). Typically the child intensely resists any attempt by others to change these routines, although the child him- or herself could choose to change them. Kanner thought this pattern of behaviour was rare and unique and separate from all other childhood conditions. Lotter (1966) carried out the first epidemiological study using Kanner and Eisenberg's criteria and found a prevalence of 4.5 per 10,000 children.

The year following Kanner's publication, a Viennese paediatrician, Hans Asperger, published his first paper on a group of children with a pattern of behaviour that had many similarities to Kanner's autism (Asperger, 1944; see English translation in Frith, 1991). Among other features, Asperger's group made social approaches but these were often inappropriate in form. They had good expressive language but used it to talk repetitively about their special interests, not for two-way conversations. Most, though not all, of the children seen had overall levels of IQ in the borderline, average, or high ranges but their profiles of skills were typically patchy.

In the 1970s my colleague Judith Gould and I carried out a study of a group of children who were living in the former London borough of Camberwell on 31 December 1970 and who were aged under 15 years on that date. Our aim was to identify children who had any of the features of behaviour that had been described as occurring in autism (Wing and Gould, 1979). All the children Lotter had identified in his study were known to have special needs and most had IQs under 70. At the time when we were carrying out our study the great majority of children with special needs were in special schools, so we confined our search to this population. We decided also to include in the study all children classified as severely learning disabled (IQ under 50), whether or not they had any of the features of autism. We used a brief screening interview with nearly 1,000 children in special schools and pre-school units for children with any kind of disability, physical or psychological. The total number of children we found with any aspect of autistic behaviour, plus those with IQs under 50 without any autistic behaviour, was 173.

We collected detailed accounts of the children's behaviour and developmental skills from their parents and their teachers or nursery nurses. From this data emerged the finding that there was a group who had, in one form or another, impairment of the ability to interact socially with other people. It was as if they lacked the social instinct that, as Darwin originally pointed out, is inbuilt from birth in humans and other mammals because it is essential for the survival of the species. Kanner (1943) wrote in his first paper, 'We must assume that the children have come into the world with innate inability to form the usual, biologically provided affective contact with people.' Sadly, he later moved away from this view of autism and instead blamed the parents' methods of child-rearing, though eventually he rejected this idea (see his collected papers, Kanner, 1973). In our study we found that, when this social impairment was present, social communications and social imagination were also impaired. The earliest outward indication of the development of imagination is pretend play, including role play. This is the precursor of the ability to imagine how another person might think and feel; the absence of this ability has been called 'mind blindness' (Frith, 2003). The social imagination problem also impairs the ability to think flexibly and to foresee the consequences of one's actions. We referred to these three impairments as the triad. This 'triad of impairments' was closely associated with a narrow, repetitive pattern of interests and activities.

Among the 173 children studied we found 74 who had this triad of impairments, although only 7 had previously been diagnosed as autistic. We were able to identify a few children who fitted Kanner and Eisenberg's strict criteria (1956) for early infantile autism. We also found another few who fitted all the details of Asperger's descriptions (Asperger, 1944). However, the great majority had mixtures of features from the two named groups plus a variety of other untypical behaviours. There was no neat dividing line between those who fitted Kanner's or Asperger's descriptions and the others who did not.

The study took three years to complete. Over that time our ideas gradually evolved. We began by believing that the children fitting Kanner's criteria would be clearly separated from all the rest. We ended by rejecting this view completely. Instead, we developed the concept of a spectrum of autistic disorders, comprising widely varied clinical pictures. The only thing that holds the group together is the presence of the triad of impairments.

Other previously held ideas also had to be changed. As mentioned above, Kanner had originally believed that his so-called syndrome was unique and separate from all other childhood disorders. We found that the triad of impairments could occur together with any other physical, developmental or psychiatric disorder. Kanner also considered that children with early infantile autism were all of potentially normal intelligence. We now know that the triad can be found in children and adults of any level of intelligence, from profound learning disability up to genius level. These enormous variations in the clinical picture can make recognition of the presence of an autistic spectrum disorder very difficult. To make matters worse there are as yet no physical or psychological tests that can be used to diagnose the presence of the triad of impairments. The diagnosis has to be made on the pattern of development of skills and behaviour from infancy onwards. Because of the absence of any physical signs, during the 1940s and 1950s, when psychodynamic theory was particularly influential, it was widely believed that autism was due to upbringing by cold, distant, intellectual parents. Research from the 1960s onwards has shown that autistic spectrum conditions are due to untypical patterns of brain development, in most cases dating from before birth (Wing, 1997). There is now strong evidence that complex genetic factors are important, although it is likely that various types of environmental events as yet to be identified, often operating prenatally, can influence the final clinical picture. As a result of the research work that has been done in this field, autistic spectrum disorders are now recognised as developmental disorders (Volkmar *et al.*, 2005; Frith, 2003).

Prevalence

Changes in ideas on the nature of autistic disorders have resulted in changes in estimates of prevalence. When more recent studies began to show higher and higher rates, well above Lotter's estimate of 4.5 in 10,000, there was talk of an 'autism epidemic'. All kinds of causes, including diet, atmospheric pollution, the stress of modern life, and the measles, mumps and rubella (MMR) vaccination were suggested. Careful study of all the factors involved has shown no evidence for any of these theories and indicates that the main reason is the widening of the criteria consequent upon the development of the idea of the autistic spectrum (Wing and Potter, 2002). The recognition that autistic disorders can occur together with any other condition and be associated with any level of ability has also contributed. The growth of interest in and services for people with autistic disorders has considerably increased the chance that a diagnosis will be made and not missed, as often happened in the past.

What is the prevalence of the whole autistic spectrum? Our brief screening schedule was based on the behaviour found in typical autism and missed the more subtle features. This was because we did not become aware of Asperger's group until we had finished the screening phase of the study. We therefore missed children with this pattern of behaviour when we screened schools for those with emotional and behaviour disorders, children with physical disabilities, schools for 'delicate' children. We also missed any who might have been in mainstream schools. We found that the prevalence among those with IQ under 70 was 4.9 per 10,000 for children who fitted Kanner and Eisenberg's criteria. This was very close to the rate found by Lotter. The prevalence of the whole autistic spectrum among those with IQ under 70 was 20 per 10,000. Ehlers and Gillberg (1993) carried out a very small but intensive study in Gothenburg, Sweden, of children aged from 13 to 17 years with IQ of 70 and above. They found a prevalence of 35 per 10,000 children fitting their criteria for Asperger syndrome and a further 35 per 10,000 who had social impairment but did not completely fit either Kanner's or Asperger's syndromes. If the rates found in Camberwell and Gothenburg are added, this gives a total prevalence of 90 per 10,000 children with autistic spectrum disorders of any level of IQ. This is among the highest rate found. A number of studies have been carried out in recent years producing a wide range of rates, which have tended to be higher the nearer to the present time that the studies were carried out. The Medical Research Council (2001) suggested that the best estimate for the whole spectrum is 60 in 10,000. This is a considerable advance on the 4.5 in 10,000 found by Lotter (1966).

Educational problems and needs

Whatever other disabilities are present, it is the triad of impairments that is the major determinant of educational needs. Each of the impairments and the repetitive pattern of activities can be manifested in a wide variety of ways. Any combination of manifestations of the triad can occur together with any combination of other developmental, physical or psychiatric conditions. Certain combinations are rather more common than others and I shall use these to illustrate the educational problems and needs among children with autistic disorders. I must emphasise that these groups shade into each other and children can change in their clinical pictures in different environments and at different ages. For example, a child can fit Kanner's early infantile autism as a young child, but change to fit Asperger's descriptions by later childhood (Wing, 2002).

Because interest in autism began with Leo Kanner's descriptions of the subgroup among the whole spectrum, the pattern of behaviour he described is now considered to represent typical autism. It is this clinical picture that the general public tend to associate with the term 'autism'. Such children are socially aloof and indifferent to people they do not know, although most are more responsive to their parents and others who are very familiar to them. They tend to dislike approaches from people they do not know and actively isolate themselves as much as they can. Most of them have no or very limited expressive language. They use what speech they have to satisfy their needs or sometimes to remark on things that interest them, but not to engage in two-way conversation. They tend to echo words or phrases they hear and to repeat phrases they have heard in the past. Their comprehension of language is very limited and literal. They are unable to compensate for their problems with speech by using gesture. They find gesture and other body language as difficult to use and understand as speech. They have minimal or no pretend play and no grasp of what toys represent in the real world. For them, events occur without rhyme or reason. They have no idea why things happen, why people appear and disappear, why they are made to do all sorts of incomprehensible things. It is not surprising that they want to hold on to objects that are familiar and they want the same events to happen in the same way over and over again without the smallest variation. Changes in familiar routines and objects cause intense distress and often temper tantrums together with aggression to self or to others. Although often delayed in acquiring motor skills, by school age children in this group are usually well able to walk, run, climb and to escape at speed from situations they dislike.

The committee chaired by Mary Warnock envisaged a common set of goals for all children: independence, enjoyment and understanding. The aim for children with disabilities should be to help them make progress, however limited, towards these goals (Warnock, 2005, p. 17). For children with autism who are socially aloof and indifferent, education has to begin with the basic skills of self-care, slowly increasing understanding and use of verbal and/or non-verbal communication, and visuo-spatial and practical skills. Even more important is the gentle encouragement of the child to tolerate simple social contact with others. To be successful, teachers must have a deep empathy with children with these problems and a high level of skill in the specialised teaching methods that have been developed (Jordan and Jones, 1999; Mesibov *et al.*, 1994). *Given this ideal type of teaching*, how much progress can be made beyond these basic skills depends on the innate potential of the individual child.

Putting children with these problems in the class in a mainstream school exposes them to a noisy, brightly lit, ever-changing environment that they find terrifying. Providing a one-to-one teaching assistant is usually of no help at all. It is very rare for someone with the training and skill needed to teach children with autism to work as a teaching assistant.

To make any educational progress, children with these problems need their own space in a small, highly organised classroom with enough experienced and skilled teachers to provide adequate one-to-one teaching time for each child. Most in this group have moderate or severe learning disabilities and make limited educational progress. A small minority have average or high ability, though with the typically patchy profile of skills. Given the right kind of help they may make considerable progress.

One of the arguments put forward by those in favour of educational inclusion for all disabled children is that such children benefit from the social life in a mainstream school and from the role models provided by typically developing children. The trouble with this argument is that children with this type of autism are completely indifferent to other children, or find them very frightening, and have no ability and no desire to copy them. It is reasonable to ask why one should put a vulnerable child through the ordeal of mainstream schooling, making their anxiety and social isolation much worse, because of the theories of idealists who have no knowledge of or empathy for children with autism.

Another subgroup among children with autistic spectrum disorders comprise those who are passive in social interaction, at least in a school setting. Instead of being aloof to others and moving away from physical and social contact, these children passively accept approaches from others, although they do not initiate approaches for themselves. They usually have more useful expressive language than the aloof children but their understanding is almost always lower than their speech would suggest. They may appear to have some pretend play but observation shows that this is usually an empty copy of other children's play. They are also likely to have better self-care and practical skills then the aloof group. They are less inclined to have tantrums and to become aggressive in response distress. They too want routines and people and things around them to remain the same, but their reaction to change is usually less dramatic than in the aloof group.

This type of child can be seen as ideal for placement in a mainstream school. They may accept such a placement without evident protest. Typically they sit quietly, give no trouble, and the school staff assume that all is well. Some of these children are indeed content to attend a mainstream school, at least at primary stage. However, others in this group, while showing no outward sign in school, are very unhappy and distressed. The evidence is to be found at home. Some shed their passivity on entering their home and become difficult, even aggressive in behaviour. In the mornings of schooldays, they make their unwillingness to go to school very clear and parents have a hard time getting them dressed, fed and ready for the journey to school. What is astonishing is the way in which, at some point in the transition from home to school, the cloak of passivity returns and the school staff see what they think is a contented child. Depending on their level of ability, such children make some educational progress but at the cost of inner turmoil and intense distress for their parents and family. Quite often, if parents report the difficulties they are having at home, which are in such contrast to the child's behaviour in school, the parents are blamed for the way they are managing their child and the problems drag on without any solution. Children in this group, if they experience stressful situations over a long time, are especially vulnerable to developing catatonia-like conditions in adolescence or adult life (Wing and Shah, 2000). If they are moved to a small specialist school that suits their needs, most passive children settle happily.

The third group, with 'active-but-odd' social interaction, the closest to Asperger's descriptions, are perhaps the hardest to understand. They are the children who make spontaneous approaches to other people but these are inappropriate, one-sided and without regard for the feelings and interests of the people approached. The reasons for the approaches are not social. The children wish to talk repetitively about their special interests, for example the movement of the planets or events in a favourite soap opera, or to ask an endless series of questions on the same topic: 'What kind of car have you got? What colour is it? How many miles does it do to the gallon? Is it automatic? What is the engine size? Do you drive it on the M4?', and so on. Children in this group usually have an extensive vocabulary and adequate grammar but, as always in autistic spectrum disorders, their comprehension is lower than their expressive language would lead you to expect. Some have little or no pretend play, but some copy other children and some have an imaginary world of their own, often copied from books, films or television, which is rigid and repetitive in form and is not shared with other children. It is a constant source of surprise how real such imaginary worlds appear to be to these children. More than one child of this kind has lived in a fantasy of being Batman and more than one has jumped from a height assuming they will fly, with inevitable consequences that they did not anticipate. These children's repetitive activities are manifested in such fantasy worlds or in their intense concentration on their special interests, rather than resistance to change in objects and routines. The inability to foresee the consequences of actions is characteristic of all children with autistic spectrum disorders, but is most obvious in this group because of their active but inappropriate social behaviour. This causes them many problems in school. They say what they think in class and will tell the teacher if they think he or she is wrong. Some have a high level of skill in, for example, maths, and will point out any errors in the teacher's calculations without hesitation. A good teacher should be able to cope with this (though not all are mature enough to do so, with unhappy consequences for the child), but frank outspokenness does not tend to please age peers. Many active-but-odd children are the targets of bullying, especially in secondary school. Children in primary school tend to be tolerant but those in their early teens have an unerring ability to detect socially odd behaviour and can be merciless in their response. While some children in this autistic spectrum subgroup are oblivious of teasing, others suffer severely. However, they rarely complain, not even to their parents, but suffer in silence. This is a remarkable example of the autistic lack of understanding of the purpose and value of inter-personal communication, and the lack of any empathy or expectation of empathy from others.

Another type of problem for children in this subgroup also arises from the combination of an intense concentration on their special interests, their lack of social sense, and their inability to foresee the consequences of their actions. Some of the children work hard and do well in a few subjects that interest them but refuse to bother with those that they find boring. No amount of encouragement, cajoling or scolding from teachers or parents makes any difference. They cannot see any point in doing anything they do not find interesting.

Some children with active-but-odd behaviour cope in mainstream with few problems while others suffer a great deal. They benefit from the individual teaching and understanding to be found in specialist schools that offer the appropriate level in the academic programme. Clare Sainsbury, who has Asperger's syndrome, has written a detailed, moving and fascinating account of the educational problems and needs of children with this type of autistic spectrum disorder (Sainsbury, 2000). Clare writes that she was academically able but that she found the other children in her mainstream school difficult to understand, confusing and frightening. She quotes comments from her primary school reports that show how much she, in her turn, puzzled, worried and exasperated many of her teachers, though she does write that some good teachers were sympathetic. She tried to cope by keeping away from other children and finding some comfort in the fantasy that she was an alien from another planet. She thought that one day she would be rescued by a spaceship that would take her to a place where there were other people like her. As the years went by she realised that this was not going to happen. It was not until she was 20 years old that she was diagnosed with Asperger's syndrome and at last understood why she had always felt so different.

The final group comprise those who have little skill or interest in social interaction but have learnt enough basic social conventions not to appear strange in company. They are of high ability, usually in one or two specific areas, have good self-care and practical skills and have an equable temperament. They make only the necessary social approaches and get on quietly with their schoolwork, so do not aggravate their teachers or become the butt of other children's teasing. Other children may regard them as 'little professors' and admire them for their knowledge in their special field of interest. These are the most likely to succeed in and even enjoy mainstream schooling.

Despite the variations in the manifestations of autistic spectrum disorders, all the children have certain features in common. Over-sensitivity to sensory input affects most children with these disorders, even those with the highest levels of ability. Loud noises, bright lights, and being touched or hugged, are particularly likely to cause distress. It would be difficult to ensure that these stimuli do not occur from time to time in classrooms in mainstream schools.

The comments of teachers and verbal exchanges with students can be a source of distress to children with autistic disorders who have a very literal understanding of speech. Many of the children, even those with excellent expressive speech, are significantly slower than typically developing children in processing the meaning of words they hear. Verbal joking with play on the meanings of words can confuse and frighten them. For example, one child was terrified by his teacher who pretended to be a monster from outer space in the context of a discussion of science fiction, to the delight of the other children in the class. He told no one of his fear, and his terror of the teacher lasted for years until finally he spoke of it to his parents, who were able to explain the teacher's behaviour in a way the boy understood. It would be hard to forbid such imaginative activities in the classroom, which are enjoyed by typically developing children. Bullying and teasing, whether verbal or physical, can make play time a nightmare for a vulnerable child. From the point of view of the other children in the class, temper tantrums or screaming by the child with an autistic disorder is very disruptive to lessons.

Whatever their level of ability, all children with autistic spectrum disorders need specialised techniques of teaching if they are to be able to learn. The daily programme must be highly organised so that the children always know what will happen. Their literal understanding means that abstract ideas have to be presented in a simple, concrete form. Visual presentations of the daily timetable and the content of the subjects to be learnt are essential. As already emphasised, children with autistic disorders are intensely absorbed by their special interests and many are unwilling to attend to anything else. One of the skills of an experienced teacher in this field is to encourage learning through linking with the child's special interests. To take a simple example, a child who is fascinated with railways may be helped to begin to understand arithmetic by counting, adding and subtracting toy engines. Teachers also have to realise that, when they address the whole class, even the most able child with an autistic disorder tends not realise that they are included in the general instruction. The child must be specifically included in the way the instruction is worded. All of these techniques require a high level of understanding of the individual child as well as experience, imagination and ingenuity from the teacher. It would not be easy to provide all this for one child in a large mainstream classroom.

Some children with autistic spectrum disorders have been placed in special schools primarily intended for other types of disability. This can pose as many problems as mainstreaming unless appropriate special provision is organised. Particularly unsatisfactory is placement of a child with autistic disorder within a school for children with emotional and behaviour disorders. The child concerned may be the terrified victim of bullying or else try naively to fit in with a group and become the one who gets caught and blamed for the anti-social behaviour of the rest.

Factors making for success in mainstream schools

The attitude of the school staff and their willingness to adapt to the individual needs of children with autistic spectrum disorders is of great importance. Proper leadership from the adults in charge has a major influence on the way the other children in the school behave towards a vulnerable child. The formation of a 'circle of friends', who are willing and interested in helping a vulnerable child, can be of great benefit to those taking part in the circle as well as the child concerned. All this is much easier to achieve in a small school, in contrast to a comprehensive school with very large numbers of students.

However, it is factors within the child that are the most crucial in determining success or failure in mainstream placement. The child's level of ability is closely associated with the progress that she or he makes. Children with autistic disorders, just like typically developing children, have their own personalities. A child who is calm and cheerful by temperament will find it easier to adapt. But above all other considerations, if the child with an autistic spectrum disorder *decides* that he wants to attend mainstream school like other children, he is likely to cope despite any difficulties and to make good progress. On the other hand, those who intensely dislike and fear mainstream school are unlikely to benefit from the experience. Even the most able children with autistic disorders may find mainstream school intolerable. Mary Warnock writes about children with autistic disorders:

> It is essential that we raise the question what their 'inclusion' in mainstream school amounts to and whether it is experienced by them as good. The reality seems to be, in many cases, that it is experienced as a painful kind of exclusion.
>
> (Warnock, 2005, p. 43)

Quoting from a conversation she had with me, Mary Warnock also writes: 'The fact is that, if educated in mainstream schools, many such children are not included at all. They suffer all the pains of the permanent outsider. No political ideology should impose this on them' (p. 45). Some carry the distress and fear into adult life and some are filled with a bitter resentment, which can lead to depression and self-destructive behaviour or, in extreme cases, aggression to others.

Conclusions

Special schools are needed and will continue to be needed for many, though not all, children with autistic spectrum disorders. There are children at very different levels of ability for whom mainstream schooling is a nightmare and a denial, not a fulfilment, of their human rights. Some children do well at some subjects in mainstream school but need the specialist provision for other subjects. Some need specialist provision at some stages in their lives but could cope with mainstream school at others. Some would be happy and able to learn in a specialist unit within a mainstream school. Some can attend mainstream school but to do so they need varying degrees of individual support and teaching. Finally there are some children who can cope with mainstream school full-time with minimal or no special support and are happy in this environment. What is needed by all those involved, administrators, teachers and parents, is imagination and flexibility and a genuine understanding of each child concerned.

In the last section of her pamphlet, 'The ideal of inclusion reconsidered', Mary

Warnock makes an eloquent plea for a realistic, non-dogmatic, child-centred view of inclusion. She argues that all children should be included in a common educational project, not that they should necessarily be included under the same roof.

Why do we not find out from the children themselves what kind of schooling is best for them? Many children with autistic disorders cannot express their feelings in words, but skilled observation of their behaviour at home as well as at school, in the playground as well as in the classroom, is the best guide to the effect that school is having upon them. The issue of mainstream versus special education has such a profound impact on autistic children's lives that their day-to-day experiences, rather than our ideology, should be our guide.

References

Asperger, H. (1944), 'Die "autistischen psychopathen" im kindersalter', *Archiv für Psychiatrie und Nervenkrankheiten*, 117, 76–136

Ehlers, S. and C. Gillberg (1993), 'The epidemiology of Asperger syndrome: a total population study', *Journal of Child Psychology and Psychiatry*, 34, 1327–50

Frith, U. (1991), 'Asperger and his syndrome', in U. Frith (ed.), *Autism and Asperger Syndrome*, Cambridge: Cambridge University Press, 1–36

Frith, U. (2003), *Autism: Explaining the Enigma*, Oxford: Blackwell

Jordan, R. and G. Jones (1999), *Meeting the Needs of Children with Autistic Spectrum Disorders*, London: David Fulton

Kanner, L. (1943), 'Autistic disturbances of affective contact', *Nervous Child*, 2, 217–50

Kanner, L. (1973), *Childhood Psychosis: Initial Studies and New Insights*, Washington, DC: Winston

Kanner, L. and L. Eisenberg (1956), 'Early infantile autism, 1943–1955', *American Journal of Orthopsychiatry*, 26, 55–65

Lotter, V. (1966), 'Epidemiology of autistic conditions in young children: I. prevalence', *Social Psychiatry*, 1, 124–37.

Medical Research Council (2001), *MRC Review of Autism Research*, London: MRC, 18

Mesibov, G., E. Schopler and K. Hearsey (1994), 'Structured teaching', in E. Schopler and G. Mesibov (eds.), *Behavioural Issues in Autism*, New York: Plenum

Sainsbury, C. (2000), *Martian in the Playground: Understanding the Schoolchild with Asperger's Syndrome*, Bristol: Lucky Duck Publishing

Volkmar, F., R. Paul, A. Klin, and D. Cohen (eds.) (2005), *Handbook of Autism and Developmental Disorders* (3rd edn), vols 1 and 2, New York: Wiley

Wing, L. (1997), 'The history of ideas on autism: legends, myths and reality', *Autism*, 1, 13–23

Wing, L. (2002), *The Autistic Spectrum*, London: Constable and Robinson

Wing, L. and J. Gould (1979), 'Severe impairments of social interaction and associated abnormalities in children: epidemiology and classification', *Journal of Autism and Developmental Disorders*, 9, 11–29

Wing, L. and D. Potter (2002), 'The epidemiology of autistic spectrum disorders. Is the prevalence rising?', *Mental Retardation and Developmental Disabilities Research Reviews*, 8, 151–61

Wing, L. and A. Shah (2000), 'Catatonia in autistic spectrum disorders', *British Journal of Psychiatry*, 76, 357–62

4 Speaking as a parent
Thoughts about educational inclusion for autistic children

Charlotte Moore

I have three sons. George, 16, and Sam, 14, are both autistic; Jake, 8, is developing normally. George and Sam began their education career in mainstream schools, but at the ages of 8 and 6 respectively they transferred to an ASD facility linked to a local special needs school. I have never regretted my decision to make this change.

All autists are different. George and Sam are as different from each other as either of them is from Jake. The autistic spectrum covers a huge range of ability, and besides, each individual on that spectrum has their own unique character. George and Sam both recognisably have the classic 'triad of impairments' – of communication, social interaction and social imagination – but the ways in which these impairments manifest themselves varies enormously. To take just one example: both boys have language abnormalities, but whereas George has been highly echolalic and now speaks in a clear but over-elaborate, over-literal way (he described fried bread as 'a small square piece of gold'), Sam's vocabulary is mainly confined to nouns and simple verbs, and he has poor pronunciation and significant word-finding difficulties. I have never doubted the validity of their shared diagnosis, but their symptoms, and therefore their needs, differ greatly.

It is difficult, then, to make a pronouncement about the right kind of education for an autistic child. Each case needs to be assessed on its own merits. But I am certain that a blanket policy in favour of inclusion in mainstream schools is harmful. At best it is misguided, at worst it is an immoral and ineffectual cost-cutting exercise – ineffectual because though inclusion is cheaper at the time, the emotional and behavioural problems it can cause diminish the child's level of independence, and dependent, traumatised young adults are very expensive. There certainly are autistic children who can cope with, even benefit from, inclusion. But there are many, many more for whom it is totally inappropriate. Those who advocate inclusion are often talking about what they want to be true and are ignoring reality. They argue that every child should have access to the same curriculum, should have the chance to take public examinations and gain qualifications that will fit them either for tertiary education or for the world of work. But an autistic student who has gained some GCSE grades won't truly be more employable as a result. His grades don't mean that he'll be able to cope with the independent living that a university place entails, or that he'll have overcome his rigid routines sufficiently to fit into a working environment. Autists have disabling difficulties with social interaction; these difficulties won't be lessened by passing exams.

Uniquely, autism is more a social than an intellectual handicap. A significant proportion of autists have low IQs and will never achieve literacy, numeracy or even speech. A similar proportion are extremely intellectually able and may go on to flourish in an academic environment. One of the biggest mistakes made by education authorities is to assume that academic ability automatically means that a child can cope in mainstream. 'He's eleven and he's got a reading age of sixteen – why shouldn't he go to the comprehensive?' But as we surely all remember from our own school days, to thrive at school it is far more important to have social skills than academic ones. I have come across many cases of high-functioning autistic children who have been pushed into comprehensives, spend their school days bewildered and bullied, and end up refusing to go to school altogether. They spend their days at home, isolated, glued to their computers, while their despairing parents are threatened with prosecution by the local authorities.

Yes, of course autistic children should be able to access the curriculum, if that is appropriate. But in order for an autist to 'access' anything, the environment has to be right. Simon Baron-Cohen (2003) quotes a young man with Asperger Syndrome:

> People with A.S. are like salt-water fish who are forced to live in fresh water. We're fine if you just put us into the right environment. When the person with A.S. and the environment *match*, the problems go away and we even thrive. When they don't match, we seem disabled.

The environment of a typical mainstream school is not adjusted to meet the needs of an autistic pupil in any way. It cannot be, because autistic needs are diametrically opposed to the needs of the mainstream majority. When I looked for a suitable school for Jake, I wanted the very features that would have been anathema to George and Sam. Lots of variety, educational trips, a rich and busy playground life, links with the local community, colourful displays of the children's work, whole-school assemblies, opportunities to perform and compete. . . . Jake goes to the village primary school, which provides all this and more. But for George and Sam, such an environment is overwhelming. They spent their first years in just such a school, and, despite the goodwill of staff and pupils, they couldn't cope.

Autists dislike change. An early sign of autism is often an insistence that pieces of furniture should be kept in exactly the same place, or that the same route from home to the shops should be followed without variation. In a mainstream school, especially at secondary level, the day consists of endless changes – from one classroom to the next, from gym to cafeteria to science labs. 'OK 3A, we can't use Room 16 today because it's needed for French orals, so can you all go to Mrs Baker's room instead.' This kind of instruction would present little difficulty to the average child, but could confuse a child on the spectrum to a disabling extent.

When I was doing my teacher training in 1981, we were told that we should change our wall displays at least every three weeks. For mainstream children, change is stimulating; it wakes up their brains and their senses. For autistic children, it has exactly the opposite effect. Bruno Kanner, the psychologist who first identified autism in 1943, named an intense desire for 'the preservation of sameness' as a defining characteristic of the condition. By insisting on eating food of only one colour, wearing only one kind of shirt, or watching the same video over and over again, autists seem to be attempting to keep the confusing pace of change under control. Their brains take longer to process change. If they are rushed, they overload and 'shut down', and in that state they are unreachable and unteachable. In a mainstream school they are always rushed. Of course, part of the education of autists should be to help them come to terms with change, because change is an inevitable part of life. But it needs to be taught slowly and with sensitivity. You do not teach a crippled child to walk by kicking away his crutches.

Autism is usually discussed as a mental condition. Its physical symptoms are too often overlooked, but I know that my sons' experience of the physical world differs greatly from my own. Their senses operate differently. I've never been tempted to run out into the garden in January, naked and barefoot, dip my hair into the icy water of the birdbath and flick it all over the place. I've never wanted to bang my hands on the floor until they bled. I've never had the slightest desire to eat felt tip pens or swallow deodorant or deliberately sting myself on nettles. Carpet underlay doesn't whet my appetite. On the whole, I prefer the story part of the video to repeatedly watching the credits roll. Conversely, I am not bothered by things that the boys cannot tolerate. I approach electric hand driers calmly. I hardly notice the hum of a radiator that might entirely preoccupy George. If I dislike the smell of a particular cleaning fluid or the texture of a certain garment, I can overcome my aversion; I do not have to let it ruin my day.

Autists often have sensory hypersensitivities, and the designers of mainstream school buildings do not take these into account. How can they? They are designing to a limited budget, to meet the needs of the many. Donna Williams, autistic author of *Nobody Nowhere* and other books, describes how strip lighting causes figures to shake and jump about in a way that makes it impossible for her to function. But in most schools, strip lighting is everywhere. In schools specifically designed for autistic children, dull, quiet colours are used on the walls, and floor colours are plain and uniform, to minimise problems for those who, like Sam, have difficulty with depth perception. When Sam comes to the edge of a carpet, he cannot necessarily see whether the floor beyond it is on the same level, or whether there is a steep drop. He will rock back and forth, frozen to the spot, trying to decide whether it is safe to proceed.

And then there is the noise! Schools are inevitably noisy. As Luke Jackson, the autistic teenager who wrote *Freaks, Geeks and Asperger Syndrome*, says of his unhappy experience of mainstream, 'Everything at school was so loud and so complicated'. My George spent the first six years of his life with his hands clapped over his ears. He is less sound-sensitive than he was, but certain noises, even certain tones of voice, are still too much to bear. Many autists favour hoods, or ear muffs; you'll see them pulling their jumpers up over their ears. It is not just a question of what one likes or dislikes – the wrong noises actually hurt.

The biggest barrier to learning, for an autist, is motivation. Consider what motivates a neurotypical child: the desire for praise from adults, the desire to shine in the opinion of one's peers, a reward such as a gold star or – later – a high exam grade, a boost to self-esteem from feeling 'clever', a desire to finish the job and move onto something more interesting, a desire to conform, to work because that is what everyone else is doing, a genuine interest in the subject for its own sake. Only the last of these will apply to an autistic child, and that rarely. If an autist's interest is engaged, his concentration and attention to detail can be phenomenal, but it is very hard to engage that interest. Autists do not seek approbation. They don't usually mind whether or not other people think highly of them. They may shy away from praise, because they do not like attention to be drawn to themselves. They have no competitive instinct – they don't compare themselves with others. A star, an A grade, or applause in assembly mean little or nothing, because these things are not rewarding in themselves; they are just symbols of an externally applied standard, which is of little interest. If one wants to reward an autistic pupil, one must find something that genuinely motivates that individual. At one stage, George was rewarded with sticking plasters because he had a thing about them, and being allowed to sit on the heater for one minute.

Above all, autists never do anything simply because that is the social norm. They learn very little in a group. Many people believe that if an autistic child attends a mainstream school the 'normality' will rub off on him, and his autistic behaviours will decrease. This is wishful thinking. A core feature of autism is the lack of imitative behaviour, or rather, there is an inability to learn through imitation. Neurotypical children have an innate curiosity about the way other people do things; in autists, this instinct has gone awry. Autists may imitate an action or a gesture in the same way that they may echo a phrase, but they fail to grasp the meaning underlying that action. Being with non-autistic children does not normalise the autists' behaviour; if anything, it accentuates the difference. Self-stimulatory autistic habits (humming, rocking, hand flapping, even self-harming) increase at times of stress, and if the child is in an environment he doesn't understand, stress levels will be high.

Most autistic children come from a 'normal' home environment, and that hasn't made them less autistic, so why should school do the trick? Conversely, parents fear that in an all-autistic school, the children will copy each other's difficult behaviours and the autism will intensify, but in my experience this isn't the case. Neither George nor Sam have ever copied what their classmates do in anything but the most fleeting and superficial way. Again, the instinct to imitate just isn't there.

I am not suggesting that autists should be confined to some kind of ghetto and be deprived of all contact with neurotypical children. Some, like my Sam, are socially aloof, and really do not seem to desire contact with others except to get their needs met, but others, like George, are socially 'active but odd', to use Lorna Wing's phrase. At the more able end of the spectrum there may be a desire to make friends. Such children should not be thrown in at the deep end, but should be guided and supported in the development of their social skills by patient and experienced adults.

Even the most socially responsive of autistic children need help and protection. Autists are bad at interpreting facial expressions, tones of voice, body language, irony, sarcasm and jokes. They are slow to follow the rules of games, even slower to pick up on the subtle, self-created rules of social behaviour through which neurotypical children establish their pecking order. Autists are literal-minded and prone to misinterpret. Joe, a very intelligent autistic boy I know, attended a mainstream school, but believed himself, correctly I'm afraid, to be unpopular. He asked his mother how he could make the other children like him more. 'Why don't you watch what Danny does?' suggested his mother. 'Everybody likes Danny, and he's always smiling.' A few days later, Joe asked his mother to buy him a comb. Why? 'Because I've worked out why Danny smiles a lot. It's because he combs his hair.'

Social difficulties obviously make the autistic child vulnerable to bullying. Luke Jackson states bluntly: 'All my life I have been bullied.' He points out that the ASD child is an easy target because he is often alone. He also says that the victim is unlikely to seek help; autists rarely ask for adult help for anything, partly because their 'mind-blindness' means they are unaware that the adult does not automatically know what is going on in their head. To this day, my sons don't always tell me when they've been hurt. The ASD child will not necessarily identify bullying for what it is; when you don't understand what the norms are, you don't recognise behaviour that oversteps the mark. Luke Jackson again: 'Bullies don't actually say "Now I am going to bully you." Therefore your child may not realise that the torment they are suffering is bullying.' And, in his thoughtful and fair-minded way, he puts the other side of the case: 'Some bullying may not actually be bullying! A.S. kids don't always realise when friendly messing about is actually friendly stuff.'

In *Martian in the Playground*, Clare Sainsbury, who is herself autistic, collates the experiences of many high-functioning autists who have endured bullying in mainstream schools. The conclusion is inescapable; for a pupil with an autistic spectrum disorder in a mainstream school, being bullied will become a fact of life. How could it not be so? Bullies have always existed, always will exist, and teachers – not always incapable of doing the bullying themselves – have only limited power to discover and control them. And bullies always pick on someone who is isolated, defenceless, set apart from the pack. It is argued that incorporating special-needs children teaches the other children tolerance and compassion, and that is true; I think it is good for neurotypical children to have contact with those who are 'differently abled', and I have known many children who go out of their way to be kind and accommodating. But the long-term damage caused by the bullies probably outweighs these benefits.

Why don't educationalists and politicians listen more carefully to the words that come, as it were, out of the horse's mouth? I have read many autobiographical accounts of the miseries of inclusion, but I have yet to find an account of the joys. Thérèse Jolliffe, an autistic woman who became a university academic, is unequivocal:

> I hated school. Parents of autistic children should never think about sending their children to ordinary schools, because the suffering will far outweigh any of the benefits achieved. . . . Although ordinary schooling enabled me to leave with a dozen or so O-levels and a few A-levels and then to obtain a degree, it was not worth all the misery I suffered . . . I was frightened of the girls and boys, the teachers and everything there. I was frightened of the toilets and you had to ask to use them, which I was not able to do; also I was never sure when I wanted to go to the toilet anyway. . . . When I attended a place for autistic people, life was a little more bearable and there was certainly less despair.
>
> (Jolliffe *et al.*, 1992)

What, then, is the most desirable educational path for an autistic child? There is no easy answer, but here are some ideas. Early intervention is important. Better diagnostic techniques mean that autism is now being picked up in very young children, but there is often a significant delay between the diagnosis and the start of meaningful educational intervention. This delay means not only that the child is being denied the right kind of help, but also that he may be harmed by an unsuitable approach.

I believe that mainstream nurseries are almost always bad for autistic toddlers, who tend either to retreat to the wendy house and pull a blanket over their heads, or become a restless, disruptive satellite to the activities of the other children, tipping up paint, chewing wax crayons and breaking off the knobbly bits of jigsaws. The unsuitability of such a placement causes unnecessary stress for the staff, the other children, and for the autistic child himself. But no group of parents needs a break from their children as badly as the exhausted mothers of autistic three- and four-year-olds. There are two answers to this problem. One is to set up a therapy programme in the child's own home, run on lines such as Applied Behavioural Analysis. It takes three or four adults to run a programme like this; tutors come to work with the child on a rota system, using a specially equipped room, such as a spare bedroom. With such intensive intervention, the child often makes dramatic progress. Indeed, autistic children who prosper under this system are sometimes able to move on to mainstream school relatively smoothly. (For more information about ABA or other interventions, contact PEACH on 01344 882248 or the National Autistic Society on 020 7833 2299.)

The drawbacks are that running such a programme is very expensive. Tutors can be hard to find, and the burden of organising it is carried by the parents. In a small house or flat it can be difficult to find a peaceful space for teaching. And though the parents don't have to do the teaching themselves, the child does not actually leave the house, so the break is not a complete one. An alternative is a nursery (later, a school) run on ABA lines, such as the Tree House school in North London or the Step by Step school near East Grinstead. Here, a small number of children will be taught one-to-one in a calm environment; tasks will be broken down into small stages, the child will be rewarded ('reinforced') for success – and the rewards will be whatever genuinely motivates that child. Such schools are obviously expensive too, but effective intervention in autism requires very high staff ratios – there's no way round that.

In short, all autistic children should either follow a home therapy programme or attend a special-needs nursery from the moment of diagnosis. Much progress can be made with very young children, before they become 'closed in' by the rigidities of autism. But special-needs nurseries are in woefully short supply. My Sam spent a year in one, and made excellent progress. But this nursery was then closed, for the idiotic reason that as it could serve only a small number of children its existence was unfair.

After pre-schoolers, the autistic group most poorly catered for by our education system are the academically able teenagers. Most special schools cannot provide a high enough level of academic teaching; most mainstream schools cannot provide enough social education and pastoral support. The answer could well be ASD units attached to mainstream schools, so that the ASD teenager can access the academic abilities of a large body of staff, but be based in a secure, supportive environment where one-to-one help could fill the gaps in social and self-care skills that come naturally to neurotypical children. Such units do exist, but they are in short supply.

George is now 16; soon, he'll have to leave the ASD facility which he loves. This is because all the state schools in our part of the country finish at 16, just as all the primary schools stop at 11. But autistic children develop at very different rates from neurotypical ones. Emotionally, George is at about a five-year-old level. It is ironic that he has to leave school just as, in some senses, he is ready to begin it.

We are lucky; we have a fully funded place for him in a private special-needs college not far from where we live. He will be there for three years, but I very much doubt whether, at 19, George will be ready for 'the real world'. I have spoken to many parents whose autistic children are in their thirties and forties, and they all agree that learning and developing continues into adulthood; there is no cut-off point. This leads one to think that an extended educational programme could be the best way of maximising autistic potential. It sounds strange, but I would be delighted if George and Sam could still be in school in ten years' time.

To sum up, then, the majority of autistic children need to be educated in a specially adapted environment by a large number of well-trained, committed staff. A balance has to be achieved between respecting the autistic need for 'aloneness' and encouraging the child by slow, small steps to engage with the neurotypical world. Such teaching requires patience and dedication, but it's a fascinating and rewarding task. Autism is interesting, especially if you don't have to live with it 24 hours a day. The government should hugely increase the amount of training on offer; there should be a recruitment drive to encourage people to engage with autism, whether on the level of occasional babysitting or as a full-blown teaching career.

There is an enormous amount of public interest in the subject. When George was diagnosed, 12 years ago, the condition was little known; now, the media is full of it. Incidence is believed to run at 1 in 100 – and that means that an awful lot of salt-water fish are floundering in fresh water. Badly handled, autism causes infinitely harmful knock-on effects in terms of stress, exhaustion and depression in the families of those affected. It does not have to be this way, but to get things right requires time, effort, money, and recognition that, of all the conditions that go under the heading of 'special needs', autism is the one most accurately described as 'differently abled'.

References

Baron-Cohen, Simon (2003), *The Essential Difference: Men, Women and the Extreme Male Brain*, London: Allen Lane

Jackson, Luke (2002), *Freaks, Geeks and Asperger Syndrome*, London: Jessica Kingsley

Jolliffe, Thérèse, Richard, Lansdown, and Clive, Robertson (1992), 'Autism: a personal account', *Communication*, vol. 26 (3)

Sainsbury, Clare (2000), *Martian in the Playground*, Bristol: Lucky Duck

Williams, Donna (1992), *Nobody Nowhere*, New York: Random House

5 'Jigsawing it together'

Reflections on deaf pupils and inclusion

Joy Jarvis

The reflections in this chapter are based on my experience as a teacher, advisory teacher and teacher educator in deaf education. The duration of this experience coincides with Mary Warnock's involvement in the field of special educational needs (SEN). As she began her inquiry into provision for 'handicapped children and young people' I started teaching in mainstream schools. By the time the 1981 Act had been passed, I was taking up my first post in a 'partially hearing unit' attached to a mainstream school. It is interesting to explore changes in deaf education over these past thirty years.

Mary Warnock's pessimism about the current situation in special education perhaps leads her to underestimate the great strides that have been taken in providing education for all children. When I started my first teaching job, with a class of forty 8- and 9-year-olds, I had a pupil who could not write his own name. When I sought advice and support from the head teacher, he responded that I needed to realise that some children were 'slow' and that there was nothing to be done about it. Looking back, I see how far we have come since then and appreciate the role that Mary Warnock has played in this progress. Now, with new ideas about the funding and responsibility for education being considered, we need to consider with Mary Warnock how we can best provide for all children within an appropriate educational framework.

Developments in the fields of deafness and education

In the past thirty years much has changed for deaf children. Technological developments such as digital hearing aids, cochlear implants and miniature radio systems have given more deaf children than ever before the chance of hearing spoken language. Newborn hearing screening, whereby deafness can be detected in the first few days of life, enables the early fitting of hearing aids, support for families from teachers of the deaf and the development of language by young deaf children. Deaf children should therefore be more advanced in terms of communication skills and conceptual development when they reach school age than would have been the case previously. Another development has been the identification of signed languages as languages in their own right, not inferior communication systems, and the recognition that for some deaf children British Sign Language

(BSL) should be their first language. The acceptance of BSL as one of Britain's languages in 2003, and its rising profile in the media, is leading to its being seen as a 'different' way of communication, rather than a badge of deficit.

These developments, which have taken place outside the education system, should have led to deaf children having more opportunities to participate in both school and society. The statementing process, in which there are many flaws, as Mary Warnock has identified, has nevertheless given many deaf pupils an entitlement to equipment and support. The issue here has been more about local implementation of the process, with different types and levels of support dependent on geography and local funding. With a low incidence condition such as deafness, the ability of a local authority or London borough to maintain a range of appropriate provision for deaf pupils is limited. Equity in relation to provision is a concern for those involved in deaf education.

Another concern for those of us who work in deaf education is the way in which the concept of inclusion has been interpreted to mean mainstreaming. The Code of Practice statement 'The special educational needs of children will normally be met in mainstream schools or settings' (DfES, 2001, p. 7) demonstrates the government's approach to inclusion as concerned with location. The number of special schools for deaf pupils has reduced over the past thirty years, and currently over 70 per cent of deaf children attend mainstream schools or resource bases or units in mainstream schools (Fortnum *et al.*, 2002). The nature of unit provision has also changed. When I first started working in a unit context, the deaf pupils spent most of their time with teachers of the deaf and their deaf peers. Now the situation is more likely to be one of placement in a mainstream class with in-class support provided by teachers of the deaf or teaching assistants. The majority of deaf children attend their local schools with support from teachers of the deaf and/or teaching assistants. This type of placement has been questioned as follows: 'The British Deaf Association has very strong objections regarding the widespread placement of individual children in local mainstream [schools].' (BDA, 1996, p. 7). Why should there be this concern from the BDA and from many teachers, families, ex-pupils and current pupils? The answer lies in the nature of deafness and its effect on communication. Communication lies at the heart of education, as well as personal and social development.

Academic issues

> I reckon that half of school for me is actually figuring out and jigsawing together what is said.
>
> (National Deaf Children's Society, 1990, p. 19)

These words from a deaf pupil about her mainstream secondary school illustrate the fundamental problem for deaf children in hearing contexts: they do not have full access to information. This may be about the content of a lesson or the latest peer group gossip. Without this access they cannot always be fully included in the sense of fully participating in learning. This pupil was responding to a questionnaire designed to gather pupils' perspectives on attending mainstream schools at a time when the key concept was one of 'integration'. In this context a pupil might have support to do the 'jigsawing', to put together the puzzle of what was happening in school. Now the key concept is 'inclusion', which means that it is the responsibility of the school to include the pupils, to do the 'jigsawing' for them. Is this happening? In 2002 I was part of a research team that interviewed deaf secondary-age pupils about being educated in mainstream schools (University of Hertfordshire, 2002). We found that some schools did attempt to change the way the teaching was undertaken to include the deaf child, but in many cases the child was still doing the 'jigsawing', with support from a teaching assistant, communication support worker or teacher of the deaf. The way lessons were taught was not fundamentally changed to meet the needs of the deaf pupil.

Two examples from lessons I have observed illustrate this point.

> Jack and Emily are five-year-old deaf children sitting on the carpet with 20 hearing children while their mainstream teacher reads them the story *Six Dinner Sid*. The story is about a cat that tricks a number of families into thinking he belongs to them, thereby acquiring meals from each household. At the end of the story his duplicity is revealed.
>
> The deaf children's attention alternates between the teacher's face and the pictures in the book she is holding up. They can't see both at the same time so when they look at the pictures they can't use lip reading to help them understand the imperfect auditory signal. The language used by the teacher is beyond the comprehension of both Jack and Emily who have delayed understanding of sentences and reduced knowledge of vocabulary in relation to their hearing peers.
>
> The hearing and the deaf children enjoy the story but are gaining different information from it. The deaf children see a series of individual pictures with cats, people and houses. They don't appreciate the sequential nature of the events or the reasons for them. When she has finished reading the story the teacher asks questions to check the children's comprehension. She differentiates her questions. She asks Jack to tell her the colour of the cat, a question he answers successfully. Hearing children are asked about reasons, consequences and the meaning of the title.
>
> Subsequent discussion after the lesson reveals that the teacher is pleased with the way the deaf children were included in the lesson and that she reports that she always differentiates her questions to meet different levels of ability, as recommended in national curriculum and strategy documents.
>
> In this example, the way the lesson was presented meant that the deaf pupils were unable to gain full understanding of the story. This was perceived by the teacher to be an issue of 'ability', a term which is often used to label a child, rather than to describe current attainment in a particular context. It is the children who are having to 'jigsaw together' the puzzle of the lesson and who are not fully included in the lesson.

The second example comes from a secondary school.

Emma is in a year 8 geography class. She is highly motivated and has read a chapter in her textbook to prepare for this lesson. Pupils are set by ability and Emma is in a low set because her English is not as developed as hearing children of the same age and because she has difficulty following the lessons. She has a communication support worker with her for most lessons, who uses BSL to translate what the teacher is saying. Emma shifts her attention between the maps the teacher is pointing to and the CSW who is signing the information. A number of geographical terms are used which neither Emma nor the CSW fully understand.

Group work begins. Other pupils talk quickly and the CSW tries to indicate what is being said by each of them. He takes notes that Emma can look at later. She tries to follow what is happening in the group, but can't join in because the discussion has moved on. There is no opportunity for her to initiate or lead any of the discussion.

At the end of the lesson the CSW writes the homework in Emma's book. The teacher reports that he is happy to have deaf pupils in his class because a CSW can interpret so they fully understand. When asked about group work, the teacher notes that he cannot slow it down to accommodate one child, partly because other children might mess about and partly because he would not be able to cover the curriculum. Also he was praised in a recent inspection for the pace of his lessons that kept everyone on their toes.

Again the deaf child is responsible for putting the pieces of the lesson together, this time with the help of an adult who is not the teacher. She does not have full access to the lesson, particularly the group work. She is assumed to be unable to work at a more conceptually difficult level. Additionally she has an adult supporting her most of the time, making independent learning more difficult. This necessity to have help to understand communication that is understood by the rest of the class can lead to the deaf pupil having a poor self-image. Social and emotional issues related to mainstream placements are a particular concern.

Social and emotional issues

At a hearing school you . . . always have to work towards being the same as the others, but you never get there.

(NDCS, 1990, p. 19)

This statement was made by the pupil who talked about the 'jigsawing' nature of her activity in lessons. It illustrates issues of identity for deaf pupils in mainstream schools. This theme is explored by the Deaf Ex-Mainstreamers Group. This is a group of deaf people who have experienced mainstream education and who feel that their experiences adversely affected them. They have written about their feelings of isolation in a mainstream school when they couldn't communicate with hearing pupils. They also argue that by not having access to deaf culture, because they lacked deaf peers and deaf adult role models, they are cut off from the deaf community. They suggest that provision should be large enough to create a deaf cultural community, and therefore advocate special schools or large units in mainstream schools (Deaf Ex-Mainstreamers Group, 2004).

What is the social situation for deaf pupils currently in mainstream schools? In our 2002 study of pupils' perceptions of attending mainstream schools most of the participants talked about the importance of friendship and saw it as a key aspect of school life. Communication between deaf and hearing peers was seen as an issue and some deaf pupils preferred to have deaf friends for this reason. Some deaf pupils reported being teased or bullied about their deafness, but they generally felt that this was dealt with by staff. Some deaf pupils were positive about attending a hearing school: 'I like both deaf and hearing. I have made lots of new friends and they're being very nice,' reported an 11-year-old boy. However, a 12-year-old stated, 'For me it's a bit difficult to make friends because when they talk I can't hear them so they're not interested in talking to me'.

School ethos was identified as significant in research by the Royal National Institute for Deaf People's on what constituted good practice in the education of deaf pupils (Powers *et al.*, 1999). A positive attitude of staff and pupils to diversity, and the modelling of good practice in relation to individuals' differing needs, allowed minority pupils to feel included. In our own study pupils spoke positively about some teachers' deaf awareness. One 13-year-old girl reported, 'There's nothing to be ashamed of, being deaf in this school.' None, however, mentioned having deaf adults in their schools, although it is a policy in some areas to involve deaf adults, particularly in relation to the development of sign language skills. It is unusual for a pupil in a mainstream school to have a teacher who is deaf, while this might be expected in a school for deaf children. I remember a few years ago one of the deaf teachers on the course I run for teachers of deaf children undertook a placement in a mainstream school with a resource base. The deaf and hearing pupils and the mainstream teachers assumed he was a teaching assistant as they had never met a deaf teacher before. This lack of staff diversity will influence how all those involved perceive deafness and the potential life choices of deaf young people.

Inclusion for deaf pupils?

> Integration would make life much easier for many people, combining their ideas and hopes. But parents and teachers must know how the children feel.
>
> (NDCS, 1990, p. 14)

This quotation, from a 17-year-old deaf pupil, highlights the issue of idealism and reality that Mary Warnock considers in relation to some pupils' experiences in mainstream schools. Inclusion is an ideal relating to social and political ends, and as Powers (Powers *et al.*, 2002, p. 232) has pointed out, there 'is often a strong sense of political correctness in discussions on inclusion'. In these discussions the notion of inclusion usually relates to location. This is emphasised by legislation which assumes that mainstream schools should be the first choice of provision. This idea of inclusion as mainstream placement affects the way schools work with children in classrooms. For example, in the first classroom scenario I described, Emily and Jack would have been more included in terms of being able to understand the story if they had been able to have some pre-teaching through individual or small group work outside the classroom beforehand, with an adult with expertise in the field of deaf education. However the mainstream school's head teacher believes that 'it is not inclusion if children are taken out of the classroom'. For deaf children, who need specific support with linguistic and conceptual development in a quiet context so that noise amplified by hearing aids does not interfere with understanding, this concept of inclusion limits what they can achieve educationally.

A key issue, as Mary Warnock states, is to come to a shared understanding of inclusion. If it is to include mainstreaming as a priority then schools cannot remain as they are, unless individual children are to be disadvantaged by being placed in a less than optimal learning environment. Policies such as a prescribed curriculum, prescribed teaching approaches and league tables based on academic achievement militate against innovating to meet individual needs. For example, as Wearmouth and Soler (2001, p. 115) have noted, there is a dilemma for some teachers of children with literacy difficulties, 'whether to include them in the Literacy Hour in the name of equity or to exclude them because the pedagogy is inappropriate to their learning needs'. (This is an example of the 'dilemma of difference' discussed by Mary Warnock in her 2005 pamphlet, and also in Chapter 12 of this book.) Most deaf children will have issues with literacy owing to linguistic delays. While an approach to teaching reading based on phonics may be useful to some deaf children, most can identify print but need more understanding of vocabulary in order to know what the words mean. If inclusion is seen as using the same teaching approach for all children, then this is unlikely to meet individual learning needs.

The meeting of individual needs requires expertise in particular fields. This has been threatened, as Mary Warnock notes, by the reluctance to label children; so-called labels may identify the fields of expertise from which children are likely to benefit. In the field of deafness it is also threatened by policies that are not specifically to do with SEN, but have a significant impact on practice. Delegation of local education authority budgets to schools has had a detrimental effect on services for deaf children in many areas, and this has been noted by the inspection service (Ofsted, 2003). Services for deaf children can provide support for children, families and schools, but if they are too small or subject to fluctuating budgets they cannot provide a quality service. The emphasis in government policy is often on the outreach service potential that exists in special schools, failing to acknowledge the expertise of specialist teachers working for LEAs and London boroughs who can work with children from diagnosis.

Delegation of unit or resource base funding to schools has also diminished the effectiveness of some of this provision. From being part of local provision, the unit becomes detached from the network of people with experience of working in this field. Teachers of the deaf can become isolated professionally and lack the guidance of an experienced head of service. This is particularly problematic when teachers are appointed to run units or resource bases without being qualified or experienced in the field. This occurs because the funding for training to be a teacher of the deaf is limited to those already working with deaf pupils, unless they are prepared to pay for their own one year full-time equivalent course, which is rarely realistic. One worrying trend that I have noticed in the 13 years I have been running a course for training teachers of deaf pupils is an increase in the number of teachers coming to the course having been appointed as teacher-in-charge of a delegated unit. Having been unable to appoint a teacher of the deaf, as they are in short supply, a school appoints a teacher who may be interested in the field but who will need to learn a great deal in a short period of time. This process would be less difficult if there was a local service from which to gain support.

In some cases teachers of the deaf are working on their own to try to develop provision in a context where the head teacher is satisfied that the provision is already appropriate. So, for example, in both the schools in which the scenarios above were set, the head teachers of the school were happy that the contexts were inclusive because the pupils were in the classrooms and making progress. Due to lack of expertise head teachers may well have fairly low expectations of what deaf children can achieve. Teachers of the deaf, on the other hand, would expect Emily and Jack to be able to give reasons and explanations, and, if they were unable to do this, would be likely to attribute the problem to the teaching rather than the child. Teachers of the deaf are often not helped to effect change by school inspectors who, lacking experience in the field, report that provision is appropriate in areas that the teachers see as anything but.

An issue in this area of expertise is an understanding of BSL. Teachers without expertise in the field may well assume that, if they are able to sign to a limited level, then they can include all children in all sessions by using some signs. The idea that BSL is as complex as a verbal language is not understood. It is unlikely that a teacher who had attended an elementary class in Mandarin would feel confident to teach all subjects though that language, but I have met head teachers who assume that a beginner's sign language certificate is sufficient to enable full communication between themselves and a deaf child. They may also fail to appreciate that the pupil him- or herself may be at an early stage in their development of BSL. In the secondary school scenario, the geography teacher assumed that Emma was obtaining though sign interpretation what the other children were hearing. However, deaf children of hearing parents are likely to have limited BSL even when they reach secondary school, owing to lack of opportunities to use the language in a range of contexts with different adults. They will need specific teaching of BSL outside mainstream lessons. The Communication Support Worker may also have limited BSL, because of lack of training opportunities. He or she may also lack subject knowledge. In the case of the CSW working with Emma in geography, he had expertise in art, drama and music, but timetabling difficulties and shortage of staff meant that he was supporting in geography, maths and science lessons that year.

The concept of expertise is important in relation to the adults who are likely to be working most with pupils in mainstream contexts: mainstream teachers and teaching assistants. Educating people in the field of deafness requires effective, ongoing training and support. Without this teachers are likely to assume, as they did in the two scenarios, that deaf children are being given opportunities to learn when they are being denied these opportunities. Teachers of the deaf, whose concern is the education of the children in their care, will argue that children are included in an educational context if they have good, appropriate teaching and a communication context in which they can thrive personally and socially. They need contacts with other deaf children and deaf adults. This could be provided by a mainstream school, a unit or a special school. Some mainstream schools do educate deaf children well by adapting their provision to meet the individual needs of the pupils. They use the expertise of teachers of the deaf and build in effective planning and liaison time to enable all those who are involved to work together effectively. They ensure that deaf children can meet together, even if this is only for clubs or by email link, and they include Deaf culture as part of the curriculum. This requires a great deal of commitment and investment in time and resources. The RNID's *Review of Good Practice in Deaf Education* (Powers *et al.*, 1999) identified a number of excellent mainstream and unit provisions that included deaf pupils both academically and socially. In my own research and experience I have seen deaf pupils thriving and achieving in mainstream and unit contexts. I have also seen children who are unhappy, lonely or achieving little academically. As Mary Warnock says, in order for some children to be included fully in a context, that context needs to be a special school. This should be available as a first choice, not as a last resort.

Ways forward?

Mary Warnock argues that it is time for a new inquiry into the provision we make for children with special educational needs. As she says, we must develop a shared understanding of inclusion that goes beyond location to an understanding of particular and individual needs. In relation to low incidence conditions such as deafness, we need to look at regional planning to enable mainstream, unit and special school provision to be organised so that the range is available to all children. The current attempt to meet the needs of all children within one education authority results in many pupils being inappropriately placed. In addition, strong support and advisory services are essential if families and mainstream schools are to provide effectively for a range of pupil needs. Schools need to be rewarded for creative approaches to learning and teaching rather than for compliance to specified formats. Government ministers should understand that they are currently giving conflicting messages to schools about what good education is about. If all children are to be included in an education system, then the measurement of success cannot be the achievement of a limited number of academic goals.

Today's deaf children have the greatest potential for participating in society, thanks to the technological and linguistic advances discussed earlier. If they are to benefit from educational opportunities, then we have to recognise the essentially specialist nature of the schooling they need and seek to provide it. This may mean placement in a special school with good links to mainstream provision; it may mean attending one of a network of properly staffed units in mainstream schools; or it may mean local mainstream placement with an ethos and teaching approach informed by knowledge and understanding in the field and supported by teachers of the deaf. It may mean attending each of these at a different stage of education. At the moment we have got it right for some children but not for others. We need to stop seeing inclusion as a debate about location, and work towards a school system that aims to provide quality education for all children, recognising that this does not mean the same education for all children.

In the past 30 years we have come a long way in our understanding of the importance of all schools celebrating diversity, and our acceptance of the rights of children to have their special educational needs met. There are, as Mary Warnock suggests, issues with current provision in the field, and these need to be addressed. Maybe we should start by taking 'location' out of the jigsaw, and consider our vision of education as a whole.

References

British Deaf Association (1996), *The Right to be Equal*, London: BDA

Deaf Ex-Mainstreamers Group (2004), *Deaf Toolkit: Best Value Review of Deaf Children in Education From Users' Perspective*, Leeds: DEX

Department for Education and Skills (2001), *Special Educational Needs: Code of Practice*, London: DfES

Fortnum, H., D. Marshall, J. Bamford and A. Q. Summerfield (2002), 'Hearing-Impaired Children in the UK: Education Setting and Communication Approach', *Deafness and Education International*, 4 (3), 123–41

National Deaf Children's Society (1990), *Young Deaf People's Views on Integration: a Survey Report*, London: NDCS

Ofsted (2003), *Special Educational Needs in the Mainstream*, LEA Policy and Support Services, HMI 556 e-publication, Ofsted

Powers, S. (2002), 'From Concepts to Practice in Deaf Education: a United Kingdom Perspective', *Journal of Deaf Studies and Deaf Education*, 7 (3), 230–43

Powers, S., S. Gregory, W. Lynas, W. McCracken, L. Watson, A. Boulton and D. Harris (1999), *A Review of Good Practice in Deaf Education*, London: RNID

University of Hertfordshire (2002), *Inclusion: What Deaf Pupils Think*, London: RNID

Wearmouth, J. and J. Soler (2001), 'How Inclusive is the Literacy Hour?', *British Journal of Special Education*, 28 (3) 113–19

6 The road to Marrakesh
Reflections on small schools and fragile children

William Colley

Introduction

In her recent pamphlet, Mary Warnock writes: 'in a small school there is the possibility of real, experienced inclusion [for fragile children]. Pupils know and are known to their teachers. . . . Pupils can identify with and take pride in their school' (Warnock, 2005, pp. 49–50). Towards the end of the pamphlet, she makes a stronger statement. She argues that, whether because of specific disabilities or needs arising from 'social disadvantage', some children *need* small schools. This, she says, is her 'strong conviction', continuing: 'what is needed is hard evidence to support this view. One person's conviction is not enough'.

I share Warnock's conviction about small schools and fragile pupils, and in this chapter shall explain how I arrived at this position, drawing on my experiences as both a teacher and a head teacher.

In the early 1990s, I taught at one of the largest boarding schools in Scotland, and enjoyed the trappings of our considerable academic and economic success. Classes were small, the children reasonably motivated, and there was a sense of camaraderie among staff and pupils alike that had generated an identity and a pride in the community to which we belonged. It was a privileged existence.

Our speech days were held every summer, on the cusp of the long weekend break before the bulk of the main public exams began in earnest. The whole school then gathered in a sprawling marquee on the lawn in front of the main house to hear speeches and present prizes to those who had excelled. It was all about kilts, improbable hats, flowing dresses and a real sense of occasion, heightened in part by the booming sound of our award-winning pipe band, which rendered polite conversation over the sparkling wine and canapes somewhat difficult.

Our guest speaker in 1993 was Baroness Linklater who had just, not far away, established her own school for children she described as 'educationally fragile' and who would, she said, struggle to thrive in a learning community as large, diverse, and challenging as our own. We listened as attentively as ever, applauded sympathetically at the end of her speech, and then did the same for the long line of children who rose momentarily from the proletarian ranks of the audience to collect their prizes on stage.

I doubt that any of my colleagues was any more or less indifferent than me to what was said that day. It was certainly of no relevance to us and to our school, but hers was clearly a worthy cause and we could not doubt her passion and sincerity. We wished her well, but as we left for our mid-term break later that afternoon, Baroness Linklater's views on education were left to dance in the warm breeze, among the discarded paper plates and napkins.

Less than a decade later, I was running her school.

Meeting the needs of educationally fragile children

During the decade leading up to 2002, a great deal of understanding had been acquired about the kaleidoscopic range of intellects and personalities that pass through the doors of schools. Each colour and hue had been thrown into sharper focus by advances in technology that yielded new understanding of children and the difficulties that many of them face in our neurotypical world. For those among us with the professional humility to reconsider long-held prejudices and beliefs, what was most shocking was the realisation that such difficulties were not evident in a small fraction of children, but in a disturbingly large minority: possibly as many as one in five.

The New School was set up for children who experienced such difficulties, whether or not they had a 'label' like Asperger's Syndrome, ADHD or Tourette's. One of our challenges was to acknowledge that the way in which people tend to address behavioural difficulties – the simplistic use of punishments and sanctions to drive home the 'universal truth' that every action has a consequence – was in fact very primitive, irrelevant, and even damaging to the youngsters we encountered. They were the blunt instruments of a technologically impoverished age, and things had to move on if we were to ensure that our school was fair and just. Many of our pupils were strange and eccentric individuals, who for some reason chose not to subscribe to the social norms demanded by communal living, and who often cast themselves adrift at 14 or 15. They were the 'loners' of Sula Wolff's memorable and ground-breaking book (1995).

What I know now is that, for many of those youngsters, their life paths since school will have been punctuated by unhappiness and depression, and a sense of not quite fitting in wherever they may happen to be. For others, disengagement from education will have led to social marginalisation and civil transgressions, leading to a bleak path through the youth justice system.

Prior to my appointment at the New School, one boy had changed my own understanding of the atypical learner, almost overnight. He threw into sharp focus my ignorance of learning difficulties and exposed the weakness of a school built on the flawed logic of success in teaching to the middle. We will call him Adam.

Adam was ten when he arrived at the mainstream school where I was teaching. He was a prickly character from the start and it was not long before he was having tremendous difficulties in settling in to school life. In fact things became very bad very quickly. Adam erupted at the slightest comment, misinterpreted comments made by fellow pupils, hid in small cupboards and found any change in routine extremely difficult to cope with. He appeared permanently tense, as if everyone was out to get him and spoil his enjoyment of school life, and he was as selfish as a 3-year-old, oblivious to others and to the impact that his tantrums had on those around him. We were soon facing the probability that we would have to lose him because his behaviour was so challenging, erratic and bizarre that he was having a very negative affect on his peers and on colleagues who tried to teach him. It would have been a very easy decision to justify. We just did not have the skills to cope.

On the same day that I tried without success to contact his parents in America and break the news, I chose to search for clues to explain his rigid behaviour, volatile temper, egocentricity and lack of empathy. I trawled every website I could find and devoured each book that came my way. Within the space of a few hours, I believed that I knew not only why Adam was struggling to cope, but why at least six or seven other pupils under my care were facing problems of a similar, but not as obvious, nature.

It was a Damascene moment and one that led to a dramatic change in my professional outlook and future career. We decided with the support of a few close colleagues, and despite the overt hostility of others, that we should try to keep Adam, and indeed that it was our duty to do so. It was not a decision based on the romance of a rescue fantasy, but on the 'certainty' that he and we could succeed, if we developed the knowledge and the skills to help him overcome the difficulties that he faced.

What became clear over the next few months was that there was nothing that we could do to alter Adam himself. It was his environment that had to change. Just as the 'fragility' of a wine glass can be measured in terms of its position in the place where it is standing, rather than qualities inherent in its construction, so with Adam it was the environment that would determine whether or not he could succeed at school. The glass in its cabinet is safe and secure. Adam needed a safe environment in order to build a level of resilience that would later allow him to engage with others in a mutually beneficial way and to leave the cabinet behind. We as teachers were a part of his environment, and we too had to change by revising the rather simplistic assumptions that we had tended to make about human behaviour.

Many years before all of this I had, as a final-year student at university, cycled alone from London to Marrakesh at the height of summer and with the Saharan heat spilling down through North Africa and into southern Spain. On crossing the straits of Gibraltar, I found myself in an alien land in which every gesture and expression that had served me in France and Spain suddenly had no resonance. I was mobbed by youths, spat at by vendors and chased by those who tried to sell me huge watermelons by the roadside as I cycled past. The ride from Ceuta to Marrakesh was lonely and depressing, and I rarely glanced up to admire the beauty of the arid landscape. I suddenly found myself as an alien in a world that I could not begin to comprehend or communicate with.

I recognised in Adam that he was cycling that road every time he walked through the boarding house or into a classroom, and living in a hostile world that he could not begin to understand without considerable support. Nor could those around him understand why living as part of a community, with all of its interaction, negotiations and posturing, was so difficult for him. Over the next few months we did all we could to understand Adam, and the patterns in his behaviour that were beginning to emerge. We tried to see the world the way he did, and to cycle that Marrakesh road with him.

We released ourselves from the need to make moral judgements about his behaviour, and developed instead the analytical skills to explain why things went wrong when they did. We began to plan for him and to help him avoid the difficulties that had in the past led to eruptions and temper tantrums.

In time, and after many ups and downs and times when we thought that we would lose him, he began to settle, and episodes of difficult behaviour became less frequent and more predictable. By the time I left the school three years later, and he moved up into the senior school, there were even some colleagues who felt, like we did, that he should remain in mainstream education. We felt that the battle had almost been won, even though his future at the school continued to hang by a thread.

Adam, like so many others we began to recognise within the school community, straddled the gap between the need for 'normal' schooling and the need for more specialised provision. Our failure at that time was in attributing challenging behaviour to selfishness and immaturity, and in attempting to use crude disciplinary measures to address problems that were more profound than we could comprehend. Not only did we not possess the knowledge and skills fully to understand the difficulties he was facing, but our mindset was simplistic in identifying causation, and geared primarily towards those who were already destined to succeed.

For mainstream school to work for Adam it, and not he, had to change. We had to recognise the need for additional support, but we also had to learn how to change our own perceptions and abandon the deficit model of the challenging learner. We needed staff who had the insight to discern patterns in his behaviour that were associated with known conditions such as ASD and ADHD. They needed to be skilled and knowledgeable, but also willing to embark upon a significant reassessment of their own ingrained attitudes towards difficult pupils and behaviour in general. They had to offer unconditional support to Adam, no matter how remote and unwelcoming he could be, and in turn be given the same level of support by those in positions of higher authority within the school for the sympathetic actions that they took.

We also saw in the school a need to improve very significantly the way we communicated information about children, so that all staff could understand why certain approaches were taken, and conventional ones ignored. We were assisted at this time by a very supportive and determined headmaster who was prepared to give us the time we needed to make a difference. The school was not big, but changing attitudes was always going to be an uphill battle. It is often the case that successful schools are harder to improve than those that know they need to change.

During his early years at school, Adam was caught for a time in the eddies and backwaters of the mainstream system, but he pulled through with the support of sympathetic and knowledgeable staff and is now an example of how the inclusion of complex youngsters can work. He has passed his GCSEs with flying colours, performed on stage in school productions, and will go on to university where his academic potential, at least, should be realised. I doubt that life will be particularly easy for him, but he has developed a level of social competence that at one stage looked beyond his reach.

The case for small schools

When the call came through inviting me to apply for the post of head teacher at the New School, I was ready for a change, and for the challenge of running a school designed for the Adams of this world. The battles and paradigm shifts that had enabled Adam to survive in a mainstream environment had engendered in me an ambition to try elsewhere and with children whose needs were at least as demanding as his.

My job was to secure the future of the school by making sense of the term 'educationally fragile', and by convincing those who make decisions about the education of children with complex needs that the environment of the New School was what many of their youngsters needed. The concept of educational fragility was considered vague and romantic by many. Many assumed, incorrectly, that the school offered itself as a place of refuge and sanctuary, rather than of learning. My view was that this was certainly a community for learning, but also a place where children could develop and strengthen a sense of who they were and what they could do. It was a therapeutic environment in which individual resilience could be enhanced, and learning could be promoted. After all, effective learning requires confidence in who one is and where one is going. It requires a preparedness to take risks and sometimes to fail. Perhaps the best way to understand the concept of educational fragility is as a debilitating excess of fear. The fragile learner is, for whatever reason, *afraid* to learn, and afraid of much else besides. It is fear that underlies much of the challenging behaviour that characterises children like Adam.

An important feature of schools like the New School is their determination to allow children to fail, by providing a 'safe' environment. Failure is an important part of personal development, and social competence can occur only when resilience is built by learning to overcome adversity. So the props and prosthetic supports that allow a child to enter the school for the first time must be withdrawn before they become a permanent scaffold on which the child leans for the rest of his life.

Children must learn to cope with failed relationships and learn to repair them. They must learn to tease and be teased and to recognise in themselves their own strengths and weaknesses, and their value to those around them. Humour can be a powerful tool for affecting and expressing change, but only when used in a secure and trusting relationship.

The New School provides an environment in which children who might otherwise be excluded from the opportunities to do so can grow and form as individuals in much the same way that others do in mainstream schools. We do not shirk our responsibilities to challenge children, but do so with the skills that are needed when addressing the complex problems they bring with them. And we ensure that they leave us ready for the next stage in their lives.

After working with 'fragile' learners for the last six years or so, I have concluded that inclusion should be regarded as a worthy sentiment and a goal for many, rather than a dogma driving structural change within all schools. Inclusive societies are healthier and more humane than those that discriminate against difference and disability, and we, as individuals, must learn to respect the diversity of personalities and intellects that humankind has generated. But we must also recognise that we have yet to arrive at a definitive ideal for what the inclusive school system should provide.

A great deal can be achieved in mainstream schools. They can employ staff with special skills and expertise for meeting special educational needs, and they can liaise with other institutions which embody such expertise. But what they cannot do is be small and on a scale that falls within the grasp of the fragile learner. They cannot, therefore, offer the range of experiences that many fragile learners need for the full development of their capacities and sense of self. As laudable as the drive towards full inclusion may be, the time has not yet come when the special schools should close their doors. Too many children are still cycling that road to Marrakesh.

References

Warnock, Mary (2005), *Special Educational Needs: a New Look*, London: Philosophy of Education Society of Great Britain

Wolff, Sula (1995), *Loners: the Life Path of Unusual Children*, London: Routledge

7 Diversity and choice for children with complex learning needs

Will Spurgeon

In returning to the debate about inclusion (Warnock, 2005), Mary Warnock rightly reflects that the current education system, and the ideology that underpins it, belong to a very different world from the one her committee described in 1978. There are more diverse organisational arrangements, often created by schools themselves. Formal and informal relationships between schools and their communities have improved. And there have been significant changes in the role of local authorities and the degree of prescription from successive national governments.

Though much has changed, there is no indication of a shift in Warnock's basic ideas about the meaning and purpose of education. She does not reject the belief on which the 1978 report was based, that all children, irrespective of their abilities or disabilities, should be encouraged to aspire towards the same educational goals, namely independence, enjoyment and understanding. Rather, she invites us to consider the rich range of provision that has been created over the last 30 years to realise this concept. In particular, she is concerned that children should be permitted to choose the provision that best serves their educational and (indistinguishably in many cases) emotional interests.

The radical review for which Warnock calls in her 2005 publication should not in my view lead to a sterile and polarised argument about placement. The issue is not about two competing models, mainstream versus special provision. Instead it is an opportunity to show how the education system has matured to offer those with the most complex needs a choice. Those who try to polarise the debate by insisting on mainstream provision for all are in effect trying to deny such a choice to children with special needs. Instead of going to a special school if this is what they (or their parents) want and believe they need, they are to have only one option, mainstream provision, irrespective of its suitability. Indeed clear evidence to the effect that some children are not well served by mainstream education frequently falls on deaf ears. (The launch of Mary Warnock's 2005 pamphlet is a case in point.)

Radical inclusionists – people who want to abolish special provision – often argue that pupils in special schools are excluded and discriminated against. In this chapter I take the opposite view, arguing that a child who wants and possibly needs a special school may be excluded and discriminated against if denied such a school. If a school provides a happy, healthy atmosphere for living and learning, children who go there generally feel privileged to do so, and above all, feel included at the school. If this is not the case, they are free to go elsewhere.

In this chapter I shall discuss Marshfields School, near Peterborough, the school of which I am head. Marshfields is both a special and a specialist school. It is also, in my view, an inclusive school, given certain refinements of the concept of inclusion. Inclusion is not in my view simply about where a student is educated; rather it is about the nature of a person's learning experiences. I believe that the most inclusive setting for any student is the one that has the most positive impact on his or her learning.

For most students, this is unquestionably a mainstream setting. However, there are students who, for a number of reasons, thrive more completely in a different environment. This claim is not simply an attempt at self-justification. Since all schools have become data-rich and are subject to exacting evaluation from within and without, it is an empirical claim, which can be tested. I believe that the evidence will bear it out.

Full inclusionists, or special school abolitionists, should look at evidence that is rooted in school practice. This evidence should be drawn from the planned, formal aspects of school life as well as the less predictable, informal and more subjective elements. My experience has shown that a specialised environment can have a profound, positive effect on certain students both formally and informally. Researchers should compare special and mainstream schools with reference both to academic achievement and to qualitative factors relating to social, emotional and personal development.

Inclusion is not a matter of school life alone. We spend a considerable period of our lives in school, but this is negligible compared to the length of our lives typically spent in the wider community. Education is of worth in itself but it is also a preparation for the day that the young person leaves school and endeavours to become an independent adult in the world beyond school. Again my experience, based on evidence of students leaving school, demonstrates that some specialised environments provide a more complete support structure to bring this about. This turns the ideology of full inclusionism on its head, since the idea that mainstream experience is a necessary prerequisite of later successful inclusion in the community is one of its mainstays.

There are other, equally valid principles, working with and not against inclusion, that should help to shape the education system. A key tenet of government thinking, as expressed in the White Paper (DfES, 2005), is the promotion of diversity and choice. Schools strive to create cultures that endorse common principles but also show unique characteristics that meet the demands of their particular communities. Parents and students seek to find the school that most closely matches their own expectations of a community where they can flourish. This might be about academic excellence, but it could also be about the ethos of the school, the breadth of curriculum provision or the specialist opportunities that such a school affords. Few would question the right of parents and students to choose. The argument of this chapter is about the importance of protecting this right for those with complex needs.

Finally, a practical consideration influences my views. I am frequently confronted by parents and students who are distraught at their experiences of failure in local schools. The casualties of full inclusion are numerous, and this is why schools like Marshfields are heavily over-subscribed. For the sake of these students we need to remain a vibrant and successful school. If this means that we deny resources to others and inhibit progress to a different model, then so be it. I make no apology.

Marshfields School

Marshfields is a predominantly secondary day school for approximately 180 students aged 10 to 19 years who have complex learning needs and other associated difficulties. The students who have complex social, emotional and behavioural difficulties number 35 per cent, and 40 per cent of students have some kind of language impairment or communication difficulty. All the students in key stages 2, 3 and 4 have a statement of special educational need. Key stage 5 provides for the needs of an even more diverse group of students, who can enter with or without a statement. Every student who is admitted to the school has already had a significant experience of mainstream education.

Marshfields has a history of successful innovation and is involved in a number of local and national initiatives. It has developed a wide range of community partners which, in turn, allow a dynamic relationship between students on the school's roll and those in other establishments as well as interaction with business partners, public services and voluntary agencies. The school's work has been recognised by a number of prestigious awards, including the School Achievement Award, School Curriculum Award, Healthy Schools Award and Investors in People Award. It is included in the 2005 list of the most successful schools, published by Ofsted. This is the third occasion on which the school has been named by Oftsed, a privilege achieved by only 24 schools nationally.

In September 2003, Marshfields won specialist school status as a specialist technology college. This status has transformed an already successful school into a centre of excellence that meets the needs not only of the students on its roll, but also of staff and students in its wider family of schools and community partners across the region. In this chapter I shall explore some features that make Marshfields significantly different from a mainstream school. These features have a profound impact on the learning experiences of students, and are repeatedly referred to by parents when they choose to send their children to the school.

School ethos

Marshfields' mission statement says that students are seen as individuals who are valued for themselves. They have an individual identity that defines them in positive terms according to the contribution that they make to school life, rather than negatively in terms of their disability or learning need. This ethos is established and maintained by a staff whose focus is on treating students in this unique way. It can be sustained because the school is small enough for every student to be known intimately, and for all staff to be guided and supported in bringing this about.

This outstanding inclusive ethos has a positive effect on students' learning. Students are very happy to be in school, as seen in their impressive attendance records and their attitudes to school life. They behave well both in and outside the classroom. They are engaged in school life, and show a remarkable work ethic. Most importantly, students display a very high degree of confidence and self-esteem. This is directly related to their sense of belonging and the degree of staff support that they receive. As a result of this inclusive ethos, students enjoy considerable progress. This stands in stark contrast to their experiences earlier in their school careers.

Student population

With the exception of the sixth form, it is not possible to win a place at Marshfields without a statement of special educational need. The students have a diverse range of learning needs, but all are associated with the development of literacy and numeracy skills. They also have common challenges relating to their personal or social development. Finally, they have all had experiences of failure in their neighbourhood schools.

On admission to Marshfields, they become an equal member of a community where their learning needs are not seen as the most important thing about them. They are able to identify immediately with others who have had a common experience of school life. While each student brings a unique set of characteristics to the school, they are more readily described by their similarities than their differences. It is an enormous relief to them to feel similar to others; this is shown both by the remarkable changes in their attitude to school and in the explicit statements they make.

This sense of unity has a number of effects on learning. Perhaps the most impressive influence is the willingness on the part of students to take a risk. The pressure they feel is a positive encouragement to make progress, as it is with their peers elsewhere. Their earlier, mainstream experiences had been of an entirely different nature: that of protecting their self-esteem by avoiding failure, ridicule, social exclusion. This did not promote risk-taking but caution and fear, often leading to withdrawal from the learning activity entirely.

School organisation

Students enter a school setting that has been created specifically for them, rather than a system that they are required to adjust to and where they are at the margins. The organisational arrangements are aimed at promoting the learning of all students, rather than being devoted primarily to interests of the more able majority, as in many mainstream schools. Marshfields has no learning support units or separate SEN departments. It does not have to rely on streaming or setting in order to differentiate learning objectives so that they become relevant to all students within a year group.

Class sizes are limited to twelve. Each class is supported by a fully qualified, experienced teacher and a learning support assistant. This arrangement provides an optimal setting for dynamic relationships between students, so that they can both learn from each other and have frequent opportunities to receive individual support, as and when they require it.

In such small classes, each student can receive individual attention and praise for the most appropriate of reasons. They can have their moment in the spotlight through their educational achievement. Since this leads to immediate praise, a cycle of success is quickly established. This, in turn, transforms each student's own expectation about their life in school.

The school is two-form entry. With a sixth form of 50 places, this creates a school population of 180. The school is under constant pressure to expand, but the governors have consistently refused to accept this. They believe that part of the reason for the success of the school is its small size in terms of the total population, and not simply in terms of class sizes. This enables the school to maintain its underpinning ethos in all areas of school life. It also ensures that every student is an individual who is recognised and valued by all members of staff, and not just those with whom they come into immediate contact. Finally, it makes it possible to include every student fully in both the planned and the informal aspects of school life, within and beyond the campus.

Teaching and learning

The quality of teaching is fundamental to the standards that are achieved across the school. This is not unique to Marshfields. What are important are the skills and knowledge of the staff in working with students with complex needs. The staff have secure subject knowledge which is then combined with an expertise about making that knowledge accessible to students with these sorts of needs. They become expert in both dimensions. They are well trained in maintaining high standards of behaviour, particularly in the levels of motivation and expectations within students. Students know that they are in a class to learn but also know that the tasks have been created precisely for them. As a result, they are more fully engaged as active learners in relevant and meaningful learning tasks.

This is a far more difficult proposition in a mainstream setting, where class sizes are considerably bigger and the range of student abilities so much greater. Typically, in a mainstream secondary classroom, a teacher may be confronted by students operating at National Curriculum levels which are more than four levels apart. The pace of lessons inevitably will be faster; the step from one task to another will be greater; and the opportunities for teachers to return to earlier skills for 'over-learning' will be reduced.

In order for students with complex needs to succeed in mainstream classrooms, most schools will need to enhance their provision. At the least, this has resource implications. Many schools win extra funding, often in the form of extra hours provided by a teaching assistant, to enrich the classroom environment. However, this can be a further barrier to learning and inclusion. Learning may be inhibited because, being supported in their learning by the assistant, they have less direct time from the teacher. Their opportunities for inclusion are impaired because dependence on an adult exacerbates their difference from so-called 'normal' children.

Specialist school status

Marshfields was awarded specialist school status as a technology college in September 2003. This has further transformed the ability of the school to promote the learning of its students, and offers an effective model for other special schools across the country to keep pace with the current improvement agenda.

The specialist schools movement aims to build a network of innovative, high-performing secondary schools in partnership with business and the wider community. The expectation is that this will lead to higher standards both in these schools and in the wider community. Schools work together at all levels to share good practice and provide mutual support and challenge. They develop a particular identity through their chosen specialism, while maintaining a broader framework in line with the demands of the National Curriculum. Special schools offering secondary provision are entitled to apply, selecting either a curriculum specialism, like other secondary schools, or an SEN specialism.

In winning this status, Marshfields can present itself on equal terms with other successful secondary schools. It can reasonably argue that there is no distinction in terms of vision, aspiration or impact and so can be the first, best choice for some students rather than a compromise or last resort. Furthermore, the specialist school model provides a framework where special schools can overcome concerns about isolation, since the model demands a community dimension that formalises a relationship between the special school and its family of schools and wide community partners.

Since the successful bid, the school has dramatically improved its staffing and learning resources from an already high base. They are now regarded by Ofsted as excellent. The accommodation is also outstanding, and fit for its purpose as a provider of secondary education. When parents and students view the school, they do not talk about their experience of visiting a special school but are delighted that it is just like the best of the local secondary schools.

Returning to the rationale set out at the beginning, the school uses measures of impact on a student's learning as a reason to justify its existence. Students of all ages, irrespective of their ability or type of learning difficulty, achieve well. The students' success is attributable to consistently high-quality teaching and to the strong work ethic. Since the school became a specialist technology college, there has been a further steady increase in the standards reached.

Status has enabled the school to extend a curriculum that was already broad-ranging and well differentiated so that now it is very good, with excellent opportunities for enrichment. The school has emphasised those specialist subjects that are believed to be the most important in preparing students for life beyond school. Furthermore, this coherent and integrated development of the four specialist areas of maths, science, design technology and information and communication technology have helped to secure cross-curricular thinking skills relating to problem-solving. In addition to the expected National Curriculum subjects, students benefit from a wide range of applied learning experiences. This is especially true of life skills that can be taught explicitly rather than having to rely on their being 'caught' through informal experiences beyond the school, as is the case for most students.

Becoming a technology college changed Marshfields profoundly. This was not an add-on or simply an opportunity to increase annual funding, welcome as this is. The most important change was in this school's relationship to others. The school moved from *ad hoc* and informal links to a formalised partnership with a family of primary, secondary and special schools that led to a shared vision, common priorities for future action, joint training and a pooling of resources. Students now move between schools or work alongside each other on projects of mutual benefit. This ensures that the students at Marshfields have a specialised environment, dedicated specifically to meeting the core of their needs, but with opportunities to test their learning in a wider range of settings and alongside their peers. They are able to take advantage of these opportunities because of the progress they have made in this specialised setting, particularly in their emotional strength, confidence and self-esteem.

The community dimension of the school's work goes beyond the needs of students in the family of schools. Staff, parents and governors from within and beyond the school have access to the school's facilities, and use these both to enhance their own skills and to broaden their understanding of the needs of students with complex learning difficulties. The school extends this service to individuals, and their representative voluntary groups, that have ongoing learning needs in adult life.

Community-based learning

I have discussed the way in which specialist school status strengthened the role of Marshfields within its community. This involved building on a history of very successful practice relating to community-based learning. While partnerships have been formalised, this dimension has been a significant aspect of provision that has supported the successful transition of students from Marshfields to the world beyond school. As a result, community links are now excellent.

The school prepares students very well for the next stage of their lives, whether in education or employment. It is clear that the ultimate goal of the school is to educate students so that they can occupy a meaningful role within the community and make a valid contribution once they have left. Voluntary work through initiatives like the Millennium Volunteers Scheme, as well as compulsory work experience, are all parts of the vision.

The sixth form is the most developed and impressive aspect of this vision. The school offers post-16 provision to students who may or may not be statemented. Some are already on the school's roll; others join the school from other secondary schools following completion of statutory schooling. The school offers courses at three levels: foundation and intermediate, and a partnership course through a federation with the local regional college. There are clear aims and admissions criteria for each course, and clearly identified progression routes that enable students to move from a school-based environment to further education courses, training programmes and the world of work. This form of provision has been assessed by others to be a model of good practice to be shared nationally. However, this rests on the same vision as all aspects of community-based learning: that is, to create personalised learning opportunities that provide a structured process of greater inclusion in the world beyond school.

These links provide outstanding opportunities for students' personal development. Through such opportunities we reinforce our mission statement, and aim to work with the whole child, not just the academic. In other words, we aim to place him or her at the heart of the community.

Conclusion

This argument is not about competing opposites, but rather about an education system that has matured into a diverse, richly resourced and interrelated set of autonomous institutions. Each has a reason to exist in its own right, but is influenced by developments in partner establishments. This does not deny the validity of the inclusion concept. I have tried to show that special schools have become more complex organisations precisely in order to ensure their inclusiveness. The development of special schools as specialist has both raised standards and created links between schools within communities.

The notion of choice has become a controversial concept. There is concern that students will be selected by ability, and that the casualties of this process will be vulnerable students with complex needs, forced into second-rate, isolated provision. This very regrettable consequence is not my experience. Students and their parents choose us. No one is forced to attend the school. Rather, there is a sense of celebration because there is now an opportunity for the young person to flourish in an environment that is most appropriate to their needs. This is not leading to a reversal in the inclusion of students whose needs can be best met in the neighbourhood school. Marshfields remains successful because it is a specialist environment, developed to enhance the complex needs of a very specific group. At the same time, the school is formally involved in a dynamic relationship with the wider educational community, drawing from and contributing to the greater good.

If a young person wins a place at the Royal Ballet School to promote her skills in dance, or at the Royal School of Music to become a more accomplished cellist, there is unbridled joy. This is seen as a truly positive achievement. The same reaction should arise for a young person winning a place at this school. In my view it is the same process at work.

References

DfES (2004), *Removing Barriers to Achievement – the Government's Strategy for SEN* (White Paper), London: DfES

DfES (2005), *Schools – Achieving Success* (White Paper), London: DfES

Ofsted (2004), *Special Educational Needs and Disability: Towards Inclusive Schools*, London: Audit Commission

Warnock Committee (1978), *Special Educational Needs (the Warnock Report)*, London: DfES

Warnock, M. (2005), *Special Educational Needs: A New Look*, London: Philosophy of Education Society of Great Britain

Part 2

Philosophical and practical perspectives on inclusive education

8 Dilemmas of inclusion and the future of education

Brahm Norwich

Introduction

In *Special Educational Needs: A New Look*, Mary Warnock critically surveys concepts, values and practices in the special education field. In one respect, of course, she is well placed to do this: she chaired the well-known 1978 committee that introduced the concept of special educational need and paved the way for inclusive education as we know it. In other respects, however, this recent contribution is puzzling, betraying a lack of familiarity with current educational policy and debate. She writes, for example, that despite the expectations of the Warnock Committee that about 2 per cent would require a statement, 'the actual figure was around 20%' (Warnock 2005, p. 13). There is confusion here between the wider group of those considered to have special educational needs (about 16–20 per cent) and those with more significant needs who receive a statement (about 2–3 per cent). She states that there are 'gradations of need which our early thinking did not adequately address' (ibid., p. 13), ignoring what was said in her own report about the range and degrees of special educational needs. She also seems unaware of what is generally accepted nowadays about these gradations. There is no reference to non-statement special needs, nor to the DfES's recent attempt to define SEN in terms of broad categories for monitoring purposes.

On the question of inclusion, there is further confusion. Warnock rejects the idea that educational inclusion means having all children 'under the same roof' in favour of the idea that it means 'including all children in the common educational enterprise of learning, wherever they learn best' (ibid., p. 14). She also insists that the feeling of belonging is an important part of her concept of inclusion, but she does not explain how this relates to the notion of inclusion as being engaged in the common enterprise of learning. It is also notable that, despite what seem like negative comments about inclusive ideology and inclusion taking a 'foothold in society', she does not comment on specific government policy towards special schools. Since the Green Paper (DfEE, 1997) which set out the New Labour policy on SEN, it has been clear that government sees a continuing role for special schools. Though there has been an overall national decrease in the proportion of children in special schools from 1983 to 2001 (Norwich, 2002), with some local education authorities showing striking decreases over this period, the latest figures indicate that about 1.3 per cent of children are in special schools and that there are no LEAs who do not run or use special schools for children in their authorities (Ofsted, 2004).

In short, Warnock does not seem to be responding to current government policy or to overall patterns of policy and practice change. Her language and approach (such as her reference to the 'disastrous legacy' of the 1978 report) are antagonistic without reflecting the complexity and actualities of policy and practice. In an important sense there is a resemblance between her approach and that of some of her critics. The Centre for Studies on Inclusive Education, for example, argued in a response to the Warnock pamphlet that 'the right of disabled children and young people to inclusive education' should be defended (CSIE, 2005). Warnock's position is portrayed as representing 'bad integration', not 'inclusion which means changing schools so all children can flourish' (ibid.). Unfortunately this position is based, as I am arguing Warnock's position is based, on generalities. Rights are defended without recognition of the need to balance some rights against others. There is talk of 'special school survivors' but no mention of people with disabilities who are positive about special schools. It is claimed, falsely, that DfES research shows that effective inclusion improves achievement for all pupils/students (see Chapter 12, by Dyson *et al.*, in this book, for details of the study in question). The authors refer to the 'social model [which] draws on the thinking of disabled people and underpins all inclusive education'. This suggests, implausibly, if not disrespectfully, that all disabled people think alike. Contributions to this book demonstrate how far this is from being the case.

Both the CSIE and Mary Warnock from their opposing positions fail to grasp the multi-dimensional nature of concepts like inclusion and disability. 'Inclusion' has a multiplicity of meanings: it can refer to being 'under the same roof', being in the same class, and/or being engaged in the common enterprise of learning. 'Disability', likewise, can refer to specific literacy difficulties, profound hearing impairments, moderate emotional difficulties and profound and multiple learning disabilities. It is possible, for example, that inclusion in the sense of being under the same roof has not gone far enough for children with moderate emotional and behaviour difficulties, but gone too far for children with profound and multiple learning disabilities. Multi-dimensional concepts do not make for easy generalisations. This chapter is a call for appreciation of conceptual complexity and its implications for educational policy.

There are different approaches to the inclusive schooling question, some of which are represented in the chapters of this book. One focuses on reviewing relevant empirical research literature that bears on the field. This has been a favoured approach in the current climate, which stresses the value of evidence-based policy and practice. Though it is a useful approach, there is a scarcity of significant studies, especially in the UK, and seemingly not much interest in funding programmes of evaluative research. Another approach is to focus on particular studies that bear on specific aspects of the field, for example LEA policy-making or the relation between attainments in schools with different proportions of children with significant educational needs. Another common approach presents details about specific 'inclusive' practices, their context, procedures and evaluation of outcomes. All approaches include some normative or prescriptive line, but they differ in the extent to which the adopted norms and values are presented as clear cut or complex and needing deliberation.

It is rare to find arguments against inclusion, as it is rare to find arguments against democracy. Disagreement occurs, by and large, in regard to the extent and nature of inclusion. Warnock supports inclusion, but a particular version of it and not another. Vaughan supports what some call full or unconditional inclusion: that which rejects the option of special schools. Warnock recognises some ideals as 'worthy' but believes that they can be taken too far and so threaten other values. This implies that policy arises from the balance of values. The Warnock–Vaughan debate is about the difference between full or unconditional and conditional conceptions of inclusive education. I do not intend to examine this difference further. My aim, rather, is to explore some recent, more visionary thinking about how an inclusion education could evolve.

Pluralist democracies and multiple values

Recent thinking about conditional forms of inclusion tends to adopt a wider perspective than that set out by Mary Warnock. It connects SEN policy to other educational issues and views disability as one of several areas of vulnerability to exclusion. The problem with this wider perspective is the risk of ignoring the specific interests of those with disabilities in education. At particular risk are children with complex difficulties and those with challenging emotional and behavioural difficulties.

Proponents of a full inclusive education, who reject special schooling as an option, ground their position in basic rights. There has been much reference to fundamental rights, such as those asserted in the UNESCO Salamanca statement (UNESCO, 1994). It is rarely noted that the statement refers to a fundamental right to education, and not to an inclusive education. Assertions of basic rights also introduce complexity and uncertainty. Children may have several, conflicting rights, and there is scope for disagreement about which should take priority. Lunt and Norwich (2000) distinguish:

1   a right to participate in a mainstream school
2   a right to acceptance and respect
3   a right to individually relevant learning
4   a right to engage in common learning opportunities
5   a right to active involvement and choice in the matter.

In addition to tensions between these rights, there can be confusion about whether a practice is inclusive or not. For example, if inclusion means participating in the same learning programmes in the same location and being accepted and respected there, then *any* separate provision, say, in a part-time withdrawal setting, could be considered exclusionary, whether or not it provides opportunities to engage in common or relevant learning for an individual child.

The problem with asserting the predominance of one kind of right is that it ignores other considerations and can be damaging to the interests of children with disabilities. The problem with recognising multiple rights is that rights are not always compatible and balancing may be required. The rights of the minorities may undermine the rights of the majorities, or the right to individual preference for educational provision in a separate setting may conflict with participation in mainstream settings. These tensions are only too evident in the current debates and uncertainties around inclusion. They arise from the fact that as a society we hold multiple social and political values that bear on education. These lead to policy and practice dilemmas.

A basic tension, recognised by Warnock in her pamphlet, arises from the desire to treat all children as the same, while also treating them as different. This has been described as the 'dilemma of difference' (Minow, 1985). Recognising difference can lead to different provision that might be poor quality, stigmatised and devalued; but not recognising difference can lead to not providing adequately for individual needs. I have argued elsewhere (since Norwich, 1993) that the dilemma of difference centres around three aspects of education:

1   identification: whether to attribute SEN/disability or not?
2   curricula: whether and when to have common curriculum programmes and when specialised programmes?
3   location: whether to place in mainstream or separate settings and have ability or mixed-ability classes and groupings within classes?

In his examination of plural democracies, Dahl (1982) argued that autonomy for individuals and organisations is desirable in democracies. It is essential for the avoidance of government coercion and for human well-being. However, it also creates opportunities to do harm: to perpetuate injustice or to foster narrow egotism at the expense of the public good. Individuals and organisations, he concluded, ought to have some autonomy but ought also to be controlled.

This tension or dilemma has several aspects. Dahl identified one of these aspects as the tension between *uniformity* and *diversity*. Diversity relates to precious phenomena like language, religion, customs and values, and represents the importance of identity, personality and culture. But uniformity is also desirable, recognised more positively as commonality, or commitment to the common good. Not all differentiation has good consequences, and in education we oppose differences in opportunities to learn in favour of entitlement to a common curriculum. In this sense, the dilemma of difference within education may be seen as part of the wider dilemma of plural democracy.

Another aspect of Dahl's democratic dilemma is the tension between the *con-*

centration and dispersal of political power and resources. Opposition to the concentration of power runs deep in more liberal democratic systems (such as in the USA), and less so in more progressive and social democratic systems. Dispersal of power is widely prized in democratic societies, but where uniform enforcement of policy is desirable, then some centralisation, argues Dahl, is required and this depends on some concentration of power.

Dilemmas call for resolutions rather than solutions. They require the balancing of tensions, accepting less than ideal ways forward, and working positively with uncertainties and complexities. However, though it is useful to recognise the dilemmatic aspects of policy in education and special education, we need to go further and consider how these balances might work out in different kinds of resolutions or settlements.

Future scenarios

In this section I describe a project undertaken by the SEN Policy Options Group to examine policy options for the education of children with special needs or disabilities. The group, which has been in existence since the early 1990s as a national network of professionals, administrators and academics interested in policy and practice in the field, has organised policy seminars and published policy papers. The spur for the project was the wider interest and use of future scenario planning and its recent application to public services, beyond its origins in the commercial–industrial sector (Schwartz, 1998). What was promising about scenario planning was not that it would be prescient about the future, but that it can give a sense of what it may feel like in that future. It has the potential to improve strategic thinking by considering multiple possible futures, and in so doing it promises to enhance flexibility and adaptability.

The aim of the workshop was to explore the scope for an educational response to two different socio-political scenarios, as a basis for evolving a view of the issues around meeting the needs of those requiring special educational approaches. The workshop was led by a very experienced facilitator from the corporate sector. The aim of the workshop was to create knowledge-based future scenarios (with a view to 20 years from now) through the participation of informed stakeholders. The scenarios were chosen from a two-dimensional map (see Figure 8.1) to represent distinct socio-political contexts. The horizontal axis represented the second of the two aspects of Dahl's democracy dilemma (concentration versus dispersal of political power and resources), and ran from state decisions (left) to parental decisions (right). The intersecting vertical axis, representing the first dilemma (uniformity versus diversity), ran from differentiation (top) to commonality (bottom). Two socio-political scenarios were formulated for the workshop: one in the top right quartile was labelled 'extended choice and diversity', and the other, in the lower left, 'inclusive citizenship'. After the workshop further work was done to identify a third scenario, which was called 'regulated choice and diversity' (see Norwich and Lunt, 2005, for the full report about the project).

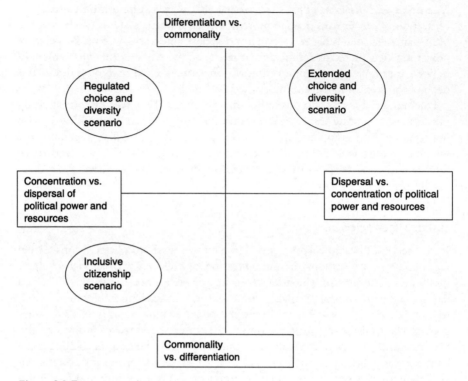

Figure 8.1 Future scenarios.

The poles defining the two dimensions in Figure 8.1 focus on one or other of the poles of the dilemmas. One end represents an emphasis on one pole with the other pole involved but in a secondary way; the other end represents the reverse relationship. This is meant to indicate that the poles do not stand for simple either/or situations, but rather a balance towards one or other pole. For example, commonality cannot be detached from some degree of differentiation.

Figure 8.2 shows that the scenarios were formulated in stages starting with the general socio-political features. From these general features, vision statements about the school system were formulated to be consistent with the socio-political orientation. Finally, those aspects concerned with SEN/disability were formulated in terms of the general school system.

The 'inclusive citizenship' scenario in Figure 8.1 involves a strong state role with the focus on common good and culture. The 'extended choice and diversity' scenario involves a market style system, with a key role for non-state providers and minimal state role. And the 'regulated choice and diversity' scenario sets limits to diversification through the state moderating user and provider competition. In the following sections, I describe the scenarios in greater detail.

General features of scenarios

- Finance for basic welfare/education services
- State/public and private sector roles
- Culture/user behaviour
- Organisational development
- Provision variations

Specifying scenarios of general school system

- Workforce/skills
- Content of learning
- Teaching and learning (pedagogy)
- Organisational structures
- Funding
- Partnerships/relationships
- Accountability (including stakeholders)
- Assessment

Specifying scenarios in terms of SEN/disability

- Identification and areas of SEN
- Curriculum and pedagogy
- Additional resources
- Legal and organisational basis for additional resource allocation
- School specialisation including future of special schools
- School admissions and exclusion
- Internal school/centre organisation: grouping, settings, support
- Raising standards

Figure 8.2 Stages in building scenarios.

Scenario one: inclusive citizenship

General features of the scenario

Society is considered as a whole with a significant state role based on prescriptive procedures and a minimal private sector role. Consensus building and a common culture are a priority. State sources (high tax base) fund basic welfare and health services, with the state applying the funds. People tend to be compliant to a democratic state and users accept what is provided. There are common institutions organised in terms of democratic accountabilities. The guiding principle is that provision variations are reduced to a minimum.

Features of general school system

There is a substantial national specified broad curriculum. Content focuses on cognitive, meta-cognitive and social and citizenship aspects. There is a blending of academic and work-related learning for 14–16-year-olds. All learners are entitled to a range of 'individualised' learning experiences from an agreed set of institutions. Learners are consulted about their individual learning experiences. The state determines what counts as appropriate teaching, and justifies this in terms of evidence. There is extensive use of state-developed ICT to support multi-pace differentiated teaching, learning and assessment. The predominant model of pedagogy is objectivist and outcomes-oriented. Every learner attends a local neighbourhood learning centre/school. These centres meet high quality state standards, which are organised through regional agencies that are responsible for the planning and continuity of centres/schools. The local government role is confined to supporting school improvement.

Attendance at a state centre/school is compulsory between 5 and 16 years. There is formal monitoring of admission and attendance practices. Every child receives an appropriate learning programme in a centre/school where the intake reflects a mix of attainments and social backgrounds (this has meant the demise of grammar, single-sex, faith and independent schools).

Resourcing is differentiated by a comprehensive national model of need that reflects democratic accountability. The level and focus of spending is prescribed and monitored through the use of audit trails (funding is no longer a local government role). The state prescribes accountability mechanisms in terms of national standards. All children are assessed in terms of a range of nationally prescribed outcomes using a national and teacher-based assessment framework. The assessment system takes account of learner differences and teacher judgements are checked through moderation and by comparison with a sampling of national test results. Teachers and teaching assistants are trained to national standards and deployed flexibly to meet the full range of learning needs. The workforce is managed in terms of supply and the meeting of standards.

Features of provision for educational disabilities

There has been a significant reduction in the identification of those having educationally recognised disabilities from 16 per cent (2005) to about 5–6 per cent (2020). The SEN concept has been abandoned and replaced by tighter definitions of educational disability. Moderate learning difficulties (MLD), social, emotional and behavioural difficulties (SEBD), and mild specific learning difficulties (SpLD) have also been abandoned, replaced by new area of 'moderate mixed difficulties' to cover a minority of children previously in the three historic areas. The national common curriculum applies to all learners, except those in the profound and multiple learning disabilities range, who have an adapted functional version of the national framework. Pedagogic adaptations for other areas of disability are prescribed nationally (in terms of pace, timing, setting, group size, intensity of strategy use, adapted materials) in ways that do not undermine standards of attainment. There are centrally determined pedagogic strategies for different dimensions of educational disability, relying on 'evidence-informed' sources. Disability is one of several areas for additional compensatory resources. All areas of specified disadvantage come under the same legislative system. The comprehensive resource allocation model is based on differential need with nationally prescribed formulae. National indicators are specified and allocations are made from a central agency through the regional structure to schools and partnerships of schools/learning centres.

Schools/ learning centres are legally responsible for formulating and reviewing individual learning plans for all children (not just for disability) and ensuring the maximum possible achievement of goals. All parents can access tribunals to contest the adequacy of educational provision after non-legal disagreement resolution procedures have been used. All schools are inclusive of all children in their neighbourhood. They provide the common national curriculum with adaptations to teaching–learning approaches based on individual needs. There are no special schools (as were known in 2005), though about 1 per cent with profound and multiple disabilities are mainly in self-contained groups in separate settings in neighbourhood centres/schools. These learners have as much learning and social participation as possible with less significantly disabled and non-disabled students. Special centres exist for children with significant health conditions and children in need of social care where education services are provided. There are state regulations about admissions and the conditions under which school/centre transfers take place. All schools/centres have an intake of children reflecting a mix of attainments and social background factors. (This was the basis for the closure of single-sex, faith, ability/disability selective, and fee-paying independent schools.)

Within centres/schools, every child belongs to a mixed-ability group and learns together for at least half of their programmes. Ability and cross-age grouping is used for the rest of the time. At secondary age, mixed-ability groups reduce to a minimum of a third of the time (justified in terms of social/citizenship goals). There is much use of co-teaching, collaborative learning and peer tutoring approaches. Teachers and assistants are well prepared for co-teaching and working with mixed-ability groups. There is a requirement that within 'classes' both mixed- and cross-ability groups are used. Individuals and small groups are sometimes 'withdrawn' from the class, but not just children with disabilities. Individual and small group teaching is also practised before and after formal timetable periods. 'Extended schools' play a key role in maintaining additional provision for those with disabilities. Educational standards are defined in terms of the outcomes set in the national curriculum framework. These outcomes are specified so that progress is inclusive of all, including those with profound and multiple disabilities. There are differentiated 'national targets' for different groups that take account of social and individual circumstances. These situated targets make simple school performance comparisons difficult. However, schools not reaching these targets persistently are required to review, re-plan provision, and sometimes change staff.

Scenario two: extended choice and diversity

General features of the scenario

The state acts as an enhanced broker in a market-style system where non-state providers respond to user preferences. There is a basic national 'safety net' through the limited use of vouchers. Individuals' private funds underpin choice of provision, though this can include philanthropic support. Users act as consumers in a system with a low tax base. There is minimal state control in a system based mainly on entrepreneurial activity and individualism. This has led to new models of diverse provision, where new alliances are welcomed. Individuals exercise their preferences in a system of competition between users for provision and providers for users. Change, flexibility and customisation are the key priorities. Wide variations in provisions are tolerated within broad and minimal national standards, reflecting socio-economic diversity.

Features of general school system

Stakeholders, learners and their families determine curriculum content, which therefore reflects socio-economic, faith, regional, sectional and other differences. The state specifies only a general curriculum framework confined to curriculum design and review procedures. This framework focuses on children and young people identifying their own learning needs. Diverse curricula have been developed. The learning needs of individuals are identified as part of a process of giving learners as much autonomy and responsibility for their learning as possible. Learners have rights to participate in forming their individual learning plans, to access a rich variety of learning paths and to support informed choices. A range of learning opportunities is available, from which informed decisions about preferred teaching and learning styles and learning centres/schools are made. This includes flexible learner groupings, various sites for learning (e.g. home, work-related settings), diverse learning facilitators and modalities of learning (e.g. the extensive use of privately developed ICT). Pedagogy assumes a learner-centred self-determining model.

The state requires every learner to have an individual learning plan between the ages of 5 and 19 years. User groups (such as charities, voluntary organisations, commercial organisations, parent groups, etc.) are responsible for planning and providing continuity, quality and a range of learning opportunities. The state specifies basic general procedures for managing all learning centres/schools, which have charitable status. All learners have conditional rights to suitable learning opportunities that meet their individual needs and preferences. Providers are required to demonstrate fair entry and exclusion criteria, given their programme goals and children's learning characteristics. They are expected to have their own clear learning standards expressed in outcome terms and users' decisions and preferences are the basis for local accountability systems. There are diverse assessment systems corresponding to the range of educational programmes, managed by diverse organisations. The national assessment framework, with a strong formative focus, offers guidance and exemplars. The workforce is drawn from different backgrounds and professions. There are diverse quality assurance systems for training the workforce.

Features of provision for educational disabilities

There is no national classification of SEN/disability. It is widely believed that the proportion of identified children for specialist provision has increased. This is attributed to parental pressures, though relevant statistics are not collected nationally. There has been increased recognition of 'new areas' of disorder, for example non-verbal learning disabilities (NVLD) and disorders of attention, motor and perceptual functioning (DAMP). Identification is conducted mainly by non-state agencies that serve learning centres and institutions. The general national curriculum framework enables the growth of specific curricula and pedagogic approaches. This includes specialist 'therapeutically' orientated curricula and pedagogic approaches, which have emerged in response to parental interest in addressing functional impairments. There has also been an increase in the merging of educational and learning-based health and mental health interventions. Additional resources for specialist provision come from family income, voluntary organisation contributions and minimal state additional vouchers. The state provides a strong tax incentive for charitable donations to disability organisations, so supporting voluntary organisations' contributions to schooling. Voluntary and not-for-profit organisations play a major role in funding and providing education services for children with disabilities. These providers of special education services are held to account through user preferences and evaluations. There is no specific legal basis for redress, other than a 'duty of care'.

Specialisation is a key aspect of school organisation, which is permitted in the areas of curriculum (teaching focus and level), faith and philosophical orientation. Through the operation of parental preference, there has been an increase of dis-ability-specialised schools/learning centres (justified in terms of curriculum focus and philosophical orientation). A diverse range of organisations operate, for example, special schools/centres, specialised settings co-located with general schools, 'inclusive' schools/centres which welcome all children with disabilities and provide as much social and learning participation in general settings as possible. Providers are required by legislation to demonstrate fair entry in terms of gender and ethnicity, with limited selection in the areas of permitted school specialisation: faith, learning abilities and disabilities. Fair exclusion criteria are also required by legislation. There is a wide range of internal forms of ability grouping and learning support, depending on the orientation and kind of learning centre. These internal forms reflect the curriculum orientation and aims of the schools/ learning centres, and are justified in terms of what is required to support learning outlined in individual learning plans. Children with similar kinds and degrees of disabilities learn in distinct kinds of settings (as parents and children have a major say in placement and forms of provision). Raising standards has diverse interpretations reflecting the range and kinds of learning outcomes. There are no standard national assessment framework or tests, but well-developed assessment systems for diverse needs, abilities and interests, including children with profound and multiple disabilities (informed by a national assessment framework in the form of guidance).

Scenario three: regulated choice and diversity

General features of the scenario

The state leads and moderates the private and voluntary sector role in a system based on choice. There is some degree of mixing of private and state funds (e.g. vouchers with limits on the use of private funds). The state has a counterbalancing role to redress the negative impacts of a market-oriented system. Diverse cultures are encouraged within a loosely linked common culture. The state moderates user and provider competition and provides frameworks for organisations, in which the priority is user participation in new developments. Diversity is tolerated only within specific national standards.

Features of general school system

There is a flexible general nationally specified curriculum core, with a focus on self-determined learning and social goals. There is scope for stakeholders, learners and families to specify content and learning orientation within the broad national framework, though there is national regulation of the curriculum development process. Individual learning needs are derived from the continuous negotiations between the state-prescribed agendas and family/learner participation. This reflects a general and flexible national commitment to learning entitlements. Learners are therefore consulted about their learning needs, but negotiate in forming plans with parents and teachers. There is general national guidance about 'appropriate' teaching–learning approaches and settings. Extensive partnerships and negotiations between diverse educational organisations and providers are encouraged as a way of determining appropriate teaching approaches within national guidelines that emphasise social goals. There are also partnerships about the extensive use of ICT. This pedagogic approach assumes a teacher–learner negotiated model. Every learner is required to have an individual learning plan (from 5 to 19 years) that includes reference to the provision required to meet learning goals.

There is a mix of state-maintained and non-state schools/learning centres. More expensive centres/schools are required to provide a certain number of state-funded studentships. Regional agencies monitor and regulate overall continuity and coverage of provision. These regional agencies also delegate functions to local government for all provision in their areas. All learners have conditional rights to suitable learning opportunities that meet their individual needs and preferences. The state requires that all providers do not discriminate on the basis of gender, ethnicity, and disability for entry/exclusion to provision. Adequate common levels of funding are set by the state, through a semi-independent agency. Funding comes from mix of sources: state (significant proportion), commercial and voluntary organisation partnerships, and limited use of individual income. Providers set specific educational standards locally within the prescribed general standards framework. Providers' own monitoring and evaluation act as the basis for accountability systems, with users' evaluations and preferences also taken into account. Assessment systems relate to the diversity of local educational provision/programmes, though they also conform to the general national assessment framework, which takes account of learner differences. There are national standards for the entry and preparation of the workforce, which includes flexibilities about non-teacher groups involved in provision. The supply and quality assurance of the workforce is coordinated by a national agency.

Features of provision for educational disabilities

A national classification of educational disabilities is in operation. It was based on the multiple dimensions of educationally relevant functional impairments, learning activity limitations and learning participation restrictions, derived from the World Health Organisation's International Classification of Functioning (WHO ICF). The framework is used to standardise identification practices and to inform curriculum and pedagogic planning. The national curriculum framework, with its core focus on self-determined learning and social goals, applies to all learners. Stakeholders are encouraged to adapt or suspend elements when they have an 'alternative' framework. The national curriculum agency facilitates 'alternative' curriculum and pedagogic developments in partnership with stakeholder organisations/groups. Pedagogic diversity is also encouraged through partnerships between the agency and other groups and organisations. Adequate levels of additional resources for disability are specified as part of statutory framework for additional resourcing to address social disadvantage. There is significant funding from tax, but also from non-state organisations and family income. There are state incentives and encouragement for organisations to contribute additional resourcing. Maintained and non-state schools/centres are expected to raise funds from non-state sources to be matched by state funds. Providers are legally responsible for individual learning plans for all children, with specific requirements for children with disabilities. Local government organises disagreement resolution (between providers and parents) as part of its delegated responsibility from regional agencies.

The diversity of provision for children with disabilities gives a limited legitimacy to separate special schools/centres. Specialist provision in separate settings, that is, in special schools and classes, has to meet national statutory conditions (e.g. minimum degree of learning and social participation with the non-disabled). Interchange sometimes involves teachers and children from the general settings participating in settings designed for children with disabilities. Direct providers are not permitted to discriminate on the basis of gender, ethnicity, faith, learning abilities and disability for entry and exclusion to provision. Diverse forms of internal organisation in school/learning centres are permitted, if they are consistent with the curriculum orientation and aims of specific schools/centres and the national curriculum framework. Ability and other kinds of groupings are encouraged (cross-age, similar interests, etc.), provided they do not engender excessive social divisions between diverse children. Mixed-ability groupings are required for at least 20 per cent of formal learning times. Withdrawal of children with disabilities from mixed-ability groupings is practised, in order to provide learning support in keeping with learners' preferences. Educational standards are defined in programme-specific terms and the limited national core set of learning outcomes. These national outcomes are monitored selectively by testing national random samples. Assessment of progress within the diverse programmes has to take account of learner differences including those with disabilities.

Conclusions

These scenarios may not be easily matched to actual policies and practices; they are hypothetical constructs relating to future possibilities. However, they enable us to consider the implications of distinct socio-political visions, based in values that we can assume will be enduring over the next 15 to 20 years. The advantage of this kind of scenario approach is that it enables us to engage in holistic and inter-connected thinking about the general school system and provision for the minority identified as having SEN/disabilities. The approach adopted in this project also reflects the way in which SEN/disability policy is embedded in the general school system and the general social system.

There is no space to comment in detail about the similarities and differences across the three scenarios. But the project can be seen to illustrate, through working out in detail how the policy elements are inter-connected, that what is considered to be 'good' provision and educational 'progress' depend on the balances struck in the control and differentiation dilemmas assumed in the exercise. The detail presented above is illustrative rather than definitive. The similarities are particularly interesting, as they relate to particular issues in current policy and practice. In all the scenarios there is some retention of separate educational settings – least in the inclusive citizenship scenario, where the state prescription of commonality is greatest. In all scenarios classification systems play a key role in additional resource allocation and curriculum/pedagogic planning, though the kinds of classification are different from current models in practice. Some form of differentiation is evident in the linked question of curriculum focus and organisation across the scenarios. The current concept of SEN gives way to other related notions through focusing on some of its elements, for example, additional needs that go beyond SEN/disability, and individual planning that goes beyond statements. The system outlined in the inclusive citizenship scenario bears some resemblance to the wider concept of 'additional support needs' in the new Scottish system.

Some differences between the scenarios are also notable. Resource allocation and funding, which is clearly a key area for education, is dealt with differently in the three scenarios. The extent of partnerships and collaboration differs across the scenarios, and here the competition/collaboration tension inherent in current policy is clearly articulated. Accountability is different across the three scenarios, in its nature, purpose and extent. All scenarios envisage an assessment system in place, though the nature and accountability differ. Under admissions, all learners are entitled to an education, but there is considerable variation in choice and therefore in nature of provision.

It is also appropriate to comment on the specific forms that the scenarios have taken. The final versions were based on further work after the workshop and do not represent the positions of those involved in the original workshop. The pluralist and dilemmatic assumptions built into the exercise are evident in the specific formulations of each scenario. The scenarios reflect the different balances between commonality and differentiation and central or distributed control, but also contain some minor elements of the other opposing pole. So the versions of the inclusive citizenship and extended choice and diversity scenarios veer away from the 'scarier' versions that are heard in some political debate. The inclusive citizenship scenario is presented as 'softer' and as more participative than some versions associated with 'Stalinist' visions of an over-controlled society. The extended choice and diversity scenario is presented as having more social coherence and minimum standards than some visions of a divided, unequal and over-individualised society.

The third scenario, regulated choice and diversity, might be seen as a version of New Labour's 'third way' policies. This was not the intention, and nor does this scenario correspond with the details of recent government policy. The scenario was derived in the same way as the other two during the project. Its formulation in terms of the general school system and SEN aspects is markedly different from the changing orientations evident in recent government policies. This difference is also evident in the government's 'personalised learning' agenda. There are elements of this agenda in each of the scenarios presented here. This new policy interest in 'personalised learning' also illustrates how these imagined, interconnected and coherent scenarios contrast with the mixing of policy elements in the development of actual policy initiatives.

It is also worth discussing some responses to these scenarios at a recent policy seminar. One judgement was that the scenarios were not adventurous enough and too bound by current assumptions and influences. Others were concerned about the design of the scenarios, questioning the design principle of balancing contrary values. This was a critical point as it can be linked to the position discussed at the start of this chapter, the position that avoids and ignores multiple values and their possible tensions. This positioning can be seen to express a form of 'ideological purity' (Norwich, 1996), which reflects an exclusive commitment to a particular kind of idealised future that cannot be tarnished or moderated by other ideals or factors. If the scenario approach illustrated in this chapter is useful, it is because it helps us to envisage different kinds of futures, to exercise creative foresight and to enhance strategic thinking through greater adaptability. If it has relevance to the current debates about SEN policy, it is to understand and accept 'ideological impurity', the realisation that, in plural democracies, we need to be positive and realistic about recognising and resolving policy dilemmas.

References

Centre for Studies on Inclusive Education (2005), 'In defence of inclusion: Warnock challenges the rights of disabled children to inclusion' (personal communication)

Dahl, R. A. (1982), *Dilemmas of Pluralist Democracy: Autonomy and Control*, New Haven, CT: Yale University Press

DfEE (1997), *Excellence for All Children: Meeting Special Educational Needs*, London: HMSO

Lunt, I. and B. Norwich (2000), *Can Effective Schools be Inclusive Schools?* London: Institute of Education, Bedford Way Series

Minow, M. (1985), 'Learning to live with the dilemma of difference: bilingual and special education', in K.T. Bartlett and J.W. Wegner (eds), *Children with Special Needs*, New Brunswick, NJ: Transaction Books

Norwich, B. (1993), 'Ideological dilemmas in special needs education: practitioners' views', *Oxford Review of Education*, 19 (4), 527–46

Norwich, B. (1996), 'Special needs education, inclusive education or just education for all?', inaugural lecture, Institute of Education, London University

Norwich B (2002), 'Special school placement and statements for English LEAs 1997–2001', report, CSIE, University of Exeter

Norwich, B. and I. Lunt (2005), 'Future schooling that includes children with SEN/disability: a scenario planning approach', in SEN Policy Options group (ed.), *Future Schooling for SEN/Disability*, Policy Paper (policy seminar, 22 Sept 2005, Institute of Education, London University), NASEN website, http://www.nasen.org.uk

Ofsted (2004), *Special Educational Needs and Disability: Towards Inclusive Schools*, Ofsted HM 2276

Schwartz, P. (1998), *The Art of the Long View: Paths to Strategic Insight for Yourself and Your Company*, New York: Doubleday

UNESCO (1994), *The Salamanca Statement and Framework for Action on Special Needs Education*, Paris: UNESCO

Vaughan, M. (2005), 'Wary about Warnock', letter, *Times Educational Supplement* (17 June 2005, p. 26)

Warnock, M. (2005), *Special Educational Needs: A New Look*, London: Philosophy of Education Society of Great Britain

9   Reforming special educational needs law

Vocabulary and distributive justice

William Evans

Warnock (2005) proposes a radical review of special educational needs (SEN). If her contentions are that there should be less emphasis on inclusion, that there should be more specialist provision in small units, and that statements of special educational need should be used only as passports to those units, then her proposals are not radical enough to overcome some other difficulties the present law produces. Review of the law could usefully examine in particular two fundamental issues: the vocabulary the law of special educational needs uses; and the philosophical basis that ought to inform how the law is reformed.

The vocabulary of special educational needs

The current law of SEN is contained in the Education Act 1996, as amended by the Special Educational Needs and Disability Act 2001. The 1996 Act largely repeated provisions in the Education Act 1993, which introduced a code of practice and a statutory tribunal to decide certain types of dispute between parents and local education authorities, but otherwise substantially re-enacted the Education Act 1981. The 1981 Act was based on recommendations of the committee Mary Warnock chaired, which reported in 1978 but which had done much of its work in the mid-1970s.

Before Warnock (1978), what law there was relating to the education of pupils with impairments was an irregular patchwork of uncoordinated provisions, many confined to pupils with particular descriptions of disability. Its vocabulary was inconsistent and disorderly. In place of the ten descriptions of what were then called handicaps, Warnock (1978) proposed, and the 1981 Act introduced, generalised concepts of learning difficulty, special educational needs, and special educational provision. All were defined in terms of difference from the norm.

When the 1981 Act came into force, UK law had no concept of disability discrimination. The only statute relating to disability at large was the Chronically Sick and Disabled Persons Act 1970, which imposed a qualified duty on local social services authorities to make a limited range of services available to people with certain descriptions of disability. Apart from a code of practice, now in its second edition, a statutory tribunal to determine appeals, and an extension of that tribunal's jurisdiction over certain types of disability discrimination claim, SEN law remains much as it was in 1981, as does the vocabulary used in the legislation and hence also by those who work in SEN, in schools, the NHS, voluntary organisations, local and central government and the professions.

The key word, repeated throughout the legislation, is 'special'. Pupils with special educational needs are thus distinguished from 'ordinary' or 'normal' pupils. Their needs are assessed by methods that compare their cognitive abilities, capabilities and attainments with those of the majority of pupils. Delivery of educational provision for them will be 'special' and will often be 'differentiated'. Unlike other pupils, they will have individual education plans. Some may have statements, of whom some may attend special, as distinct from mainstream, schools. Because the vocabulary permeates the whole system, the system distinguishes pupils with SEN as 'other'.

Since 1981 popular English usage of the word 'special' has changed. In some contexts the word has been evacuated of meaning by marketing hype, for example, special offers or chef's specials. Sometimes 'special' is a euphemism to disguise the unpalatable, for example, special clinics, special forces. A school may be described diplomatically as being in special measures. Some people may use 'special' as a term of abuse, a point noted by Mark Haddon in *The Curious Incident of the Dog in the Night-time*:

> All the other children at my school are stupid. Except I'm not meant to call them stupid, even though this is what they are. I'm meant to say that they have learning difficulties or that they have special needs. But this is stupid because everyone has learning difficulties because learning to speak French or understanding Relativity is difficult, and also everyone has special needs, like Father who has to carry a little packet of artificial sweetening tablets around with him to put in his coffee to stop him getting fat, or Mrs Peters who wears a beige-coloured hearing aid, or Siobhan who has glasses so thick that they give you a headache if you borrow them, and none of these people are Special Needs, even if they have special needs.
>
> But Siobhan said we have to use those words because people used to call children like the children at school *spaz* and *crip* and *mong* which were nasty words. But that is stupid too because sometimes the children from the school down the road see us in the street when we're getting off the bus and they shout, 'Special Needs! Special Needs!' But I don't take any notice because I don't listen to what other people say and only sticks and stones can break my bones and I have my Swiss Army knife if they hit me and if I kill them it will be self-defence and I won't go to prison.

But mostly we use 'special' to distinguish: to denote difference from the norm, otherness.

Since the late 1990s UK government policy has been that so far as possible pupils with SEN should be educated in mainstream schools. Inclusion is government policy, and local education authorities are expected to implement it. Inclusion has become indirectly a statutory duty, because it is advocated in the secretary of state's code of practice, to which the 1996 Act requires everyone making decisions about a pupil with SEN to have regard. The only explicit statutory provisions, however, are those in the 2001 Act requiring pupils who do not have statements to be educated in a mainstream school as distinct from a special one; reinforcing a parent's right in certain circumstances to choose a mainstream school; and requiring those who make decisions to have regard to the secretary of state's guidance on the point.

Schools and local education authorities find it hard to implement inclusion. As Warnock (2005) noted, some difficulties are to do with inadequacy of resources for special education; some with parents objecting to their children being educated with pupils with SEN, especially those that present in challenging behaviour; some with how behaviour is to be managed; and some with the stances taken by teachers and trade unions. But in addition to and underlying all these difficulties are conflicts and inconsistencies created by the vocabulary of SEN, which is based, not on a concept, let alone a presumption, of including pupils with SEN in mainstream schools alongside their peers, but on rules which require that they be identified, distinguished, and treated differently.

While the concepts and vocabulary of SEN have remained static since 1981, the vocabulary of disability, like its politics, has moved on. SEN law, however, has not kept up: it has fallen behind its peers. Just as academic critiques of special education practices have moved from a medical model to a disability rights model, similarly much of the law relating to people with disabilities is now about discrimination, and it is under the head of disability discrimination that the law about impairments is now developing.

That suggests a way forward. Not all pupils with SEN are disabled, as the Disability Discrimination Act uses that term. Nor does every disabled pupil, as there defined, necessarily have SEN. Under SEN law a pupil with a special educational need is one with a learning difficulty, that is, the pupil 'has a significantly greater difficulty in learning than the majority of children of his age', or 'has a disability which either prevents or hinders him from making use of educational facilities of a kind generally provided'. Under disability discrimination law a disabled pupil is one who 'has a physical or mental impairment that has a substantial and long-term adverse effect on his or her ability to carry out normal day-to-day activities'. So, for example, a pupil with a mobility difficulty might be a disabled pupil but might not necessarily have a special educational need; and a pupil with a literacy difficulty might have a special educational need but might not necessarily be a disabled pupil.

Because the concepts of SEN and disability overlap, it would be helpful if laws that apply to both sets were to be consistent, and use consistent vocabulary. A review of special education law might usefully examine the vocabulary of SEN in the light of current thinking and values about disability, and might helpfully update the conceptual constructs and the terms used in SEN law, and the labels practitioners are expected to apply to pupils. A review ought to consider complete restructuring of SEN law so as to remove from the whole sphere concepts and procedures, not just words, that create otherness. That might be considered radical in comparison with current SEN law, but it would not be radical in the context of present-day discrimination law as a whole. A mildly radical possibility might be to abolish SEN law altogether as a discrete area of public law, and instead to extend the definition of disability so as to include what SEN law now calls learning difficulties, and thus to assimilate SEN into the general law of disability discrimination. The issues for parents, local education authorities, schools and tribunals would then be, not whether the pupil should be assessed or should have a statement, but whether the pupil is a disabled pupil; and if so, whether the school, the authority and the NHS have made reasonable adjustments as required by disability discrimination law. It would still be helpful to have a code of practice to give guidance on good practice, and a tribunal to determine disputes. Problems caused by inadequacy of resources would remain, but at least decisions would be made using concepts and vocabulary consistent with present-day expectations and values surrounding impairment, and inclusion would then have a coherent legal basis.

Distributive justice

To re-articulate the law of SEN in terms of the constructions and vocabulary of disability discrimination law would still beg the question of what ethical values ought to underpin the law and the code of practice, and inform decision-making. The sphere of SEN can be seen as a market, in which a supply side (schools, local authorities and sometimes the NHS) delivers a commodity (special educational provision) to a demand side (pupils, represented by parents, some of whom may be supported or represented by voluntary organisations and special interest groups, of whom some may also act as contractors for the supply side). As philosophers from Locke onwards have observed, if there were a sufficiency or a superfluity of commodities, everyone would be able to obtain what they wanted, so there would be no disputes about allocation. And as Hume (1751, p. 83) pointed out, whereas in conditions of extreme scarcity justice is likely to give way to 'motives of necessity and self-preservation', in conditions of moderate scarcity justice is required in the allocating or distributing of resources. For most forms of special educational provision demand exceeds supply, so it is necessary to have criteria for allocating or distributing the scarce resource. Concepts of distributive justice offer one philosophical basis for devising criteria of that sort.

Since Aristotle, theories of distributive justice have been based either on concepts of equality – that is, claiming fairness by treating all recipients alike – or on concepts of desert – that is, treating recipients correlatively to a chosen factor, such as merit or need. Broadly speaking, those who argue for distribution in equal shares, so that every recipient receives the same in content, quantity or value, contend that fairness consists in the supply side taking action that is identical for every recipient on the demand side. Those who favour distribution correlative to a chosen factor contend that distribution in equal shares is unfair because it ignores inequalities that pre-exist on the demand side: in the context of

SEN, rigidly equal distribution would not respond to pupils' diversity or reflect differences in the cost of meeting diverse needs.

Current UK SEN law is based on distribution correlatively with a chosen factor, that is, special educational need. Within that approach, however, it is also implicit that pupils whose needs are similar (that is, in terms of their nature, their severity, what provision they call for, and how much that costs) are to be treated alike, so that if one pupil receives more than another with similar needs, that disparity is regarded as unfair.

Because the economy of SEN consists of a mass-market supply side delivering a mass-produced product to a demand side that consists of individuals with diverse needs, it has to face what Dyson (2001) and others call the dilemma of difference. (See Chapters 8, 10 and 13 of this book.) This concerns the apparently contradictory intentions to treat children fairly as the 'same' and also as 'different' in the sense of having individual needs. The dilemma is complicated by the law and the rhetoric of government policy permitting parental choice to those who can afford it. But there is a particular difficulty that arises out of the fact that the supply side does not have the resources to meet even the demand the supply side believes it ought to meet, let alone the (sometimes exaggerated and specially pleaded) demand that the demand side actually makes.

Not only does the current law not help resolve that problem, it exacerbates it. Part IV of the 1996 Act requires local education authorities (LEAs) to make or arrange provision to meet the special educational needs of children for whom they are responsible, as that responsibility is defined in s.321 of the 1996 Act. The 1996 Act imposes a series of statutory duties on each LEA. The first, in s.9, is to have regard to the general principle that pupils are to be educated in accordance with the wishes of their parents, so far as that is compatible with the provision of efficient education and training and the avoidance of unreasonable expenditure. That wording is echoed in paragraph 3 of schedule 27, which says that if, before a LEA issues a statement, the child's parent has expressed a preference for the child to attend a maintained school, the LEA must comply with that preference unless the school is unsuitable or the child's attendance there would be incompatible with the efficient education of other children there or the efficient use of resources. There is a similar requirement regarding change of school under paragraph 8 of schedule 27. Lastly, s.316, as amended by the 2001 Act, requires the LEA to secure that, if similarly worded conditions are satisfied, the child is educated in a school which is not a special school, unless that is incompatible with the wishes of the child's parent. As it is sometimes put, at risk of obscurity and inaccuracy in certain contexts, there is a presumption in favour of mainstream placement.

Those enactments, however, are of somewhat limited application. Section 9 of the act imposes a duty merely to have regard to (as distinct from giving effect to meticulously) a general principle (as distinct from a rule mandatory in every individual case). Paragraphs 3 and 8 of schedule 27 and the corresponding s.316 as amended apply only to cases that fall within the scope of those enactments, and are in effect confined to cases where the choice is between two types of maintained provision, so they do not apply where the issue is whether the pupil should attend a fee-charging school at the public expense. Recent case law suggests that the more specific provisions in Part IV of the Act take priority over the general duty in s.9 of the 1996 Act.

In practice those principles are subservient to the expectation that the LEA will meet all the pupil's special educational needs. The LEA is required by law to deliver provision to meet the special educational needs of the pupil subject to limited considerations about the availability of resources (whether within or outside the LEA), but completely ignoring distributive justice as between one pupil and another.

Subject to the constraints of the general law and central government controls exercised under the law, each LEA is autonomous, so different LEAs may take different views about the assessment of children's similar needs and the provision those needs call for. That is an inevitable result of local authorities being local, having autonomy, being composed of members with differing party political views, and exercising discretion, in the sense of being free to make their own decisions, within the bounds of the law.

Finance dominates all decision-making. Each LEA is required by law to determine before the start of each financial year how much it will spend in the following year. The total amount is influenced by considerations such as the amount of the previous year's spending; the amount of grant allocated by central government; the ongoing commitments the authority has entered into; the amount of council tax individuals will have to pay; the political acceptability of any increase; any mandates upon which the party in control of the council was elected; the demands of all the education service, not just pupils with SEN; the demands of all the other services, not just education, for which the council is responsible; the council's own policies about financial strategy and management; and any constraints imposed by central government (which may limit the amount of any increase in council tax, the amount of borrowing, or levels of expenditure compared with nationwide targets or norms).

In practice the council (or its controlling party), having decided what level of expenditure will be incurred by the council as a whole during the forthcoming year, will then apportion that money among the various services for which it is responsible, usually by allocating a budget to each of its services. Some of the education service budget will be allocated for special educational needs, in so far as it has not all been delegated, as the government has increasingly required, to schools. The extent to which education department officials are free to vire expenditure from one head to another within what remains of the education budget will vary from one LEA to another. But broadly speaking, once the special educational needs budget has been set, there is little chance of additional money being made available during the year: the council will have strict rules about the appraisal and approval of supplementary estimates, the terms for resort to any contingency fund or reserves, and how unforeseen emergencies must be treated.

The council's education department will have comparatively little discretion in allocating its non-delegated special educational needs budget. Most of it will be committed, in the sense that substantial amounts will already have been earmarked or top-sliced for debt charges and staffing costs – the latter a particularly severe constraint, because so much local authority work is labour-intensive, and with special educational needs entailing the employment of many comparatively highly paid staff such as experienced, qualified and specialist teachers, educational psychologists and service managers. Much of the budget will also be committed because it is for children already receiving special educational provision, whose needs the LEA will have to continue to meet unless they move out of the LEA's area, cease to have special educational needs, transfer to further education, die, or otherwise cease to be the responsibility of the LEA.

As a result, most LEAs have to devise methods of distributing the comparatively small part of the budget they are in practice free to spend. Some councils do that by establishing machinery, such as a panel of professionals, for recommending or determining the amount of money, or the degree of priority, to be accorded to one pupil as against all the others. Such moderating machinery is encouraged by paragraphs 7:37 and 8:9 of the Code of Practice for decisions about whether to undertake a statutory assessment of a pupil's special educational needs or to issue a statement. Views may differ as to what is fair in any particular instance, but there is broad if grudging acceptance of decisions which are taken in the light of policies and procedures which treat like cases alike and which do not accord preference for inadequate reasons. There is similarly grudging acceptance that professional managers exercising professional judgment, independent of pressure groups or the influence of individuals or political parties, generally come up with acceptable distributions, while recognising that there is not enough money or other resource to satisfy everyone's needs or wishes.

Perhaps because of lack of trust in professional judgment, perhaps to reduce the risk of officials giving a particular child or group of children preferential treatment, perhaps because of a wish to have a process that is as transparent and open as possible, perhaps to reduce the risk of discrimination or maladministration claims, some LEAs adopt more mechanical methods for distributing provision. Provision is allocated to individual pupils depending on the nature of the child's learning difficulty, its severity, its complexity, the availability of local resources, and other considerations. Some councils operate a bidding process. Others adopt a matrix approach, so called because the distribution is in accordance with where the child is positioned in an array of needs, arranged according to description and severity, which accords to a school a determined amount of money or money's worth depending on which box or boxes in the array or matrix the pupil falls into. Such methods are openly resource-led; they do not seek to meet the needs of the individual child, but to effect a reconciliation (some would say a compromise), fair as between all the pupils for whom the LEA is responsible, between the needs of individual pupils and the resources the local authority officials have available towards meeting those needs. Its justification is political and financial realism: it starts with the propositions that whether or not the law imposes a duty on the LEA to meet all the special educational needs of a pupil, the LEA's resources are not unlimited; and that it is politically and socially unacceptable for the LEA to meet the needs of some pupils if that means it will not meet equal or more severe needs of other pupils.

Other LEAs adopt a different approach. The authority sets thresholds or criteria that an individual pupil must meet in order to receive a particular level of service, such as a statutory assessment, the issue of a statement, or the delivery of a particular type or amount of provision. Some of these tests are crude: for example, one LEA might have a rule that a pupil will not be considered for statutory assessment unless his or her performance in certain tests is within a particular centile (say, 2 per cent) of the population, a proportion given currency by mention in the Code of Practice; or unless a pupil of a given age has not attained certain literacy levels, in some LEAs irrespective of the nature of the child's learning difficulty. Other LEAs apply more sophisticated rules, with criteria or thresholds differentiated according to the type of learning difficulty the child has, and informed by a variety of other considerations, some of which contain elements of professional impression, opinion or judgment. Sometimes these thresholds are set so as to make the expenditure consequences for the LEA approximately predictable taking one year with another so that, except in an unusual case or an unusual combination of circumstances or cluster of cases, the budget is not exceeded, and there is a roughly fair distribution of resources. It is not unlawful for a council to adopt a mechanistic distribution policy so long as it is rational and the council does not apply it rigidly and thoughtlessly without regard to the circumstances of each individual case.

As a result, LEAs make decisions about assessment and provision in the light of their own policies, budgets and local circumstances. Local moderating arrangements, commended in the Code of Practice, mean that the needs of the individual pupil are considered in the light of those policies and circumstances and the profile of the LEA's pupil population. When the tribunal, however, considers an appeal from an LEA's decision, it is likely to seek to make objective determinations as to (1) the nature, severity and complexity of the pupil's learning difficulties; (2) the nature, severity and complexity of the pupil's consequent special educational needs; and (3) the response (be it assessment, statement, provision or placement) that those needs call for. In making those determinations the tribunal will look at the evidence relating to the individual pupil, not the needs of all those for whom the LEA has responsibility. The tribunal is likely to be influenced, perhaps subconsciously, by members' knowledge of what other authorities do in like cases. Rarely is the tribunal given more than the scantiest of information about the local resource context, how the local matrix or other allocation mechanism relates to it, or the knock-on effects on other pupils of a successful appeal.

As a result, the tribunal may allow appeals, so that individual pupils whose parents have successfully appealed receive more provision than other pupils in the same LEA area with similar needs. That is perceived as unfair. Once a tribunal decision has set a precedent, other parents press for corresponding provision for their child, or the LEA of its own accord may decide to increase the provision for all other pupils in the same category, so as to avoid unfairness. That may throw the whole system of distribution the LEA has adopted out of kilter; it will certainly increase the LEA's expenditure, which may have wider consequences for other parts of the LEA's education services, which may result in further injustices on the demand side. That risk is particularly acute where the tribunal orders a residential placement in a fee-charging school, the whole cost of which (not just the difference in cost between what the tribunal has ordered and what the LEA offered) will fall on the LEA.

Where for an individual pupil the LEA's provision is by any standards inadequate, and the decision of the tribunal on appeal has rectified that, justice will have been done for that child. If that results in an LEA with low standards of service improving its provision, that is a worthwhile outcome. But if it entails or results in substantial unfairness to other pupils, or between pupils with similar needs, it calls into question the fairness of the system as a whole. It is difficult to see how this problem can be resolved without primary legislation to amend the law.

So long as there is a pretence that authorities have all the resources to meet the needs of all pupils, there will continue to be decisions that result in unfairness as between one pupil and another. If SEN law were to be based on disability discrimination principles, the risk of that sort of unfairness would be reduced, because the decision would then depend on (1) whether the less favourable treatment experienced by the pupil was justified; and (2) whether the school made reasonable adjustments; in both those cases resource considerations, and comparison with other pupils with like need, can be brought into account.

While that would reduce the risk of the tribunal making decisions that upset a fair distribution, that risk would still exist, and probably to an unacceptable extent. In particular, it would continue to allow a parent, by successfully appealing to the tribunal, to throw on to the LEA the whole cost of special educational provision in the fee-charging sector. One distributive justice approach to meeting that difficulty might be for the law to be recast so that, whilst decisions would continue to take as a starting point the pupil's needs on the demand side, the law would acknowledge the scarcity of resources on the supply side and impose a cap on the supply side's liability. One approach might be to require the LEA to show that it had properly assessed need; that it had allocated reasonable resources to meet that need; that it had adopted an allocation policy (of which a survey of need and a matrix for calculating the allocation of provision might be components); that in its local circumstances that policy was in principle fair; and that its arrangements for financial delegation to schools were reasonable. It would then be for the school to show that it had not discriminated against the individual pupil. The test would be whether discrimination (a breach of certain principles of distributive justice) had occurred and, if so, how distributive justice should be restored, as distinct from how the pupil's special educational needs ought to be met.

Parents who wanted special educational provision, different from or additional to what the tribunal considered non-discriminatory, would have to make their own arrangements at their own expense, either wholly or to the extent that the cost of the parent-preferred arrangements exceeded the cost to the public of the provision adjudged by the tribunal to be non-discriminatory. Such an approach would be not inconsistent with principles of distributive justice based on concepts of equality of opportunity as distinct from equality of shares of commodity. It would also be not inconsistent with an approach to SEN based on Sen's capability theory. Sen (1992) has contended, in the context of global welfare economics, that distributive justice should be based not on attainment of primary goods but on promotion of capability to choose between, and to exercise, various forms of social functioning. Terzi (2005) has advocated that that approach could usefully be applied to disability and special educational needs in order to resolve Dyson's dilemma of difference. A review of SEN law in terms of disability discrimination and in the light of concepts of distributive justice could accommodate and be consistent with Sen's approach.

Nor would such reform be inconsistent with a rights approach to SEN. One of the functions of distributive justice is to secure fair exercise of rights in conditions of moderate scarcity, recognising the impact that the exercise of one person's rights may have on the exercise of rights by others. A discrimination law approach asserts the rights of those with SEN as against those who do not have SEN; and distributive justice adjusts the exercise of the rights of those who have SEN as against other people, including others with SEN.

At a more practical level, such an approach would also (1) avoid the pretence that public services have unlimited resources to meet all pupils' needs; (2) relieve LEAs of having to pay the whole, as distinct from the marginal, cost of meeting parental preference in the fee-charging sector when ordered to do so by the tribunal; (3) uphold the general principle that those who want services over and above what the state properly offers without unlawful discrimination should pay the difference in cost themselves; thus (4) allow a degree of parental choice, but not so as to create unfairness; and (5) maintain distributive justice not only as between diverse pupils with different needs, but also as between those with similar needs.

References

Dyson, A. (2001), 'Special educational needs in the 21st century: where we've been and where we're going', *British Journal of Special Education*, 28 (1), 24–9

Hume, D. (1751), *An Enquiry Concerning the Principles of Morals*, ed. T. L. Beauchamp (1988), Oxford: Oxford University Press

Rawls, J. (2001) *Justice as Fairness: A Restatement*, Cambridge, MA, and London: Harvard University Press

Sen, A. (1992), *Inequality Re-examined*, New York and Oxford: Russell Sage Foundation and Clarendon Press

Terzi, L. (2005), 'Beyond the dilemma of difference: the capability approach to disability and special educational needs', *Journal of Philosophy of Education*, 39 (3), 443–59

Warnock Committee (1978), *Special Educational Needs (the Warnock Report)*, London: DfES

Warnock, M. (2005), *Special Educational Needs: A New Look*, London: Philosophy of Education Society of Great Britain

10 Beyond the dilemma of difference[1]

The capability approach to disability and special educational needs

Lorella Terzi

In *Special Educational Needs: A New Look* (2005), Mary Warnock called for a radical review of special needs education and a substantial reconsideration of the assumptions upon which the current educational framework is based. The latter, she maintains, is hindered by a tension between the intention to treat all learners as the same, and the intention to treat them as different, with due attention to their individual needs. This tension is known as the 'dilemma of difference', and it is discussed in the introduction and several chapters of this book (see the chapters by Norwich, Evans and Ainscow). In this chapter, I argue that the capability approach developed by Amartya Sen provides an innovative and important perspective for re-examining the dilemma of difference, making it possible to overcome the tension at its core, while at the same time locating the debate within a normative framework based upon justice and equality.

Warnock's recent call for a review of special education has focused attention on a complex educational problem: that of conceptualising differences among children, and in particular differences relating to disability and special needs. What counts as a disability or a special need, and how this relates to a learning difficulty, is much debated in education. The debate is characterised, on the one hand, by positions that see disabilities and special needs as individual or 'within-child' limitations and deficits (the 'medical model'), and, on the other, by positions that see them as limitations and deficits of school systems, a failure to accommodate the diversity of children (the 'social model'). A crucial aspect of this debate concerns the use of so-called 'labels'. On one side are perspectives that endorse the use of categories and classification systems in the belief that these underlie differential and appropriate educational provision. On the other side are perspectives that critically highlight the possible discriminatory and oppressive use of these systems.

In this chapter, I respond to Warnock's call for a review of special and inclusive education by drawing upon the capability approach as developed by Amartya Sen. This is a normative framework for assessing inequality. It claims that the just design of social arrangements should be evaluated in the space of capability, that is, in the space of the *real* freedoms people have to promote and achieve their own well-being. Considerations of human diversity in terms of the interrelation between individual, social and circumstantial factors are central to the notion of capability. They are therefore vital for the consideration of individual well-being.

Conceptualising differences in education: disability and special educational needs

However much they differ, educational approaches to disability and special needs all address the relationship between children's diversity and the school system. My argument will be that the duality between individual and social elements is an artificial one, leading to limited and unsatisfactory conceptualisations of disability and special needs. More specifically, I will argue that perspectives emphasising individual limitations end up overshadowing the role played by the design of schooling institutions in creating or alleviating learning difficulties. Conversely, perspectives that identify schooling factors as causes of learning difficulties tend to overlook elements relating to individual characteristics.

In order to substantiate the claim that the individual/social duality is artificial, I need to distinguish between 'impairment' and 'disability'. Impairment is an individual feature, such as the lack of a limb or the loss of a function, for instance a hearing loss. It need not result in a disability; whether it does or not depends both on the possibility to overcome the impairment and on social arrangements. A disability is a functional limitation or an inability to perform some significant functionings, which in an educational context can mean a barrier to learning. Thus a hearing impairment can become a learning disability, if teaching is not appropriately provided. If teaching were conducted in diverse ways, for instance by specific methods of facilitating language development (see, for instance, Gregory, 2005), then hearing impairment would remain an impairment, but would not result in a disability. Disabilities, then, are relational both to impairments and to the design of social arrangements. They present in some contexts but not in others. A disability therefore implies an impairment, but the opposite is not always true.

This distinction is subtle but worth making. It shows how category-based positions risk overlooking the relevance of the schooling factor in determining what does and does not count as a learning difficulty. Similar considerations apply to the concept of special educational needs, as this was adopted in the UK following the Warnock Report (DES, 1978) and the 1981 Education Act. Although it aimed to emphasise the relational aspect of learning difficulties, and bring the theory and practice of special education beyond the use of categories, the concept of special educational needs not only remains a 'within-child model', but also introduces two difficult concepts, those of 'specialness' and 'need'. It presents considerable theoretical and practical difficulties for two reasons. On the one hand the concept of special need is inflationary, for there are no clear limits to what may be claimed as a 'need'. (This conceptual difficulty underlies the substantial increase, noted in recent years, in the number of children designated as having special needs.) On the other hand, the unspecified nature of the concept leads to the reintroduction of the medical and psychological categories it aimed to abolish, like 'sensory impairment' or 'emotional and behavioural difficulties'. Ultimately, the notion of special needs remains a 'within-child model' and fails to capture the complexity of disability.

Let us now consider the social model of disability, which attributes the learning difficulties experienced by some children to the failure of the school system to meet their diversity. Educationalist Tony Booth, for instance, sees disabilities and special needs as wholly socially constructed, and as neither inherent nor essential to the child. Brahm Norwich notes that, although on this view difficulties are seen as arising from the relation between the diversity of children and the school system, critical attention is directed only to the limitations of the school rather than to a comprehensive understanding of how this relation takes place. Dyson, for example, comments:

> Special needs are not the needs that arise in a child with disabilities with regard to a system that is fixed. Rather they are needs that arise between the child and the educational system as a whole when the system fails to adapt itself to the characteristics of the child.
>
> (Dyson, cited in Norwich, 1993, p. 50)

As Norwich has rightly pointed out, there seems to be an inconsistency in arguing for an interaction between child and school and then emphasising only the limitations on the part of the school (Norwich, 1993, p. 50).

Some sociologists of education maintain that disability and special educational needs are the products of disabling barriers and of exclusionary and oppressive educational processes (see Armstrong, Barnes, Barton, Corbett, Oliver, Tomlinson). They see disabilities and difficulties as caused by institutional practices, which marginalise and discriminate through the use of labelling procedures and disabling categories and methods. Categories are seen as separating and segregating children on the basis of their presumed 'abnormality'. According to proponents of this perspective, 'difference is not a euphemism for defect, for abnormality, for a problem to be worked out through technical and assimilationist education policies. Diversity is a social fact' (Armstrong and Barton, 2000, p. 34). Differences and diversity, on this view, should be promoted and celebrated.

This is not an adequate basis upon which to determine the ends of educating the child, particularly when the aim is to respect equal educational entitlements. This is more evident, perhaps, in the case of severely disabled children or children with multiple disabilities. The abandonment of categories and classifications of disability and special needs in favour of a generic celebration of differences is in itself a problematic and, to a certain extent, counterproductive position. How can policies be designed to celebrate differences, and specifically differences related to impairment and disability, in the absence of any specification of the concept of difference? In the next section I turn to the capability approach, showing how this opens the understanding and theorisation of impairment and disability to an important, relational dimension.

Re-conceptualising disability: the capability approach[2]

The capability approach is a normative framework for the assessment of poverty, inequality and the design of social institutions. It provides an answer to the question 'equality of what?' which is central to debates in political philosophy and, specifically, in liberal egalitarianism. Closely linked to this question are two further issues: first, the choice of the space in which to assess equality and, second, the kind of measurement that should be used in comparing people's relative advantages and disadvantages.

The capability approach argues that equality and social arrangements should be evaluated in terms of the theoretical space of capabilities, that is, in the space of the real freedoms people have to achieve valued functionings that are constitutive of their well-being. It maintains that what is fundamental in assessing equality is the extent of people's freedom to choose among valuable functionings. Functionings are the 'beings' and 'doings' that individuals have reason to value. Walking, reading, being well nourished, being educated, having self-respect and acting in a political capacity are all examples of functionings. Capabilities are the real opportunities and freedoms people have to achieve these valued functionings. As Sen says, 'Capability is . . . a set of vectors of functionings, reflecting the person's freedom to lead one type of life or another . . . to choose from possible livings' (Sen, 1992, p. 40). He provides a useful example that helps us to understand the distinction between functionings and capability by comparing the situation of a starving person to that of someone fasting (p. 111). The person who is starving is deprived of the capability – that is, the real effective freedom – of choosing whether to eat or to fast, whereas the person who fasts retains her freedom to choose, and hence she has the relevant capability. For the capability approach what is fundamental in the assessment of equality is 'what people are actually able to be and to do' (Nussbaum, 2000, p. 40), and hence the sets of capabilities available to them, rather than the sets of achieved functionings they can enjoy at any given time. This allows for the pursuit of individual well-being and facilitates life-planning on the basis of individual choice (Robeyns, 2003).

The evaluation of equality, however, and the comparisons of individuals' relative advantages and disadvantages within the space of capability entail the use of some kind of measurement. Fundamental to the capability metric is human diversity. Sen claims, 'Human diversity is no secondary complication (to be ignored, or to be introduced "later on"); it is a fundamental aspect of our interest in equality' (Sen, 1992, p. xi). He says that human beings are diverse in three fundamental ways. First, they are different with respect to personal characteristics such as gender, age, physical and mental abilities, talents, proneness to illness, and so forth. Second, they differ with respect to external circumstances, such as inherited wealth and assets, environmental factors including climatic differences, and social and cultural arrangements (pp. 1, 20, 27–8). Third, and fundamentally, they are different in terms of their ability to convert resources into valued functionings (p. 85). For example, a lactating woman needs a higher intake of food for her functionings than a similar but non-lactating woman. The variations entailed by such differences are central to the capability metric, and have to be accounted for when addressing the demands of equality.

What does Sen's capability approach offer in terms of the understanding of impairment and disability? It provides two main insights. The first, which draws on Sen's specific understanding of personal heterogeneities, concerns how we can think of impairment and disability as aspects of human diversity. This raises considerations concerning the relational aspect of disability, with respect both to impairment and to social institutions. The second insight concerns the centrality of human diversity in the evaluation of people's *relative* advantages or disadvantages. This has a bearing on distributive patterns of freedom, and hence on the achievement of a just society.

On the first insight: impairment, according to the capability framework, is a personal feature that becomes a disability – an inability to perform some significant class of functionings on average performed by someone's reference group under common circumstances (Buchanan *et al.*, 2000, p. 286) – when it interacts with specific social and environmental structures. Disability is, therefore, relational both with respect to impairment and to the design of social institutions. So a visual impairment becomes a disability in relation to the specific functioning of reading text on computer screens when and if no use of Braille displays and speech output screen readers is provided (Perry *et al.*, 1996, p. 4). In this case, although the visual impairment is not overcome, the functioning of reading text on screens is achieved through an alternative functioning made possible by the adjustment of the environmental design. Consider also the case of a hearing-impaired person who has lost the hearing functioning in a certain range of frequencies of sounds, which is on average detected by people. If the range of sounds undetectable by the impaired person is irrelevant to the functionings in that person's social environment, then she is not a disabled person[3] (Buchanan *et al.*, 2000, p. 287). Consider, finally, the possibility of cars in which the functioning of seeing is played, say, by a computerised monitor. In this case, a visually impaired person would be able to drive; and hence her impairment would not result in a disability for that specific functioning. True, this person would still be able to choose to drive only one certain type of car, because of her impairment, but the opportunity of achieving the relevant functioning of driving would still be available.

The capability approach provides a specific conception of disability as one aspect of human heterogeneity, without suggesting monolithic notions of diversity as abnormality. This is fundamental in overcoming the discrimination and oppression denounced by disabled people's movements as inherent to current categories of normality, abnormality and diversity. The second insight of the capability approach relates to the centrality of human diversity in assessing equality in the space of capability. In repositioning human diversity as central to the evaluation of individual advantages and disadvantages, Sen's capability approach promotes an egalitarian perspective that differs from others in that it deals at its core with the complexity of disability. It provides an egalitarian framework in which disability is evaluated in the light of the distributive pattern of relevant capability (see Terzi, 2005, p. 209). This has fundamental consequences for the design of social policies and institutions, and consequently has fundamental implications for the design of educational policies and schooling systems.

Beyond the dilemma of difference: the capability approach in education

The capability approach usefully advances our theoretical and practical understanding of disability and special educational need. I believe that it *resolves* the dilemma of difference in the way that Norwich says it needs to be resolved in Chapter 8 of this book. He writes: 'Dilemmas call for resolutions rather than solutions. They require the balancing of tensions, accepting less than ideal ways forward, and working positively with uncertainties and complexities.' How is the dilemma of difference reframed within the capability perspective? The capability approach allows the interplay between the theoretical level of defining disability and special educational needs as aspects of human diversity (the difference) and the political level of determining and providing a just educational entitlement (the sameness: treating people as equals). Differences and diversity are reconsidered in terms of functionings and capabilities, and are seen as central in the evaluation of individuals' capabilities, that is, of their effective opportunities for educational functionings. Finally, by reconsidering impairment and disability through the concepts of functionings and capability, the capability perspective conceptualises the relational aspect of learning difficulties both to impairments and to schooling factors, thus overriding unilateral understandings relating to the artificial individual/social duality and avoiding negative 'labelling'.

Conclusion

Conceptualising differences among children, and specifically differences entailed by disability and special needs, is a difficult educational problem. I have argued in this chapter that current understandings of disability and special needs are constructed on the basis of a dualism between individual and social factors. This dualism does not capture the complexity of the matter, and I have suggested that the capability approach successfully does this. It involves on the one hand a conceptualisation of disability as inherently relational and on the other the reconsideration of questions concerning the definition of difference among children within a normative framework aimed at justice and equality.

To conclude: the capability approach is a framework of thought, not an educational theory. In helping to reconcile the dualism and tensions inherent in current understandings, it paves the way for an innovative and helpful framework for re-examining special needs education and education more generally.[4]

Notes

1 This chapter is an abridged version of an article of the same title, published in the *Journal of Philosophy of Education* (2005), 39 (3), 443–59.
2 This section draws on Terzi, 2005.
3 This, however, raises the question of considering the person's capabilities, and hence the functionings she may wish to have. What if this limitation, although not relevant in her dominant social framework, still hinders the person's set of valuable beings and doings? Here the discussion leads to the aspect of preference formation and the influence of processes of ambition-affecting socialisation that are problematic aspects of the capability approach. Some of these problems have been effectively addressed, albeit within a different framework and for different purposes, in Arneson, 1999. I am grateful to an anonymous referee for pointing out this connection.
4 I am grateful to Harry Brighouse and Terence McLaughlin for invaluable support, and also to two anonymous referees and the editor for their critical and helpful comments. This paper has been presented at the Third Anglo-American Symposium on Special Education and School Reform, Cambridge, 9–12 June 2004. I would like to thank Dr Lani Florian for inviting me to take part in the symposium and the participants for insightful and useful comments. Further valuable comments were received at the BERA 2004 Annual Conference. Finally, I gratefully acknowledge the generous research funding provided by the Philosophy of Education Society of Great Britain.

References

Armstrong, F., D. Armstrong and L. Barton (2000), *Inclusive Education: Policy, Contexts and Comparative Perspectives*, London: Fulton

Arneson, R. (1999), 'Against Rawlsian equality of opportunity', *Philosophical Studies*, 93 (1), 77–112

Barnes, C., M. Oliver and L. Barton (2002), *Disability Studies Today*, Cambridge: Polity Press

Booth, T. (2000), 'Mapping inclusion and exclusion: concepts for all?', in C. Clark A. Dyson and A. Millward (eds), *Towards Inclusive Schools?*, London: Fulton

Buchanan, A., D. W. Brock, N. Daniels and D. Wikler (eds), (2000), *From Choice to Chance: Genetics and Justice*, Cambridge: Cambridge University Press

Corbett, J. (1999), *Bad-Mouthing: The Language of Special Needs*, London: Falmer Press

Gregory, S. (2005), 'Deafness', in A. Lewis and B. Norwich (eds), *Special Teaching for Special Children? Pedagogies for Inclusion*, Maidenhead: Open University Press, pp. 15–25

Norwich, B. (1993), 'Has "special educational needs" outlived its usefulness?', in J. Visser and G. Upton (eds), *Special Education in Britain After Warnock*, London: Fulton

Nussbaum, M. (2000), *Women and Human Development: the Capabilities Approach*, Cambridge: Cambridge University Press

Oliver, M. (1996), *Understanding Disability: from Theory to Practice*, Basingstoke: Palgrave

Perry, J., E. Macken, N. Scott and S. McKinley (1996), 'Disability, inability and cyberspace', in B. Friedman (ed.) *Designing Computers for People: Human Values and the Design of Computer Technology*, Stanford, CA: CSLI Publications

Robeyns, I. (2003), 'Is Nancy Fraser's critique of theories of distributive justice Justified?', *Constellation*, 10 (4), 538–53

Sen, A. (1992), *Inequality Re-examined*, New York and Oxford: Russell Sage Foundation and Clarendon Press

Terzi, L. (2005), 'A capability perspective on impairment, disability and special needs: towards social justice in education', *Theory and Research in Education*, 3 (2), 197–223

Tomlinson, S. (1982), *A Sociology of Special Education*, London: Routledge and Kegan Paul

Warnock Committee (1978), *Special Educational Needs (the Warnock Report)*, London: DfES

Warnock, M. (2005), *Special Educational Needs: A New Look*, London: Philosophy of Education Society of Great Britain

11 The challenge of meeting additional educational needs with or without statements of special educational need

Ingrid Lunt

Introduction

Warnock (2005) suggests accurately that there is (and always has been) a 'crucial lack of clarity in the concept of a statement', and a similar lack of clarity in the concept of 'special educational needs' (SEN). This lack of clarity has become increasingly problematic, as a result of the changes that have taken place over the 25 or so years after the Warnock Report of 1978 (DES, 1978). This report led to a sea change in the way that children's learning difficulties and disabilities are conceptualised, including a move away from categorisation of children based on a notion of handicap, to a 'continuum of special educational need', a commitment to 'integrate' most children in mainstream schools, and the introduction of 'statements' for the small minority of children with severe, long-term and complex needs. The force of these changes and the subsequent legislation should not be underestimated. Coming at a time of international and worldwide interest in equal opportunities, human rights, 'mainstreaming' and the growth of the 'disability movement', the report encouraged changes in attitudes to disability, a growth of provision to support pupils in mainstream schools, and an acknowledgement of all pupils' entitlement to a broad and balanced curriculum (and, from 1988, the National Curriculum). The report also aimed to ensure that children's special needs were identified and met.

However, since that time the climate has changed and major policy tensions have been created between the 1981 Education Act and subsequent education legislation and policy. Rouse and Florian (1997) suggest that 'there has been a shift from legislation and policies based upon principles of equity, social progress and altruism, to new legislation underpinned by a market-place philosophy based on principles of academic excellence, choice and competition' (p. 324). In this chapter I shall discuss some of the problems with the term 'special educational needs' and with the use of 'statements', and shall suggest that the many inherent problems in the use of statements makes this system untenable, and that we should consider alternative means to meet the needs of all pupils. Indeed, as Warnock (2005) suggests, 'the present system of statementing, however lovingly ministers cling to it . . . must be re-examined and put to a different use if it cannot be abolished' (p. 54).

The context of the Warnock Report

It may be useful to consider briefly the historical context of the Warnock Report. Prior to the report, some children were assessed and ascertained 'handicapped', and were placed in a special school according to their disability. At the time of the report, 1.8 per cent of the school population of England and Wales (1.4 per cent in Scotland) were in special schools or classes. While a very small minority of these children might be defined as having 'severe, complex and long-term needs', and in need of highly specialist provision and support, a significant majority had needs that are often associated with social, economic and environmental factors such as social deprivation (DES figures of 1978 indicate that almost 60 per cent of those identified as 'handicapped' fell into the categories of 'maladjusted' or 'educationally subnormal: moderate').

The figure of 'one in five (i.e. 20%) likely to require special educational provision' (Warnock Report paragraph 3.17) was based on surveys available at the time, in particular the Isle of Wight survey (Rutter *et al.*, 1970). Although no estimate was provided in the report for the number of children who would be 'recorded as requiring special educational provision' (i.e. having a statement), it is clear that this was intended to be a tiny minority such as the number receiving special provision at the time (about 1.8–2 per cent). Nevertheless, although arbitrary, the figures '2 per cent' and '20 per cent' quickly achieved almost mythical and certainly administrative significance following the report (e.g. Gipps *et al.*, 1987), and led to an expectation that about 20 per cent of all children would have SEN and therefore need additional support. The push for 'integration' and placement in ordinary schools meant that the majority of pupils with SEN were expected to attend mainstream school. However, notwithstanding the somewhat arbitrary nature of the estimates provided by the report, a review of international developments by Pijl and Meijer (1991) concluded that 'countries seem to agree that at least 1.5% of the students are difficult to integrate on a curricular level in regular education' (p. 111).

The Warnock committee was set up in 1974 at a time when the education system in the UK was in the expansionist and optimistic mode of 'post-war welfarism'. However, even by the time the report was published in 1978, forced economies began to cut into the education service, and the newly elected Conservative government in 1979 began to develop a very different approach to public services, including the introduction of market-style reforms, based on individualism, competition and cost-effectiveness, introducing a 'bleak contradiction' between the aspirations of the report and subsequent legislation. Thus the 1981 Act, implemented in 1983, had to be introduced in a very different social, political and economic context from that which prevailed when the Warnock committee was set up almost ten years earlier. Subsequent legislation (in 1988, 1993, 1996, and 2001) has consolidated policy in the same direction.

The 25 years since the 1981 Act have seen major changes in the education system in the UK. While the 1981 Act itself led to a significant increase in awareness of SEN in schools, and in support services within local education authorities, it was implemented without additional funding, and schools were expected to 'integrate' pupils with SEN with little preparation or support (Goacher *et al.*, 1988; Wedell, 1990). The introduction in 1988 of the National Curriculum, local management of schools, and competition between schools for pupils had considerable impact on LEAs' and schools' ability to support pupils with SEN (Evans and Lunt, 1994; Lunt and Evans, 1994), and resulted in an increase in the number of pupils identified as having SEN and in those excluded from school. Monitoring of trends towards greater inclusion by the Centre for Studies on Inclusive Education (e.g. Swann, 1985; Norwich, 2002) has shown a gradual reduction in the numbers of pupils in special schools, although the number of special schools has remained almost constant; however, there has been an increase over this period in the number and percentage of pupils with statements, and in the overall number identified as having SEN, and each survey reports worrying variation within and between local authorities across the country.

While many of these developments are due to broader changes in the educational climate in the UK over the period, such as financial cuts, the introduction of competition between schools and the prescriptive nature of targets and accountability, they are also a result of the lack of clarity in the concept of special educational needs and in the concept of the statement. This lack of clarity has resulted in a growing number of pupils identified with SEN and increasing pressure from schools and parents for statements as a means of unlocking scarce resources, rather than a consideration of how schools might be organised to meet the diverse needs of the pupils in the community.

Special educational needs

The Warnock Report introduced the term 'special educational needs':

> seen not in terms of a particular disability which a child is judged to have, but in relation to everything about him, his abilities as well as his disabilities – indeed all the factors which have a bearing on his educational progress
>
> (para. 3.6)

The definition of 'special educational needs' used in successive legislation to this day is in terms of learning difficulties: 'Children have special educational needs if they have a learning difficulty which calls for special educational provision to be made for them' (1981 Act and subsequent legislation). This, as Wedell (1990) pointed out, 'must take a prize for circularity'.

This concept of 'special educational need' aimed to move away from medical 'within-child' terminology to an approach that was both relative and interactive. This meant that the needs of children were to be considered with respect to the strengths and weaknesses of other children and over time, and to the nature of their environment, including the home and the school, and the community. However, the 'relative' nature of the definition meant that children's SEN depended crucially on the nature of the classrooms and schools that they attended.

Evidence published at about the same time (Rutter *et al.*, 1979) demonstrated clearly that schools make a difference to pupil outcomes, a finding that has been confirmed and studied extensively over the past 25 years as part of school effectiveness and school improvement research. This means that a pupil's needs are relative to other pupils in the school and depend on the organisation, curriculum and pedagogy of the school and its capacity to meet pupil needs; one school may identify as having special educational needs (and in need of additional support) 20 per cent or more of its pupils, while a school serving exactly the same community may identify as few as 2 per cent. Pupils' needs are also interactive in the sense that pupils interact with their environment, other pupils, teachers and other staff; this interaction may be positive or negative or, as Wedell has suggested, 'compensatory', in the sense that factors in the environment may 'compensate for' factors within the child or vice versa.

However, as Warnock (2005) points out, 'the concept of need covers a wide spectrum', ranging from the tiny minority of pupils with severe, complex and long-term needs to a now growing number of pupils for whom mainstream schools find it difficult to provide, and whom they therefore 'label' as having SEN, and in need of additional resources, or something different from that 'generally provided'. This wider definition of SEN and the continuum associated with it had the benefit, at the time, of raising awareness of the wide range and complexity of children's learning needs, and encouraging schools to develop ways of coping with pupil diversity, but it brought the disadvantage of creating a further category (SEN) of pupils in mainstream schools who were in some way different from the 'majority of children'.

The expression 'special educational needs' has long been seen as problematical (cf. Norwich, 1993, 1996). The problem was identified by the Audit Commission (1992): 'as the 1981 Act does not define its client group it is very difficult for LEAs to implement it consistently' (p. 1). The term has come to be used on the one hand as part of the practical administrative arrangements for meeting the needs of pupils with learning difficulties and on the other hand as a form of diagnostic explanation for poor pupil attainment. However, as an administrative category it has been misused, as evidenced by the growing numbers of pupils identified, and as a diagnostic explanation it encourages a focus on individual children rather than the learning environment. In both cases it has begun to attain similar negative connotations to those attached to 'handicap', although the administrative need for some form of categorisation has led the revised Code of Practice (DfES, 2001) to differentiate four areas of function:

- communication and interaction
- cognition and learning
- behaviour, emotional and social development
- sensory and/or physical needs.

This reflects the 'dilemma of identification' or, as Dyson puts it, the fundamental contradiction in the UK educational system between an 'intention to treat all learners as essentially the same and an equal and opposite intention to treat them as different' (Dyson, 2001). The relativity of the concept of SEN means that if schools are not flexible and able to adapt to meet the needs of the range of pupils, the numbers of pupils who are designated SEN (i.e. who are unable to fit into the existing system of curriculum, pedagogy and organisation) will increase; this may also create unintended consequences of perverse incentives for schools, where additional support and resources appear to follow the numbers of individual pupils identified with SEN.

Returning to this contradiction, on the one hand, if we were to abolish the concept of special educational needs and treat all learners as essentially the same, there would be no formal system for acknowledging that some pupils need greater support than others; in an ideal world the corollary to the abolition of categorisation and a commitment to inclusion would be a system of providing for pupil diversity, through organisational and pedagogic adaptation, in an inclusive learning environment. On the other hand, treating learners as different, and identifying some with SEN, runs the risk of giving permission to identify growing numbers as different or as 'someone else's problem'; as the numbers of pupils with SEN increase, the school's tolerance of pupil differences decreases. This suggests that the term SEN has probably become too general to be useful, and the previously useful formulation of the wide continuum of SEN has served the purpose required of the time.

Given the inextricable relationship between the concept of SEN and the concept of a statement, many of the difficulties that result from the concept of SEN arise logically also in relation to the use of statements of SEN, and in particular over the level of SEN that should 'trigger' a statutory multi-professional assessment and statement.

Statements

Statements were introduced by the Warnock Report as 'a system of recording as in need of special educational provision those children who . . . are judged by the LEA to require special educational provision not generally available in ordinary schools' (3.31). However, this definition crucially depends on there being an agreed notion of what is or should be 'generally available' in mainstream schools; the lack of such a notion has severely undermined schools' and local authorities' ability to agree which children with what level of need require a statement.

The report also suggested that this system of recording could provide the means of 'safeguarding the interests of the minority of pupils whose needs cannot be met within the resources generally available in ordinary schools', and statements ('records of need' in Scotland) formed a central part of the statutory assessment process of the 1981 Act.

The relative and interactive definition of SEN meant that it was virtually impossible to indicate the level of need where a child required the LEA to 'determine the provision' and needed the 'protection' of a statement. This led to huge variation across the country in the numbers of pupils identified with SEN and the numbers issued with statements, in part because of a lack of agreement over the provision that could be expected as normally available in mainstream schools. Nor was there clarity in the original formulation as to the purpose of the statement: these included variously listing on a register, safeguarding rights to provision or resources, and analogously 'protecting' pupils (from possible neglect or lack of provision), or labelling as 'special' and as therefore deserving of 'special' provision or resources, or specifying the kind of provision to meet needs. With the change in social, political and, crucially, financial climate, statements rapidly became used as vouchers to gain access to increasingly scarce resources, with the result that numbers of statements increased year on year.

Ten years after the introduction of statements, the House of Commons Education Committee (House of Commons, 1993) highlighted the lack of clarity in the term 'special educational needs' and the fact that the open-ended commitment inherent in the statement procedure faced LEAs with unlimited demands to be met by limited resources.

> Since schools have no financial incentive to make provision for pupils who are hard to manage and teach, the only way they can attract finance for provision, in addition to formula funding, is to have the child made the subject of a statement; as a result the LEA becomes responsible for the cost of the additional educational provision.
>
> (para. 20)

At about the same time, the Audit Commission and school inspectors (Audit Commission, 1992) identified what they saw as 'serious deficiencies' in the way in which children with SEN are identified and provided for. These included the lack of a definition of SEN, and a lack of criteria for issuing a statement, which led to enormous variation in provision within and between LEAs. The system of statements imposed on LEAs an 'open-ended obligation to an ill-defined population', and the vagueness of most statements did not afford protection for particular provision. By the time of the follow-up report in 1998, the number of children with a statement had risen by 35 per cent since 1992 (Audit Commission, 1998), while the proportion varied between the 12 LEAs surveyed in the report from 0.8 per cent to 3.3 per cent of the pupil population.

The most recent report (Audit Commission, 2002) identified a further increase of 10 per cent since 1997 in the numbers of pupils with statements to a total of 3 per cent of the pupil population of England and Wales. Statutory assessment was said to be a

> costly, bureaucratic and unresponsive process which may add little value in helping to meet children's needs . . . statements lead to an inequitable distribution of resources and may provide funding to schools which is inconsistent with early intervention and inclusive practice.

These inter-related problems suggest that the system of statements is in need of fundamental review, as called for both by the Audit Commission (2002) and by Warnock herself. I shall highlight six related problems with the use of statements.

Problems in the use of statements

The first problem stems from the lack of clarity as to its purpose. The statement procedure was designed to meet the requirements of accountability for allocating resources to an individual pupil, in particular in mainstream school. The Audit Commission (2002) identified three separate purposes of the statutory framework: assessment of a child's needs, allocation of resources to meet their needs, assurance that their needs will be met. However, the financial constraints within schools have led to the statement being used mainly as a means to access additional resources, bolstered by a culture of litigation and the use of the tribunal, and by the competitive nature of the education system; this has led both to an increase in the numbers of statements and to an inequitable distribution of resources.

Related to this is the second problem, the lack of criteria for initiating a multiprofessional assessment and issuing a statement, and the lack of agreement as to which children should have statements. In light of this, both Codes of Practice (DfE, 1994; DfES, 2001) have attempted to give more explicit guidance on the level of need or threshold for a statement. However, there is a major tension between individual (within-child) and normative measures (for example, using standard deviations from the mean) and measures which could take into account the interactive (and within-school) nature of SEN. This reflects a difference between a more individual and a more school-based concept of need and provision. This lack of clarity contributes to the enormous variation across the country and leads to the 'postcode' lottery by which there is a fourfold difference (ranging from 1.1 per cent to 4.8 per cent in 2003) in the proportion of pupils with statements in different authorities (Pinney, 2004).

The third problem relates to the UK's continued provisional commitment to inclusion. It seems clear that the original intention of the Warnock Report was that statements were for the tiny minority of pupils (then) in special schools, those whose needs were so severe, complex and long-term that they required highly specialist provision. However, the wider concept of SEN led to pressures to provide statements for growing numbers of pupils whose needs were not necessarily so 'severe, complex and long-term' as to have been previously thought to warrant a special school, or highly specialist provision. The enhanced resources of special schools guaranteed pupils' rights to additional resources, but if the same pupils were educated in mainstream schools, a system was needed to protect their entitlement to specialist provision. The maintenance of a strong special school system alongside the mainstream schools means that considerable resources are locked within the special school system, parents have to make a choice and, crucially, schools are not required (or resourced) to adapt to become fully inclusive schools meeting the full range of pupil diversity (Lunt, 2002). As Dessent (1988) put it, 'the problem with statements is that, by focussing on assessment procedures, we pay lip service to the identification of individual needs while the system remains largely unchanged, and dominated by existing provision' (p. 44).

A fourth problem relates to funding, and to the very changed context in which schools find themselves now as compared with the early 1980s. Given the fact that, in education as in other public services, there will be unlimited demands made on limited resources and priorities are contentious, there have been understandable attempts from parents and schools to use the system to gain access to scarce resources. This can lead to inequitable distribution of resources, as LEAs are faced with demands for expensive provision for individual children. Statements now constitute one of the few ways in which additional funds may be gained for individual pupils, and they also transfer responsibility for provision from the school to the LEA. This in turn may lead to unintended consequences and perverse incentives as schools identify increased numbers of pupils (with SEN and for statements) in order to gain a greater share of scarce resources, or they become less willing to admit pupils with SEN because of their perceived adverse effects on schools' performance in the league tables.

This highlights a related problem, that statements encourage the identification of individuals and focus resources on individuals rather than on classes or schools, emphasising the needs of the '2 per cent' as opposed to the '20 per cent'. The use of tribunals encourages this, and gives the local authority an open-ended commitment that potentially skews the allocation of resources and leads to inequitable distribution of resources. This means that tribunal decisions may impose on local authorities financial commitments in respect of one particular pupil which undermine wider decisions and strategic planning in relation to schools as a whole, and which thwart initiatives for prevention, early intervention and more inclusive practice across the wider authority.

Finally, the cost of producing a statement has been estimated as over £2500, and as pointed out by the Audit Commission (Pinney, 2002) 'as 36,000 new Statements were issued in 2000, we estimate that local authorities in England and Wales are spending over £90 million annually on statutory assessment and writing Statements', money which could arguably be spent on meeting children's needs. Put starkly by Dessent (op. cit.) 'in an educational climate of contracting resources, the few resources available to an LEA may come to be spent upon manning [sic] the bureaucracy of statement production' (p. 42). These costs also involve considerable delays for pupils concerned while the bureaucratic process is completed and frequently the pupil is placed 'in a limbo' without provision awaiting a decision.

The way forward

If there were an obvious way forward this would have been identified before now. The challenges for meeting pupils' SEN and for equitable distribution of resources are considerable. Evans and Lunt (1994) articulated a number of principles which remain relevant, including:

- The principle of transparency and clarity for allocating resources. This enables local authorities to meet the accountability requirement and ensures the widest understanding of resource distribution.
- The principle of rational and coherent planning across the continuum of SEN provision. This enables local authorities to enhance the capacity of schools to prevent learning difficulties from developing, or at least to intervene at an early stage.
- The principle of minimal individual identification of pupils. The proportion of children for whom an individualised approach to resourcing is appropriate is very low, and funding needs to be used to enhance the wider capacity of schools.
- The principle of differential resourcing of schools to reflect differences in pupil needs (through a proxy such as free school meals or through moderated school audit).

In a recent project to explore the impact of LEA strategies to reduce reliance on statements (Pinney, 2004), 56 authorities were counted that had reduced the number of statements by delegating resources to schools and building their capacity to meet a wider range of SEN. The research suggested four key strands to LEA strategies to reduce reliance on statements:

- developing a clear strategic approach and engaging all partners (parents, schools, other agencies)
- realigning resources and responsibilities
- capacity-building in schools
- monitoring progress and providing assurance to parents.

These are crucial elements in reducing the number of statements to a minimum. Gray and Dessent (1993) and Moore (1999) have presented approaches to resource allocation that aim to minimise the use of statements and which are based on distributing the majority of SEN resources to schools, with weightings reflecting predictable intakes of pupils with SEN, and with contingency funds available for unpredictable needs. There is currently a major opportunity for LEAs to develop clear and transparent systems for differential resourcing, which clarify levels of provision to be made by schools and which enable greater accountability to the local school community, and responsive monitoring to ensure equity of provision, support and assessment.

A major factor in achieving an equitable resourcing system (bearing in mind finite resources) is involvement of key stakeholders, in particular parents. Studies which have focussed on parents' views of the statutory assessment procedures (c.g. O'Connor *et al.*, 2005) suggest that parents are broadly satisfied with the statutory procedures. A key requirement therefore is to devise a system that gains the confidence of parents and which enables parents and local authorities to reach agreement as to the provision required without recourse to costly statutory assessment and even more costly tribunal procedures. As Florian (2002) suggests, 'the challenge is to separate the protection offered by the Statement from the means by which that protection is offered' (p. 167). While statements continue to exist, it is difficult to see how this challenge can be met, given the power both of vested interests and of professional inertia.

However, current moves for the integration of children's services provide a real opportunity for local authorities and schools to work together and create collaborative systems based on schools and communities which ensure that resources are targeted to those in greatest need, both schools and individuals, and that there is coherent and strategic planning to provide for the most vulnerable young people.

Conclusions

In this chapter I have tried to show how the achievements of the Warnock Report and subsequent legislation were of their time and indeed marked a major step forward. Statements, in particular, constituted a device which served a much-needed purpose at a time when a different view of provision prevailed, and when moves to greater 'integration' and 'inclusion' of pupils with SEN required the dual function of 'legal protection' and specification of provision and resources. Since that time the context has changed and, as Pinney (2002) states, 'the statutory framework no longer reflects the reality of today's system of education'. If the system of statements continues to exist, it needs to be restricted in its function (to legal protection) and its scope (to about 1.5 per cent of the child population). If it ceases to exist there has to be a way to redeploy resources systemically and strategically to build the capacity of mainstream schools to meet the needs arising from the widest possible range of pupil diversity, and to protect the support for the vulnerable and tiny minority of those with severe, long-term and complex needs, particularly those in mainstream schools. Warnock's call for a fundamental review of the statutory system is timely and most appropriate: it has served a valuable purpose, and we need to move forward towards a system of providing for SEN which is suitable for the twenty-first century, and in particular for the needs of the pupils in a school system very different from that of the 1970s and 1980s.

References

Audit Commission (1992), *Getting in on the Act: Provision for Pupils with Special Educational Needs*, London: HMSO

Audit Commission (1998), *Getting in on the Act: A Review of Progress on Special Educational Needs*, London: Audit Commission

Audit Commission (2002), *Statutory Assessment and Statements of SEN: In Need of Review?*, London: Audit Commission.

Department for Education (1994), *Code of Practice on the Identification and Assessment of Special Educational Needs*, London: DfE

Department for Education and Skills (2001), *Special Educational Needs Code of Practice*, London: DfES

Dessent, T. (1988), *Making the Ordinary School Special,* Lewes: Falmer Press

Dyson, A. (2001), 'Special needs in the twenty-first century: where we've been and where we're going', *British Journal of Special Education,* 28 (1), 24–9

Evans, J. and I. Lunt (1994), *Allocating Resources for Special Educational Needs Provision,* Stafford: NASEN

Florian, L. (2002), 'The more things change the more they stay the same? A response to the Audit Commission's report on statutory assessment and statements of SEN', *British Journal of Special Education,* 29 (4), 164–9

Gipps, C., H. Gross, and H. Goldstein (1987), *Warnock's Eighteen Per Cent: Children with Special Needs in Primary Schools,* Lewes: Falmer Press

Goacher, B., J. Evans, J. Welton and K. Wedell (1988), *Policy and Provision for Special Educational Needs,* London: Cassell

Gray, P. and T. Dessent (1993), 'Getting our act together', *British Journal of Special Education,* 20 (1), 9–11

House of Commons Education Committee (1993), *Meeting Special Educational Needs: Statements of Needs and Provision,* London: HMSO

Lunt, I. (2002), 'The challenge of inclusive schooling for pupils with special educational needs', in C. Campbell (ed.), *Developing Inclusive Schooling,* London: Institute of Education

Lunt, I. and J. Evans (1994), 'Dilemmas in special educational needs: some effects of local management of schools', in S. Riddell and S. Brown (eds), *Special Educational Needs Policy in the 1990s: Warnock in the Market Place,* London: Routledge

Moore, J. (1999), 'Developing a local authority response to inclusion', *Support for Learning,* 14 (4), 174–8

Norwich, B. (1993), 'Has special educational needs outlived its usefulness?', in J. Visser and G. Upton (eds), *Special Education in Britain after Warnock,* London: David Fulton

Norwich, B. (1996), 'Special needs education, inclusive education or just education for all?' inaugural lecture, London, Institute of Education

Norwich, B. (2002), *LEA Inclusion Trends in England 1997–2001,* Bristol: CSIE

O'Connor, U., R. McConkey, and B. Hartop (2005), 'Parental views on the statutory assessment and educational planning for children with special educational needs', *European Journal of Special Needs Education,* 20 (3), 251–69

Pijl, S. J. and C. J. W. Meijer (1991), 'Does integration count for much? An analysis of the practices of integration in eight countries', *European Journal of Special Needs Education,* 6 (2), 100–12

Pinney, A. (2002), 'In need of review? The Audit Commission's report on statutory assessment and statements of special educational needs', *British Journal of Special Education,* 29 (3), 118–22

Pinney, A. (2004), *Reducing Reliance on Statements: An Investigation into Local Authority Practice and Outcomes,* Department for Education and Skills

Rouse, M. and L. Florian (1997), 'Inclusive education in the market place', *International Journal of Inclusive Education,* 1 (4), 323–36

Rutter, M., J. Tizard and K. Whitmore (eds) (1970), *Education, Health and Behaviour,* London: Longman

Rutter, M., B. Maughan, P. Mortimore and J. Ouston (1979), *Fifteen Thousand Hours: Secondary Schools and their Effects on Children,* London: Open Books

Swann, W. (1985), 'Is the integration of children with special needs happening? An analysis of recent statistics of pupils in special schools', *Oxford Review of Education,* 11 (1), 3–18

Warnock Committee (1978), *Special Educational Needs (the Warnock Report)*, London: DfES

Warnock, M. (2005), *Special Educational Needs: A New Look*, London: Philosophy of Education Society of Great Britain

Wedell, K. (1990), 'Children with special educational needs: past, present, future', in P. Evans and V. Varma (eds), *Special Education: Past, Present and Future*, Basingstoke: Falmer Press

12 But what about the others?

Patterns of student achievement in inclusive schools

*Alan Dyson and Peter Farrell with
Frances Gallannaugh, Graeme
Hutcheson and Filiz Polat*

As the current debate (Cameron, 2005; Warnock, 2005) shows, the question of how children identified as having special educational needs (SEN) are best educated remains highly contentious. In particular, the idea that children with significant levels of need can successfully be 'included' in mainstream schools continues to be met with scepticism in some quarters. This is despite the long history that inclusive provision (in this sense) has in some parts of England (see, for instance, Hackney, 1985, and Stakes and Hornby, 1997) – a history which predates the Warnock Report (1978) by some years. In part, this is because the inclusion debate is founded on questions of principle and fundamental social values. However, that debate also raises questions that ought to be answerable from empirical evidence – questions such as whether children identified as having SEN attain more highly in special or mainstream schools, where their social skills develop most rapidly, where they themselves feel happiest, and so on. Unfortunately, these different types of questions are not always clearly differentiated, and, even where they are, the research evidence is not always as robust as one might hope.

This is the case, for instance, in terms of the impact of inclusive provision on children who are *not* identified as having special educational needs. In particular, are the learning opportunities of such children compromised in such a way that their learning outcomes are poorer than they might have been in less inclusive schools? This question sometimes generates more heat than light in England, not least because of the New Labour government's commitment to developing greater inclusion at the same time as pursuing vigorously the goal of driving up standards of attainment in schools (Armstrong, 2005; Dyson, 2005). For the most part, progress towards this latter goal has been monitored by aggregating students' attainments at the school level in order to construct 'school performance tables' (latterly, 'School and College Achievement and Attainment Tables', available at http://www.dfes.gov.uk/performancetables/). Not surprisingly, therefore, many teachers and head teachers are concerned about how the presence of students identified as having SEN – many of whom will also be low-attaining – will impact on their schools' standing in these performance tables.

It does not help that in one sense the impact of students with SEN is all too obvious. Insofar as they have low attainments, their presence inevitably depresses the mean level of attainments in their schools. However, this is quite different from saying that the presence of such students interferes in some way with the ability of their peers to learn and achieve. There is, in fact, a small but important research literature on this issue (see, for instance, Affleck *et al.*, 1988; Block and Zeman, 1996; Hunt *et al.*, 1994; Obrusnikova *et al.*, 2003, Rankin *et al.*, 1999; Sharpe *et al.*, 1994; Tapasak and Walther-Thomas, 1999). Our own systematic review of this literature (Kalambouka *et al.*, 2005), aimed at assessing both its main findings and the strength of the evidence supporting those findings, was able to identify little convincing evidence to suggest that inclusive provision had any negative effects on either social or academic outcomes for students without special educational needs. In particular there were no studies reporting negative outcomes for the majority of pupils in school or class when pupils with physical and/or sensory and communication difficulties were included. However, the research base which supports these conclusions proved to be limited in a number of respects. It is, for instance, skewed towards primary schools, with some suggestions that there might be more negative outcomes in secondary schools and when students with emotional and behavioural difficulties are maintained in the mainstream. Moreover, all the evidence comes from outside the English context and is based on relatively small-scale studies, often in schools that are exceptional precisely because of their inclusiveness.

It is difficult to generalise from this evidence to likely effects in the English context where inclusion (as defined here) is a system-wide phenomenon involving large numbers of students and schools. So far as we are aware, only one attempt has been made to explore the effects of inclusion on student outcomes across the English system as a whole, but this too is limited. Lunt and Norwich sought to answer the question *Can Effective Schools Be Inclusive Schools?* (Lunt and Norwich, 1999) by analysing the GCSE performance of secondary schools with differing proportions of students identified as having SEN. They found that schools with higher proportions of students with SEN do worse in performance tables than other schools. However, with the data and analytical tools available to them, they were unable to determine whether this was because of any negative impact such students were having on their peers' learning, or simply because schools where attainments are lowest (for instance, because they serve disadvantaged areas) tend to identify larger proportions of their students as having SEN than do schools where attainments are higher. Strangely, therefore, we are in a situation where, despite decades of experience with what we now call 'inclusion', there has been no reliable evidence relating directly to the English context that can tell us what the effects of inclusion are on the majority of students in so-called inclusive schools.

The 'Inclusion and Achievement' project

It is in this context that the study we report in the remainder of this chapter was undertaken. The 'Inclusion and Achievement' project, sponsored by the Department for Education and Skills, aimed to explore the relationship between student achievement (understood in terms both of measured attainment and other forms of learning and personal development) on the one hand, and the proportion of students identified as having special educational needs in the schools attended by students on the other. The study produced a detailed technical report (Dyson *et al.*, 2004), and since it is not possible for reasons of space to do more than summarise our methods and findings, we suggest that readers may wish to access that report in order to examine some of the complexities of our work.

The study pursued its aims in two ways: the NPD analysis and the inclusive school case studies.

The NPD analysis

The study analysed the relationship between student attainment and school 'inclusivity' in the National Pupil Database (NPD) for 2002. The NPD brings together two data sets. One contains the results from national assessments and examinations for all students in assessed cohorts (school years 2, 6, 9 and 11). The other contains the Pupil-Level Annual Schools Census (PLASC) data, which records educationally relevant biographical details for all children and young people in the school system. These include information on the child's date of birth, gender, ethnicity, entitlement to free school meals (FSM), school attended and, crucially, SEN status. In 2002, this last field simply logged the 'level' of special provision made for the student (in terms of categorisation system of the SEN Code of Practice) as a proxy for the severity of his/her SEN. Subsequent versions of the NPD have been extended to include information on the broad type of SEN that the child is regarded as having.

The presence of these different types of data in the NPD made it possible to explore relationships between them. Specifically, we were able to investigate the relationship between student attainment and school inclusivity. We did this by undertaking multi-level modelling of the data. In essence this allowed us to investigate the impact on attainment of all student characteristics – gender, ethnicity, FSM entitlement, SEN status and so on – both separately and in combination. Crucially, it allowed us to investigate the relationship between the proportion of students identified as having SEN in the child's school and that child's attainment. We could do this in 'raw' terms, as Lunt and Norwich did, using attainment as the dependent and school inclusivity as the dependent variable. However, we could also account for the impact of the other student characteristic variables and determine whether there might be an 'inclusion effect' over and above the effects of those other variables. Moreover, our data were genuinely system-wide, relating to over 2 million students and including primary- as well as secondary-school students.

The inclusive school case studies

We not only wished to understand *whether* there was a relationship between school inclusivity and student achievement but also *why* such a relationship might or might not exist. In other words we wanted to know how inclusivity came to impact on achievement or, if it did not, how schools were managing their inclusive provision to avoid such impacts. We therefore undertook a series of focused case studies of 'inclusive' schools.

Full details of the methodology for these studies are provided in the project report (Dyson *et al.*, 2004). In brief, however, we worked in 16 schools that were identified because they had a high proportion of students with SEN (relative to other schools with similar levels of FSM entitlement) and which reflected a range of geographical, local education authority (LEA) and socio-economic contexts. Twelve of these schools also had overall very high levels of student attainment (again relative to schools with similar levels of FSM entitlement); four of the schools had below average levels of student attainment. The case study schools were selected primarily because of the make-up of their populations rather than because of any exceptional commitment to inclusive principles or trail-blazing work in inclusion. In this sense, they were typical of many such schools in England rather than representing the more exceptional schools often reported in the research literature (Dyson *et al.*, 2002).

Field work in each school was highly focused rather than broadly ethnographic. It purposely sought evidence that might indicate a link between the way in which the school managed inclusion and the achievements of its students. Specifically, we undertook: interviews with head teachers and other staff; analysis of school documentation (statistical analyses of school population and performance, reports from Ofsted, reports to governors, school test results etc.); focus studies of students with higher levels of SEN provision (i.e. at School Action Plus or with statements in the Code of Practice [DfES, 2001] system); and informal observations of classrooms and out-of-class school life. (The SEN Code of Practice (DfES, 2001) requires schools to make extra or different provision for pupils who do not make 'adequate progress'. School Action (the first response) could be further assessment, different teaching materials or extra adult support. School Action Plus (the second response) is required when the child still does not progress adequately; it means obtaining help or advice from the LEA's support services, or from health or social work professionals.)

Findings

Two main findings emerged from our analysis of NPD, about the impact of inclusion on attainment and school-level variation.

The impact of inclusion on attainment

We found a small, negative and statistically significant relationship between school inclusivity and the attainments of students when all other factors on which we had data were taken into account. The figures in Table 12.1 show the effect in our data that a 1 per cent increase in the inclusivity measure has on the attainment measure at each key stage (the four periods of schooling ending in years 2, 6, 9 and 11). For the purposes of our analysis, 'inclusivity' was defined in terms of the proportion of students in a school for whom provision is made at School Action Plus or above (as defined by the SEN Code of Practice [DfES, 2001]). These are students with moderate to high levels of need whose provision depends in part on inputs from beyond the school. There is, therefore, some sort of external valid-ation of the schools' identification and definition of their needs. The attainment measure is the 'average points score' (APS), which is simply a way of aggregating and averaging out the test and examination attainments of students at school level. We also show here the 'percentage score', which shows the effect of inclusiv-ity as a percentage of available points. This takes into account the fact that differ-ent numbers of points are available at each key stage and enables a comparison to be made as to the relative size of the effect (e.g. KS1 marks are out of 25, whereas KS4 marks are out of 64).

Table 12.1 shows that students in more inclusive schools tend to attain at marginally lower levels than students in less inclusive schools, even when other factors are taken into account. It is important to remember that, because our data are at individual student rather than at school level, this is not simply the mathe-matical effect of adding more low-attaining students into the calculation of a school's performance. Moreover, this effect is different at different key stages and is more marked in the secondary than in the primary phase. On the other hand, our analyses suggested that the effect seems to be reasonably evenly distributed across schools with different proportions of students identified as having SEN. We could find no 'tipping point' beyond which the scale of the effect became significantly more or less marked.

Some care needs to be exercised in interpreting these findings. First, what we are looking at here are *statistical* effects within our data. The fact that there is a statistical relationship between inclusivity and attainment does not of course mean that the relationship is *causal*. Although, therefore, an increase in the inclu-sivity measure is associated with a decrease in the attainment measure, this cannot

Table 12.1 The effect of a 1% increase in the inclusivity measure on the attainment measure

	Effect on APS score	*Effect on percentage score*
Key stage 1	−0.025	−0.100
Key stage 2	−0.045	−0.115
Key stage 3	−0.288	−0.505
Key stage 4	−0.529	−0.827

be taken to imply that adding more students with SEN to a school's existing population would necessarily have a negative effect on the attainments of that population.

Second, the statistical effect is actually very small. Even at key stage 4, it is less than 1 per cent of the available score and at the other key stages it is less – very much less in the primary phase. Put another way, schools need to have quite large differences in the relative size of their SEN populations for there to be noticeable effects on attainment levels. Hence, a secondary school of 1000 students whose KS4 attainments were 5 per cent lower than a similar-sized school might on these figures be expected to have some 60 (6 per cent) more students with moderate to high levels of SEN than its counterpart. Likewise, a primary school of 300 students with attainments 5 per cent lower at KS1 than another school might be expected to have an improbable 150 (50 per cent) more students with high-level SEN.

The small size of this effect is confirmed by other analyses we were able to carry out. From our data, it was possible to calculate value added scores – essentially, the difference between the actual change in a student's attainment between different assessment points and the median change that is made by students starting at the same level. These showed a similarly small negative relationship with school inclusivity. Specifically, for every 1 per cent of students in a school with SEN provision at School Action Plus or with a statement, we can typically expect average student value added scores in the school to be lower by the following amounts:

KS1–2	0.02 points
KS2–3	0.11 points
KS3–4	0.03 points

We were also able to explore the relationship between student attainment and inclusivity at LEA level – inclusivity in this case being defined in terms of the proportion of children for whom the LEA was responsible and who were educated in mainstream schools. Here we could find no significant relationship at all between the variables.

School-level variation

We have reported the findings above in terms of average effects on students of the inclusivity of their schools. However, when we examine the effects at school rather than at student level, an interesting picture emerges. Figure 12.1 illustrates these effects for one key stage (KS3), though the others are similar. It shows the relationship between school inclusivity and APS aggregated at the school level.

Two features are immediately apparent. First, the higher the level of inclusivity of a school, the lower the APS of that school. This is to be expected since in this analysis factors other than inclusivity are not controlled. As with the Lunt and

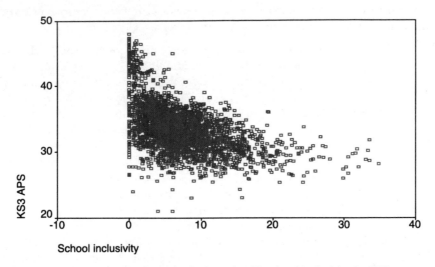

Figure 12.1 The relationship between APS at school level and inclusivity for KS3.

Norwich analysis, therefore, it is reasonable to suppose that schools with large proportions of students with SEN are also schools serving more disadvantaged and generally low-attaining students. Second, however, there is considerable variation in the inclusivity–attainment relationship at school level. In other words, it is very difficult to predict one of these variables from another: schools which are highly inclusive may also be high-performing, and low-performing schools may well not be particularly inclusive. The implication is that, even if there is an 'inclusion effect' that is more than a statistical artefact, there must be other factors at work at school level which are powerful enough to override this effect in many cases. This school-level variation underlines the importance of examining processes within schools which might link inclusion to outcomes for students. It is to this that we now turn.

The case studies

Our case studies focused on schools that were all highly inclusive in terms of the proportion of students identified as having SEN relative to other schools with similar levels of FSM entitlement. By including some schools where levels of attainment were relatively high and others where they were relatively low, we were able to explore the extent to which the two groups of schools had developed different practices or forms of provision which might account for these different outcomes. Our focus throughout was on the relationship between inclusion and student outcomes. We were not, in other words, trying to establish the *overall* 'effectiveness' of these schools.

Our case studies produced five main findings:

1 Schools which are highly inclusive manage their SEN provision in different ways, though there does seem to be a common underlying model.

Schools varied considerably in terms of their SEN populations – specifically, in terms of the 'types' of needs in those populations and how they came to be present in the school: for instance, as the result of a local policy decision to concentrate students with particular types of difficulty in the school, or because of a more general policy to maintain students with difficulties in all mainstream schools, or through 'normal' processes of recruitment. Likewise, schools differed in the ways in which they managed their SEN provision – specifically whether they had separate resource bases or classes, how the role of the SENCO (the teacher responsible for coordinating special educational needs provision) was constructed, how SEN provision was supported by other forms of provision for students with difficulties, how much time students with moderate to high levels of needs spent in mainstream classes, and how students were grouped and setted in those classes. For these reasons, the designation of a school as 'inclusive' actually tells us very little and calls into question the idea that all such schools might generate similar outcomes.

Beneath these complexities, however, there were some common features. We were able to identify a model of provision, at least in terms of a set of guiding principles, which seemed to be followed in different ways by all of the schools in our sample. The principal elements of that model were these:

- *Provision for students with special educational needs tends to be characterised by flexibility.* Students are neither rigidly segregated from their peers nor 'dumped' in mainstream classes, but are offered careful mixtures of provision in a range of settings. The precise mix is customised to the characteristics of individual students rather than being decided on a whole-group basis.
- *This customisation of provision depends on careful assessment, planning and monitoring at an individual level.* Commonly, this is part of wider monitoring systems across the whole school population.
- *Flexible provision is typically supported by the careful use of adult support.* This is provided out of the resources which the school receives for students with high levels of SEN, but also from a commitment on the part of the school to resource its SEN provision well and from the school's ability to direct its resources effectively.
- *Flexibility of provision is paralleled by flexibility of pedagogy in mainstream classes and by high-quality teaching in non-mainstream situations.*
- *Schools typically have a commitment to the principle of inclusion which is shared by a large proportion of the staff.* This does not necessarily have to be highly ideological and may take the form of a commitment to doing the best by all children. It tends, moreover, to coexist with a sense of the practical difficulties of educating a wide range of students in the same setting.
- *Alongside strategies directed towards students with SEN, high-performing schools also have strategies directed towards raising achievement more generally.* Some of these are likely to be instrumental (i.e. aiming directly at enhancing

measured attainment and school performance), but others will be directed at underlying capacities and achievements and some will include students with SEN.

Interestingly, we were not able to identify differences between higher- and lower-performing schools in terms of their adherence to this underlying model. There were some indications – but no more than this – that lower-performing schools were able to achieve slightly lower levels of flexibility than their higher-performing counterparts. However, in all important respects the two groups of schools managed their SEN provision in much the same way.

2 Inclusive schools tend to share an ethos which is positive and welcoming but which may also have a strong achievement orientation.

The broad commitment to inclusion was also reflected in the ethos of the schools. This was certainly about warm and respectful personal relations – but not simply about these. These schools also took the drive for raised achievement seriously and saw that drive as applying to all their students, including those identified as having SEN.

3 Classroom practice in inclusive schools is recognisably like 'good' practice everywhere.

Two features of the classroom practice we saw were striking. Amid a great deal of teaching which struck us as likely to be effective, we saw nothing that was *other than* 'good practice'. We did, however, see how familiar techniques were used to enhance the sorts of flexibility and individual responsiveness which also tended to characterise the structure of provision in these schools. Teachers changed and mixed these strategies to match what they saw as particular students' needs at particular times. This is part of the overall flexibility of approach on which we remarked earlier.

4 Inclusive schools use a range of strategies for raising achievement.

Schools used a range of strategies for raising achievement:

- Some of them were about promoting achievement by raising the overall quality of teaching in the school.
- Some of the strategies were more instrumental, in the sense that they focused directly on raising measured attainment even though the wider impact on learning might be difficult to see.
- A third group of strategies focused on perceived weaknesses in the underlying skills and capacities of all or many of the school's population and sought to remedy these. These strategies were not specifically targeted at students regarded as having SEN, though these students might be expected to share the weaknesses of their peers and were, therefore, likely to benefit.

Although these strategies might encompass students identified as having SEN, they were neither driven by the supposed needs of those students, nor did the presence of those students hinder their implementation. For the purposes of raising achievement, students identified as having SEN tended to be treated as part of a diverse whole school population.

5 *Inclusive schools tend to accept the task of educating most students with SEN as part of their normal responsibilities. Students whose behaviour disrupts lessons, however, are seen as presenting significant challenges.*

For the most part, schools viewed the presence of students identified as having SEN simply as a fact of life, particularly where such students formed a relatively small part of a low-attaining population presenting a wide range of challenges. The commitment to inclusive principles, noted above, meant that educating these students was seen as part of the school's responsibility to its population and to the communities it served. Nonetheless, there were problems which faced teachers in their classrooms and which threatened to impact negatively on the relationship between inclusion and achievement. The issue of problems relating to behaviours which disrupted lessons surfaced regularly as the most difficult aspect of dealing with children with SEN in the context of raising attainments.

Weighing the evidence

If, then, we consider the results of our statistical analyses alongside the findings of the case studies, what do we learn about the relationship between inclusion and student achievement?

First and foremost, we were unable to find in our analyses of NPD any convincing evidence that inclusion, in the sense we are using the term here, has any meaningful negative impact on overall levels of attainment in schools. Looking at the case studies, we can see why this might be so. Inclusive schools have a range of strategies for driving up achievement that are not dependent upon or hampered by the presence of students identified as having SEN. Moreover, they do not simply 'dump' such students in mainstream classes, but rather employ relatively sophisticated systems of flexible and individualised provision. Whether such practices compromise what some would see as the fundamental values of inclusion is, of course, a moot point. In principle, however, these schools have the capacity for ensuring that the opportunities for the majority of students to learn are not constrained by the presence of students identified as having SEN.

It is indeed the case that there is a marginally negative statistical association between levels of inclusion and levels of attainment. However, the simplest explanation of this is that it represents an effect of disadvantage. Our analysis, like many before it, found a strong association between disadvantage, low attainment and SEN. Put simply, disadvantage produces both low levels of attainment and high levels of SEN. By introducing the FSM variable into our analysis, we were able to account for this effect of disadvantage to a large extent in order to see whether there was any *separate* effect of inclusiveness. However, FSM entitlement is a crude proxy for disadvantage, so it is probable that we could not control for all its effects. What looks like a small inclusion effect, therefore, may well be a small, uncontrolled-for, disadvantage effect.

It seems, then, that inclusion does not impact negatively on overall achievements even to the very limited extent our figures indicate. However, there is a corollary to this finding: there is no evidence that inclusion impacts *positively* on overall achievements. Some inclusion proponents have argued, with Skrtic (1991), that inclusion may be 'the way to excellence'. In other words, inclusive schools might become particularly skilful at responding to the individual characteristics of learners and therefore particularly effective at promoting learning. There is no evidence in our statistical analysis to suggest that this might be the case. Likewise, our case studies uncovered no especially distinctive forms of classroom practice. On the contrary, we found a wide range of performance at school level, which could not be attributed to how inclusive schools responded to their SEN populations.

Moreover, some of our more troubling findings need to be taken into account. There is no doubt that behavioural issues cause considerable concern among teachers. Given that specialist provision for students with social, emotional and behavioural difficulties (SEBD) in both special and mainstream settings continues to thrive (Ofsted, 2004) and that most disruption of which teachers complain is low level (Steer, 2005), it seems highly unlikely that these issues are the result of national inclusion policies depositing large numbers of troubled and troublesome children in mainstream schools. On the other hand, teachers' concerns do underline the importance of what we might call the 'ecology' of inclusion. It became apparent in the case studies that most schools and teachers were managing inclusive provision with considerable success, but that this was no easy task. There was a delicate balance between the demands of students identified as having SEN, the demands of the standards agenda, the resources available in school and classroom, and the skills and capacities of the teacher. So long as this balance was maintained, all was well, though teachers might nonetheless experience considerable stresses. However, it might take little to upset that balance – a particularly demanding student, perhaps, or the absence of a teaching assistant, or an increase in pressure for results. The implication is that those who manage the various factors contributing to this balance – particularly head teachers, local authority officers and national policy-makers – have to exercise considerable care to maintain a healthy ecology.

This brings us to the final implication of our study. The absence of a relationship between inclusion and overall levels of achievement in general does not mean that there may not be significant impacts in particular cases. There may be schools and classrooms where the presence of students identified as having SEN interferes significantly with the learning of other students, or where teachers use that presence to develop forms of classroom practice that are more effective for all. There is, therefore, an obligation on teachers, heads and policy-makers to ensure that local impacts are monitored carefully through a detailed scrutiny of evidence from particular schools and classrooms. While genuine debates over matters of principle are essential, and while political conflict over these principles may be inevitable, this is no excuse for disregarding evidence where it is available and relevant. The misinformed and evidence-free assertions which often emerge in this field serve only to cloud the issue. It is in the hope of contributing to a better-informed debate, therefore, that we offer this chapter.

References

Affleck, J. Q., S. Madge, A. Adams and S. Lowenbraun (1988), 'Integrated classroom versus resource model: academic viability and effectiveness', *Exceptional Children*, 54 (4), 339–48

Armstrong, D. (2005), 'Reinventing "inclusion": New Labour and the cultural politics of special education', *Oxford Review of Education*, 31 (1), 119–34

Block, M. E. and R. Zeman (1996), 'Including students with disabilities in regular physical education: effects on non-disabled children', *Adapted Physical Activity Quarterly*, 13 (1), 38–49

Cameron, D. (2005), speech to the Oxford Conference in Education, 2 August 2005, available online at: http://www.davidcameronmp.com/articles/viewnews.php?id=abf255ae1514859dda97c69dda1a35e (accessed 3 August 2005)

Department for Education and Skills (2001), *Special Educational Needs Code of Practice* London: DfES

Dyson, A. (2005), 'Philosophy, politics and economics? The story of inclusive education in England', in D. Mitchell (ed.), *Contextualising Inclusive Education: Evaluating Old and New International Perspectives*, London: Routledge

Dyson, A., P. Farrell, F. Gallannaugh, G. Hutcheson and F. Polat (2004), *Inclusion and Pupil Achievement*, London: DfES

Dyson, A., A. Howes and B. Roberts (2002), *A Systematic Review of the Effectiveness of School-Level Actions for Promoting Participation by All Students*, London: EPPI-Centre Review, version 1.1, Research Evidence in Education Library, London: EPPI-Centre, Social Science Research Unit, Institute of Education

Farrell, P. (2000), 'The impact of research on developments in inclusive education', *International Journal of Inclusive Education*, 4 (2), 153–62

Hackney, A. (1985), 'Integration from special to ordinary schools in Oxfordshire', *Educational and Child Psychology*, 2 (3), 88–95

Hegarty, S. (1993), 'Reviewing the literature on integration', *European Journal of Special Needs Education*, 8 (3), 194–200

Hunt, P., D. Staub, M. Alwell and L. Goetz (1994), 'Achievement by all students within the context of cooperative learning groups', *Journal of the Association for Persons with Severe Handicaps*, 19 (4), 290–301

Kalambouka, A., P. Farrell, A. Dyson and I. Kaplan (2005), *The Impact of Population Inclusivity in Schools on Student Outcomes*, Research Evidence in Education Library, London: EPPI-Centre, Social Science Research Unit, Institute of Education

Lunt, I. and B. Norwich (1999), *Can Effective Schools be Inclusive Schools?*, London: Institute of Education

Obrusnikova, I., H. Valkova and M. E. Block (2003), 'Impact of inclusion in general physical education on students without disabilities', *Adapted Physical Activity Quarterly*, 20 (3), 230–45

Ofsted (2004), *Special Educational Needs And Disability: Towards Inclusive Schools*, London: Ofsted

Rankin, D. H., K. R. Logan, J. Adcock, J. Angelucci, C. Pittman, A. Sexstone and S. Straughn (1999), 'Small group learning: effects of including a student with intellectual disabilities', *Journal of Developmental and Physical Disabilities*, 11 (2), 159–77

Sharpe, M. N., J. L. York and J. Knight (1994), 'Effects of inclusion on the academic performance of classmates without disabilities: a preliminary study', *Remedial and Special Education*, 15 (5), 281–7

Skrtic, T. M. (1991), 'The special education paradox: equity as the way to excellence', *Harvard Educational Review*, 61 (2), 148–206

Stakes, R. and G. Hornby (1997), *Change in Special Education: What Brings it About?*, London: Cassell

Steer, Sir A. (chair) (2005), *Learning Behaviour: the Report of the Practitioners' Group on School Behaviour and Discipline*, London: DfES

Tapasak, R. C. and C. S. Walther-Thomas (1999), 'Evaluation of a first-year inclusion programme: student perceptions and classroom performance', *Remedial and Special Education*, 20 (4), 216–25

Warnock Committee (1978), *Special Educational Needs (the Warnock Report)*, London: DfES

Warnock, M. (2005), *Special Educational Needs: A New Look*, London: Philosophy of Education Society of Great Britain

13 Towards a more inclusive education system

Where next for special schools?

Mel Ainscow

Mary Warnock's recent pamphlet *Special Educational Needs: A New Look*, has intensified the debate about inclusive education. In some ways this has been helpful; it has moved the issue nearer to the centre of the ongoing debate about the future of education in this country. Unfortunately, it has also had a negative impact, in the sense that it has tended to encourage some in the field to retreat into traditional stances.

Within these overall debates, questions about the future of special schools are particularly problematic. Should they continue to work in much the same way, attempting to provide a distinctive educational experience for groups of children seen as having similar needs? Or should they seek to develop new roles with due regard to the inclusion agenda within the mainstream?

In this chapter, I address these questions by locating the debate in an international context and considering examples of innovatory practice from the field. I conclude with some comments about the implications for national policy.

International developments

The 1990s saw considerable efforts in many countries to develop more equitable forms of schooling. The United Nations' strategy of 'Education for All' encouraged such initiatives, focusing specifically on the need to reach out to excluded and marginalised groups of learners, not least those with disabilities. Further impetus was encouraged by UNESCO's 'Salamanca Statement on Principles, Policy and Practice in Special Needs Education' (UNESCO, 1994), which provides a framework for thinking about how to move policy and practice forward. Arguably the most significant international document that has ever appeared in special education, the statement argues that regular schools with an inclusive orientation are: 'the most effective means of combating discriminatory attitudes, building an inclusive society and achieving education for all'. Furthermore, it suggests, such schools can: 'provide an effective education for the majority of children and improve the efficiency and ultimately the cost-effectiveness of the entire education system'.

Salamanca encourages us to look at educational difficulties in a new way. This new direction in thinking is based on the belief that changes in methodology and organisation made in response to students experiencing difficulties can, under certain conditions, benefit all children. Since the late 1980s a growing number of scholars in different countries have taken this new thinking forward (e.g. Ballard, 1997; Booth, 1995; Kugelmass, 2001; Mittler, 2000; Skrtic, 1991; Slee, 1996). They argue that progress towards more inclusive education systems requires a move away from practices based on the traditional perspectives of special education, towards approaches that focus on developing 'effective schools for all' (Ainscow, 1991).

This has been characterised as an 'organisational paradigm' (Dyson and Millward, 2000). It involves a shift away from explanations of educational failure that concentrate on the characteristics of individual children and their families, towards an analysis of the barriers to participation and learning experienced by students within school systems (Booth and Ainscow, 2002). Recently my colleagues and I have referred to this approach as 'school improvement with attitude' (Ainscow *et al.*, 2006), meaning:

- the process of increasing the participation of students in, and reducing their exclusion from, the curricula, cultures and communities of local schools;
- restructuring the cultures, policies and practices of schools so that they respond to the diversity of students in their locality;
- the presence, participation and achievement of all students vulnerable to exclusionary pressures, not only those with impairments or those who are categorised as 'having special educational needs'.

Within this formulation, inclusion is seen as a continuous process. An inclusive school is one that is on the move, rather than one that has reached a perfect state. It seems to me that this new thinking provides the special education field with new opportunities for representing the interests of those learners who become marginalised within existing educational arrangements.

Collaborative inquiry

With this in mind, I recently worked with a network of special school head teachers, who are all associated with the Specialist Schools Trust, in carrying out a research project to explore ways of moving thinking and practice forward. The project involved the use of an approach that we refer to as 'collaborative inquiry'. This advocates practitioner research, carried out in partnership with academics, as a means of developing better understanding of educational processes (Ainscow, 1999). Kurt Lewin's dictum that you cannot understand an organisation until you try to change it is, perhaps, the clearest justification for this approach (Schein, 2001).

The study led to the production of a series of 'accounts of practice'. These focus on ways in which special schools in different parts of England are attempting to work in partnership with mainstream schools in order to foster the development of inclusive practices. Reflecting on the accounts that were produced, it is noticeable that the schools were working in many different ways. In what follows I try to give a sense of the range of approaches we found. These differences reflect the variety of contexts and local policies within which the schools were operating. They also point to the overall lack of direction that currently exists within the field.

Setting up enclaves

Some special schools had developed arrangements whereby some of their students spend parts of the week located on the sites of mainstream schools. These experiences throw light on the potential benefits of this approach, as well as some of the difficulties. For example, staff in an urban special school that has students attending a number of mainstream schools described how the presence of young people with disabilities had opened up many opportunities for social learning among pupils within the mainstream. A senior teacher in a partner secondary school talked with obvious pride about how some of his pupils had learnt to accept youngsters from the special school. Mention was also made of how staff in the mainstream were developing more positive attitudes to these pupils.

For special school pupils involved in mainstream opportunities there was evidence of how they had matured as a result of being involved in a wider range of curriculum and social opportunities. It was impressive to see, for example, how they mixed freely and with self-confidence in the context of a large secondary school. Developments in language were seen as a particular benefit. Being required to make choices was also seen as a helpful source of social learning. It was noted too that the special school pupils had benefited as a result of being taught by a greater range of specialist teachers and having opportunities to use more specialist facilities and resources.

Parental support for these developments was said to be growing, as more and more pupils had opportunities to have positive experiences in mainstream contexts. In addition, the experience of being involved in mainstream activities was seen to be influencing attitudes of special school staff towards notions of inclusion.

At the same time, these experiences drew attention to some of the dilemmas and challenges that face those in special education as they seek to explore new ways of working within the 'inclusion agenda'. For example, this particular special school has outstanding facilities and resources, not least in terms of technology. Given this evident strength, why should parents see mainstream as a positive option? At the same time, in order to ensure the continuation of its current financial arrangements, the school needs to maintain its pupil numbers. So, what incentive is there to put more efforts in strengthening mainstream provision? Additionally, is it sensible to invest staff time in supporting individual pupils within mainstream schools if this reduces the quality of provision made for those within the special school context?

The head teacher referred to staffing issues, noting that a key strategic dilemma relates to the need to arrange staff time so that they can move between schools.

Mention was also made of wider contextual factors that can act as barriers to further development. In particular, it was noted that the government's standards agenda was tending to leave mainstream schools with less space, time and resources in order to experiment with collaborative arrangements. In addition, rigidity of curriculum and teaching approaches, and the impact of performance league tables, were also seen as problems.

Finally, it was noted that confusion about the purposes of inclusion can act as a barrier to further development, leading some in the school to argue that greater progress would be possible if there was a clearer lead from government. At present, it was argued, so much depends on the actions of individuals in the field.

Supporting individual pupils

Some special schools had developed strategies for providing various forms of outreach support for individual pupils within mainstream schools. Again, there was evidence of potential benefits and difficulties in this type of response. Staff in one school described how they had explored a variety of strategies for working with mainstream partners and how these had developed as a result of the experimentation that had taken place. While these strategies imply a number of different aims, they all seem to be driven by a concern to use specialist resources and knowledge in new ways in order to improve learning opportunities for vulnerable children and young people.

This particular special school is in a small town and acts as a 'hub' for a range of other activities within mainstream schools across the local education authority. These include the involvement of five 'advanced skills' teachers who offer support to teachers and pupils in other schools. The school also provides training for teaching assistants in the authority.

Staff in both the special and the mainstream schools spoke with obvious pride about the impact on the achievement and self-esteem of the pupils involved. There was considerable evidence, too, of impact on the attitudes and practice of staff. Interestingly, there seemed to be general acceptance that the learning was a two-way process. Specific reference was made to the impact of the inclusion activities on value-added test scores in the primary schools, and how they had strengthened practice in the secondary school in ways that had helped with post-Ofsted action plans.

Perhaps even more significant was the evidence suggesting that the work of this particular special school, including its success in gaining specialist college and, more recently, Leading Edge status, had raised the profile of the school and created a very different view within the local community of the role of special education, thus addressing Mary Warnock's concern that special schools are held in 'low esteem'. (The aim of Leading Edge partnerships [DfES, 2003] is to raise standards of teaching and learning by teaming up schools which are considered strong all-rounders with others needing support.) The head summed this up when she commented: 'We are seen as a school that can cut the mustard.' She went on to explain: 'It helps the image of the school. We are seen as less of a dumping ground and more of a place where you will find help.'

At the same time there had been striking changes in the population of pupils now placed at the school, as the mainstream had grown in its capacity to cater for children experiencing difficulties. These population changes had also been influenced by policy moves to reduce the number of pupils placed in residential provision outside the LEA.

Reflecting on the partnership arrangements with the mainstream schools, the head teacher of the special school sensed that it may have gone as far as it can go. She commented: 'They are not moving on.' In particular, she explained, despite the progress that has been made and the level of collaboration that now exists, there is still resistance to special school pupils being placed on the registers of the partner schools. She added: 'As long as it is seen as a project it's not really inclusion.'

Apparently the main concern in the mainstream is that this could have a negative impact on the schools' overall test and examination results, as summarised in the performance league tables. Also the schools are anxious about getting too much of a reputation for their special needs work, since this might lead to more requests for admission from parents of children who need additional support.

Strengthening capacity

Throughout the country there is increasing evidence of school-to-school collaboration being used in order to support improvement efforts (Ainscow and West, 2006). In some instances, the intention is that school networks will involve a new type of special schools, which will act as inclusion support centres. Such initiatives open up possibilities for special schools to strengthen capacity for inclusion within mainstream schools. Commenting on these possibilities, one head teacher noted: 'We can become the hub for a range of services, so they can't do without us.'

Any shift in responsibility would need to be accompanied by changes in funding arrangements. Specifically, funding would have to be delegated to groups of schools. This would mean that the use of the expensive and time-consuming process of writing statements to release funding from LEAs to schools would become largely redundant.

Some interesting examples of this type of arrangement are beginning to emerge. For example, a secondary special school in one urban LEA has become an area resource centre promoting the use of technology for pupils who experience difficulties in learning. This is an approach that Mary Warnock supports in her 2005 pamphlet. In another urban authority, three district partnerships of schools have been created, each of which involves one special school (now known as 'support centres'). Significant resources have been transferred to the partnerships, and teams of head teachers share responsibility for the participation and achievement of all learners in their district. Members of various support services have also been relocated on to the sites of the special schools with the intention of fostering the multi-agency work that is demanded by the government's 'Every Child

Matters' policy. This context creates new possibilities for using the expertise within the special school to benefit a larger number of pupils. It also means that opportunities for special school pupils to participate in mainstream activities can occur as a matter of routine.

In theory, the various co-located special schools that are currently being built around the country should facilitate similar merging of responsibilities and sharing of resources. For example, plans are well advanced to federate one special school with a primary and secondary school in a new building, which will cater for 1,400 pupils on a site that is designed to ensure maximum possibilities for inclusive education. This exciting development can be seen as the culmination of over 15 years of effort to redefine the role of special education provision within this particular LEA. Interestingly, the head teacher of the special school has been appointed to the post of executive head of the new organisation.

A special school in a rural district has developed a strong presence within a local network of schools. The main purpose of these activities is to help the schools to develop a much greater capacity for supporting the participation and learning of children who experience difficulties. In developing this work the head teacher emphasised the need to ensure the viability of his own school within what he sees as a context of uncertainty. He explained that this creates a strategic dilemma, in that success in strengthening mainstream provision could eventually lead to the demise of the special school.

The network, which involves 25 schools, is well established and involves a range of cooperative activities. In many ways it is an excellent example of the collaborative arrangements that the government is now seeking to encourage, not least in that its management rests with the head teachers themselves. One head explained: 'It's from the bottom up, rather than the authority saying this is what you need.'

Cooperation about special needs and inclusion is a key element within the network, and the special school is very much the lead partner. Emphasis is placed on two linked strategies: staff development and consultancy in respect to individual pupils.

Staff development takes a variety of forms, all aimed at strengthening the capacity of mainstream staff to respond to pupils experiencing difficulties. For example, the school offers full-day workshops on specialised teaching strategies. These may be offered within schools for all staff, or at the special school site for visiting groups. One member of staff argued that such training activities were valued because they were led by practising teachers. He explained: 'When we go out we speak as practitioners with credibility. It's not just theory. We tend to throw in anecdotes from our own teaching that brings it to life.' It was noticeable that quite a number of the staff have recent mainstream experience. One teacher who works on training and consultancy in relation to autism commented: 'It really helps that I was a secondary science teacher. Some of my colleagues are less confident because of not having that experience.'

The special school also organises the work of the network's SENCO (special educational needs coordinator) forum. All the schools that are involved pay an annual membership fee of £175. Training events are paid for separately. This income is used to pay for supply staff, so that special teachers can be released. One teacher commented: 'I used to get embarrassed about saying schools had to pay. Now they realise that somebody has to pay for my release.'

Consultancy is also paid for by the mainstream schools and is focused on providing advice and support to staff. Here a particularly interesting initiative involves experienced teaching assistants from the special school spending time in mainstream contexts.

The approach that this network is developing, with its emphasis on capacity building, contrasts with the work of other special schools that are more focused on pupil re-integration strategies. Of course, questions have to be asked about the impact of such approaches. In this particular case, if we accept 'take up' as an indicator, the evidence is encouraging. Apparently almost every week members of staff are involved in leading workshops for mainstream groups, sometimes for whole staffs. In addition, demand continues to increase for consultancy support in relation to particular pupils. Of course, all these activities involve schools in paying for the services that are provided.

At the same time, it is evident that progress within the mainstream varies from school to school. Commenting on this, one member of staff explained: 'Some schools are more committed to inclusion. The ones that are successful with inclusion are the ones that have management that are committed to it.' It is also worth noting that very few special school pupils spend time in mainstream lessons and none have been re-integrated into the mainstream. Finance is seen as one of the barriers to such arrangements.

An interesting feature of this work is the way in which this special school has had to re-think its internal organisational arrangements in order to allow teachers and teaching assistants to be away from their in-school duties. This involves a strong emphasis on agreed policies that encourage consistency, and team work arrangements that mean that no individual is indispensable. Staff involved in mainstream activities are also well briefed about the rationale for their work.

At the same time there are still barriers that limit progress. The school is stretched to serve a diverse population that includes some very challenging individuals. The fact that it has children from various LEAs adds to the pressure and, of course, makes it difficult to set up local arrangements for the re-integration of some pupils. Like other special schools that are engaged in innovatory activities relating to inclusion, it has to ensure its own viability, not least in terms of pupil numbers. It is also positioned on the edge of the LEA, in ways that can make it feel slightly detached.

Barriers are created, too, by the sense of uncertainty about where the LEA is heading in relation to its overall policy for special needs. Concern was expressed about the authority's attitude towards the new roles that the school has developed, particularly in relation to the dissemination of expertise about how to teach children with particular disabilities. As in other LEAs, there is also concern about how the developing outreach role of the special school fits in with the way other support services are developing. Indeed, some staff at the school feel that they are working in competition with the LEA services.

So, like other special schools that are exploring new ways of working, this school offers striking challenges for management and leadership. In particular, those who take on these roles see themselves faced with what seem like endless dilemmas. For example, in talking about the support that is provided to schools in the network, the head teacher commented: 'It's very wobbly. I feel very wobbly about what we can offer at any one time.'

Drawing out the lessons

From the examples I have presented we see evidence of three overall approaches to the development of the work of special schools. These are:

- the development of enclaves within mainstreams schools, so that special school pupils can experience mainstream curriculum;
- strategies to provide direct support for individual pupils in the mainstream who are seen as being likely for possible transfer to special provision, or vulnerable to exclusion;
- the development of new roles for the special school in strengthening inclusive practices more generally within the mainstream.

The first two of these approaches are focused on individual pupils in ways that reflect the traditions of special education practice, whereas the third approach reflects what I referred to earlier as an organisational perspective. As we have seen, each has potential to improve services for vulnerable groups of pupils and each presents difficulties and strategic dilemmas. And of course there is potential for the three approaches to be linked.

Visitors to special schools such as the ones I have described are struck by the willingness of those involved to experiment. To use a phrase mentioned earlier, they are schools that are 'on the move'. In this sense they reveal many of the features of what Senge (1989) calls 'a learning organisation', that is, an 'organisation that is continually expanding its capacity to create its future'. It is also evident that all of this has emanated from the leadership provided by particular head teachers and their senior teams. Through their energy and enthusiasm they seem to have been successful in developing cultures of creativity and risk-taking, despite the uncertainties that they face in taking this work forward.

All of this has placed these particular special schools at the centre of developments regarding inclusion within their LEAs. As we have seen, these developments have been challenging and demanding of time, particularly for the head teachers themselves. Their vision for special schools is essentially transformative, and in some cases goes well beyond anything that currently exists. It implies new thinking regarding many aspects of the work of their schools, including the forms of governance and management that will be needed, and the approaches to the curriculum, pastoral care, budgets, roles and responsibilities, and strategies for teaching and learning.

Of course sometimes the new ideas under consideration have not found favour among key stakeholders. For example, some staff in partner mainstream schools have expressed anxiety about their ability to deal with children with more severe disabilities. Similarly, some staff in the special schools are anxious about their ability to cope within mainstream contexts. As a result, the process of negotiating agreements has required persistent yet sensitive leadership and, inevitably, some compromises have had to be made in order to achieve a degree of consensus on the overall rationale for the developments.

Across all the schools there was another striking aspect of leadership that needs to be noted. This was a capacity to understand local contexts in order to determine opportunities and resources for moving thinking and practice forward, and an ability to address possible barriers to progress. The success that has been achieved is not so much about importing solutions from elsewhere; rather it involves people within the local context inventing relevant and feasible strategies that fit existing circumstances.

Running through all this are challenges regarding the management of innovation. Research suggests that, by and large, schools find it difficult to cope with change (Hopkins *et al.*, 1994). In this respect they face a double problem: they cannot remain as they now are if they are to respond to new challenges; but at the same time they also need to maintain some continuity between their present and their previous practices. There is, therefore, a tension between *development* and *maintenance*. The problem is that schools tend to generate organisational structures that predispose them towards one or the other. Schools (or parts of schools) at the development extreme may be so over-confident of their innovative capacities that they take on too much too quickly, thus damaging the quality of what already exists. On the other hand, schools at the maintenance extreme may either see little purpose in change, or have a poor history of managing innovation.

During times of stability, of course, a tendency to maintenance presents little difficulty. On the other hand, periods of profound change and uncertainty heighten the tensions that are created within maintenance-oriented systems. Our own research indicates that the patterns of organisation and practice within special schools present a particularly extreme version of the maintenance–development dilemma (Ainscow *et al.*, 2003). They are, by their nature, organisations that are particularly focused on doing everything possible to overcome the difficulties of unusual populations of learners. Therefore they have a tradition of intensive relationships between adults and children that have a particular focus on individualised approaches to learning. They also tend to have close links with families. In addition, the involvement of relatively large numbers of external support specialists from the education, social service and health departments further consumes planning time. As a result, finding time to plan for change seems to be a particular problem and, indeed, external visitors to special schools often find that there are few opportunities during the day to have discussions with members of staff.

Consequently, leaders in special education have to address the unusual management contexts created by this intensive form of the maintenance–development dilemma. In particular, they must address the question: what forms of leadership practice can enable special schools to provide high-quality education within existing circumstances, while at the same time developing new roles in relation to developments in the mainstream?

Implications for national policy

What, then, does all of this suggest regarding national policy? Recent moves have been generally successful in encouraging local authorities and schools to move in a more inclusive direction. Too often, however, special schools have been omitted from these policy initiatives in a way that has left many within that sector feeling isolated and devalued. The time is now ripe for a national lead to emerge showing how the expertise and resources within special schools can be redirected in ways that will add support to the changes taking place in mainstream schools. Such a move would, I believe, open up new opportunities for special school staff to continue their historical task of providing support for the most vulnerable learners in the education system. Interestingly, as Baroness Warnock reminds us, this was one of the recommendations she and her colleagues made as a result of the government inquiry in 1978.

Government talk of a possible 'third way' approach has been helpful in stimulating further debate about these matters in the field. On the other hand, there is a danger that if this approach leads to ambiguous messages, it will prevent the clarity of thinking that could help provide an effective lever for change (Ainscow, 2005). There is therefore a need for a clear national policy statement that will encourage further experimentation of the sort that I have described. At the same time, there is also a need for government to provide a statement of its commitment to inclusion, accompanied by a clear statement of what an inclusive system might actually look like, that could then be used to guide policy development and inform monitoring procedures.

In a recent advice note to the schools minister Lord Adonis, my colleagues Alan Dyson, Peter Farrell and I argued that any such statement should emphasise the positive benefits of inclusion for parents and children, rather than inclusion as an ideological principle to be accepted as an article of faith. Specifically, it might be useful to emphasise the distinction between needs, rights and opportunities. All children have needs (e.g. for appropriate teaching), but they also have the right to participate fully in a common social institution (a local mainstream school) that offers a range of opportunities for them. The current system too often forces parents to choose between ensuring that their child's needs are met (which often implies special school placement) and ensuring that they have the same rights and opportunities as other children (which, according to the Salamanca Statement, not to mention a considerable consensus of public opinion, implies mainstream school placement). The aim therefore should be to create a system where these choices become unnecessary.

We also argued that the government should emphasise the idea that inclusion is about the development of mainstream schools, rather than the reorganisation of special schooling. The aim has to be to increase the capacity of all mainstream schools, so that, like the best schools today, they can meet the needs of all children, while offering them similar rights and opportunities. This has implications for a changed role for special schools in the medium term and the disappearance of special schools entirely in the longer term. However, it is vital to note that the disappearance of the bricks and mortar of special schools does not imply the disappearance of the skills, attitudes, values and resources which those buildings currently contain.

Finally we stressed that the education of children with 'special educational needs' should be seen as part of a wider set of issues relating to the education of all children who experience difficulties in school and, ultimately, of all children. This led us to conclude that the distinction between 'SEN' and 'non-SEN' children is a largely outmoded one, which ignores the considerable developments that have occurred in the system's ability to identify and respond to a wide range of difficulties.

Some final thoughts

The experiences of the special schools described in this chapter offer many reasons for optimism. They suggest that where those involved are prepared to think and act in new ways, they can make significant new contributions to the development of a more inclusive education system. While these experiments are still at the early stages of development, they offer leads as to how successful strategies might evolve. At the same time, it is important to stress the importance of analysing local contexts, recognising that an approach that works in one place may not be easily transposed to another location.

Those in leadership roles in special schools have a key role to play in providing leadership for such developments at the local level. They will therefore need support in learning how to develop, within their schools, organisation, cultures that encourage experimentation and collective problem-solving in response to the challenge of pupil diversity. Such cultures are necessary for an effective response to the increasingly challenging populations within the special schools. It may well be that they are also the most important gift that the special education community can offer to the movement towards more inclusive forms of education.

Acknowledgements

I would like to acknowledge the contributions of the head teachers who were my co-researchers in the project described in this chapter. Thanks must also go to my colleagues Alan Dyson, Peter Farrell and Andy Howes, who contributed to the development of the ideas that are presented, and to Vivian Heung and Kiki Messiou, who commented on an earlier draft.

References

Ainscow, M. (ed.) (1991), *Effective Schools for All*, London: Fulton

Ainscow, M. (1999), *Understanding the Development of Inclusive Schools*, London: Falmer Press

Ainscow, M. (2005), 'Developing inclusive education systems: what are the levers for change?', *Journal of Educational Change*, 6 (2), 109–24

Ainscow, M., T. Booth and A. Dyson with P. Farrell, J. Frankham, F. Gallannaugh, A. Howes and R. Smith (2006), *Improving Schools, Developing Inclusion*, London: Routledge

Ainscow, M., S. Fox and J. O'Kane (2003), *Leadership and Management in Special Schools: A Review of the Literature*, Nottingham: National College for School Leadership

Ainscow, M. and M. West (eds) (2006), *Leading Improvements in Urban Schools*, Buckingham: Open University Press

Ballard, K. (1997), 'Researching disability and inclusive education: participation, construction and interpretation', *International Journal of Inclusive Education*, 1 (3), 243–56

Booth, T. (1995), 'Mapping inclusion and exclusion: concepts for all?', in C. Clark, A. Dyson and A. Millward (eds), *Towards Inclusive Schools?*, London: Fulton

Booth, T. and M. Ainscow (2002), *The Index for Inclusion* (2nd edn), Centre for Studies on Inclusive Education

Dyson, A. and A. Millward (2000), *Schools and Special Needs: Issues of Innovation and Inclusion*, London: Paul Chapman

Hopkins, D., M. Ainscow and M. West (1994), *School Improvement in an Era of Change*, London: Cassell

Kugelmass, J. W. (2001), 'Collaboration and compromise in creating and sustaining an inclusive school', *Journal of Inclusive Education*. 5 (1), 47–65

Mittler, P. (2000), *Working towards Inclusive Education*, London: Fulton

Schein, E. H. (2001), 'Clinical inquiry/research', in P. Reason and H. Bradbury (eds), *Handbook of Action Research*, London: Sage

Senge, P. M. (1989), *The Fifth Discipline: The Art and Practice of the Learning Organisation*, London: Century

Skrtic, T. M. (1991), 'Students with special educational needs: artifacts of the traditional curriculum', in M. Ainscow (ed.), *Effective Schools for All*, London: Fulton

Slee, R. (1996), 'Inclusive schooling in Australia? Not yet', *Cambridge Journal of Education*, 26 (1), 19–32

UNESCO (1994), *Final Report: World Conference on Special Needs Education: Access and Quality*, Paris: UNESCO

Warnock, M. (2005), *Special Educational Needs: A New Look*, London: Philosophy of Education Society of Great Britain

14 Visions for the Village

A new framework for inclusive learning

Dela Smith

Introduction

The Education Village in Darlington is one of the first of its kind to be built under the Private Finance Initiative (PFI). Opened in April 2006, it brings together pupils from two mainstream schools (Springfield Primary School and Haughton Community School) and one special/specialist school (Beaumont Hill School and Technology College), with an integrated leadership and management team supported by a single federated governing body. It caters for 1,400 pupils from the age of 3 to 19, with lessons taking place in state of the art facilities that cater for diverse needs. It is a unique learning environment that builds capacity in order to raise standards, deliver inclusive education, and ease transition at all levels, particularly from key stage 2 to 3. Workforce reform is at the heart of the vision, as is community partnership and the 'Every Child Matters' agenda.

My aim in this chapter is to share with the reader the vision on which the Education Village in Darlington is based. The Village differs significantly from other 'co-locations'. Architecturally as well as educationally, the special school stands at the *centre* of the process, rather than as an adjunct. The vision came first, with the building providing the expression of the educational philosophy behind the vision. According to this philosophy, all children can benefit from being educated on a single site and as a single community. Special attention has been paid to children with complex learning needs who are often considered most reliant on special schools.

In addition to catering for the full range of students, our vision includes the use of the school for research and development. It embraces a town-wide inclusion strategy and provides an integrated leadership model for the system as a whole. We hope that this approach will remove the sense of secrecy and shame often associated with the special school.

The developments to date have attracted national attention from both local authorities and schools as they seek to develop their proposals for the government's 'Building Schools for the Future' initiative (2004). Special schools have also shown a keen interest in our approach at a time when the special education system is under a great deal of scrutiny from the politicians and educationalists alike.

Inclusion: sharing the responsibility

The rationale for the Village is that, despite the agenda for the development of special schools, the systems that currently operate around special educational needs do not provide an adequate lever for system change or leadership beyond a single institution. The inclusion debate has been well rehearsed over the last three decades, and continues to be a live issue. It has included discussions about whether special schools can support an inclusion agenda, or whether they perpetuate segregation. Special schools certainly exist as a resource for mainstream schools, providing much-needed expertise for pupils with complex needs. I shall argue, however, that the inclusive philosophy is best expressed in a context that meets the needs of *all* pupils, with and without special needs. It must be fit for purpose and fully resourced. It must fully avail itself of the expertise of the special school.

In its Green Paper *Excellence for All Children* (1997), the government stresses that pupils with special needs should, wherever possible, receive their education in a mainstream school, and join their peers in the curriculum and life of the school. Despite this worthy guidance, there is no clear indication of how it should work in practice. It has been left open to interpretation, and the radical changes required to make a real step change have not been widespread.

Beaumont Hill School and Technology College is the special/specialist school at the heart of the Education Village. Despite long-standing and productive partnerships with mainstream schools in Darlington, Beaumont Hill has found it difficult to build on its good practice and developments, and to extend inclusion opportunities for more complex pupils. Despite excellent support from the local authority the school became convinced that the only way forward was to base their provision right at the heart of mainstream, and to be part of an inclusive system. This opportunity came with the chance to rebuild the school through a Private Finance Initiative.

There have been many changes in the organisation of schools in recent years. Partnerships have emerged in the form of federations, networks and extended schools clusters, and the government's 'Building Schools for The Future' programme has supported the physical realisation of these partnerships. With these changes have come opportunities to reconceptualise education, that is, to rethink the basic purposes of schools. We took such an opportunity when we placed Beaumont Hill at the centre of the Village instead of rebuilding it in splendid isolation.

It is true that no matter how well developed or sophisticated special schools' outreach programmes are, the fact that most special schools remain totally separate from the mainstream system mitigates against their potential to influence the wider agenda in any sustainable way. The 'mainstreaming' of special educational needs issues into government strategy has been helpful, but attempts to develop whole-scale approaches, for example, 'P Levels' for benchmarking purposes, have progressed slowly, and the least able pupils have generally continued to have their needs met in separate provision, where the responsibility lies with the special sector.

Central to the inclusion debate is the sharing of the responsibility for our most complex pupils in the context of the community and the agenda of the Children's National Service Framework. (This framework was published by the Department of Health on 15 September 2004, partly as a response to the death of Victoria Climbie in 2000. Launched by Dr John Reid, it sets aspirations for improvement across health, education and social care for women, children and families.) We cannot simply overlay old and tired approaches onto this new and radical approach to sharing for all children the 'five outcomes', as outlined in the Children Act 2004, of being healthy, staying safe, enjoying and achieving, making a positive contribution, and achieving economic well-being. We must acknowledge the pupil as the most important unit of the organisation rather than the classroom, school or school system. This is personalisation in action, and personalisation is synonymous with inclusion as I use the term here.

It is worrying that the most challenging pupils in special schools fail to be involved in longer-term sustainable inclusion arrangements, or fail to have access to the same opportunities as those whose inclusion is not hampered by the barriers to learning we ourselves perpetuate in our schools. This is possibly due to heavy resource requirements, which can include specialist provision and adapted classrooms, but, more critically, it involves an adapted approach to timetabling across the needs of all pupils. It is this small but significant number of pupils, therefore, that will remain in special schools, many of them 'isolated by location', as a result of their high resourcing needs which are 'additional to' those which are normally provided in a mainstream classroom.

The process of inclusion needs to be one that engages the hearts and minds of all concerned. This is not meant sentimentally, but the education of hard-to-teach pupils who do not improve the performance tables does not provide the best motivation for schools to include them. Many schools do not want to change a recipe for success that places them high on the performance table. Schools which are struggling to raise their game feel compromised by the inclusion of pupils who make little or no contribution to the A*–C examination grade measures of success. Value-added scores do help for all pupils, but the system is an uneasy one to manage, and intervention programmes can frequently be aimed at those pupils who need to reach the targets. This is not a criticism of mainstream schools, but an attempt to outline the dilemma they can find themselves in. It suggests that a radical review is required.

The vision for the Village

> The Education Village will be radical and innovative in the pursuit of excellence. It will raise standards for all, in a fully inclusive community with a single integrated system of governance and management. There will be a spectrum of service provision within the Village and the Village will be a resource for the whole community and the borough of Darlington.
>
> (Outline Business Case, Darlington Borough Council)

Our vision for the Village addresses systemic issues of ownership and capacity-building by planning for, and sharing responsibility of, all children under one roof. There has been criticism that the Village may represent 'one big special school', but we hope and believe that this is not the case.

As I said, the Education Village consists of three schools operating as one inclusive organisation under one roof. It therefore provides all-through schooling, with wraparound childcare provision and state of the art facilities to meet the specific resource requirements of the most profoundly disabled pupil to the most gifted and talented. All areas of the Village are available to all pupils, and a single timetable establishes each child's right to a broad and balanced curriculum.

In order to ensure a cohesive approach, the three schools share a single federated governing body that has a complete overview of the three schools. The federation plan and carefully structured committees guide the governance strategically. The three schools have a single budget, and have developed an innovative and radical integrated leadership and management structure that reflects the values of the Village and enables the delivery of the five outcomes for children. The leadership team have worked very closely with the Hay Consultancy Group in order to identify a fit-for-purpose leadership structure for the Village that is, we believe, future-proof.

Opening doors: a school for everyone

The original idea was to replace Beaumont Hill special school, a highly successful special school. This school has demonstrated a pro-active 'outward-looking' approach to supporting inclusion work in the context of a borough-wide inclusion strategy. It has also maintained and raised high standards of achievement for all pupils, while endeavouring to offer high-quality advice and outreach support to schools.

There is no doubt that the specialist designation of the school has made a major impact on the school's ability to manage all of this process. Particularly helpful has been the context of the mainstream agenda provided through the Specialist College Trust, and also the networks around specialist schools and Leading Edge partnerships (the DfES initiative to raise standards of teaching and learning by teaming up strong all-round schools with others needing support). This has provided rigour and pace to the work of the school as well as high standards of achievement for all its pupils.

This successful activity demonstrates that the school has had a great deal of opportunity to influence the other schools with which it works. However, as long as it continued to operate in isolation, the responsibility for the most complex pupils remains in the domain of the special school with limited opportunities for leadership learning around SEN in other schools. The reverse is also true, and the learning from mainstream colleagues and their practices is not always readily available or, more importantly, *transferable* across contexts. It was for this reason that the schools sought a radical approach to the rebuilding of Beaumont Hill School.

The challenge of system change

No matter how much this excellent outreach work develops (and many special schools have risen magnificently to the challenge), without the opportunity for system change the impact on opportunities for further inclusion will remain elusive, and only by adopting an integrated approach within the universal service of education will special schools be able to make any real impact on their mainstream colleagues. There is a real and continuing problem around the perceived 'mystique' of special schools.

As the scheme for the rebuilding of Beaumont Hill progressed, it became clear that to recreate and reposition the school in a co-located situation would neither progress the contributions that the school could make to the inclusion agenda, nor release the potential to begin the system change required. The challenge for the Village therefore lay in the transformation of systems in order to support *all* learners in the light of the 'Every Child Matters' agenda, and to build leadership capacity in order to address the wider brief for the Village. The early aspirations for the Village reflected the new 'Every Child Matters' agenda faithfully, and running all through this was the opportunity for workforce reform.

It should be stressed that the Village is not a 'one size fits all' solution. Rather, it reflects a diversity of provision and a delivery model to meet needs based on personalised learning. In order to provide a supportive framework for change, the approaches to governance, leadership and management, resources and curriculum taken by the three schools required review. We were determined to do things 'differently and better'.

A special school's effectiveness runs the risk of being viewed as 'bolt on' as long as special schools continue to operate in their current way. Co-location is a step forward in bringing the two sectors together, and excellent examples are emerging across the country, but it may not be enough to ensure real context change, in order to build capacity and place special schools in a position of strength. No matter how strong the schools' links are with mainstream partners, there is still no automatic access to facilities, teaching, activities or other pupils. All this is usually subject to negotiation, and frequently agreed only if arrangements do not cause undue changes or disruption to the receiving school's organisation.

A further issue for special schools is that, because of their size, they lack the capacity to further their outreach work while 'holding the fort'. This is partly helped by funding the special, specialist schools to carry out advice and support to mainstream in their chosen category, whether it is subject specialist or in the newly developed special schools category.

Developing a common enterprise of learning in a new building 'fit for purpose'

The Outline Business Case for the Village was submitted in 2002, and referenced two major government documents that were published at the time. These were the DfES 2001 White Paper, *Schools Building on Success*, and the government's policy agenda on special educational needs in the 1999 Green Paper *Excellence for All Children* (and the subsequent document *Meeting Special Educational Needs: A Programme of Action*).

Clear success criteria for the Village were identified at this stage, and a cross-cutting set of criteria based on the necessity for the three schools to work closely in partnership in order to raise achievement for all.

The process of working with the bidders and their individual designs was time-consuming and lengthy. However, when we finally arrived at the stage of preferred bidder, we had a building that reflected our inclusive principles and educational philosophy. Over the ensuing year, the staff from the three schools worked closely with our new partner Kajima International to plan and design the internals for the new school.

The resulting Village now has all the facilities under its roof it needs in order to meet the requirements of all pupils. It is designed around a village green which will provide a central focus for community activity. There is a 'sacred space' on the village green that will act as a base for a multi-faith chaplaincy. Facilities include sensory theatres, light rooms and ball pools, swimming and hydrotherapy pools, dance and drama studios. There is a fully equipped bistro for enterprise and vocational work and a virtual reality studio that will enable cross-curricular developments such as village radio. The specialist secondary facilities reflect the specialist designations of the schools, and the design technology facilities are industrial-standard. There is the provision of primary food technology room, and a magnificent learning resource centre with a 'floating deck'. The single ICT platform has both wired and wireless technology in every room, and will ensure access to a virtual learning environment for pupils, staff and parents alike.

The primary phase is fully integrated with the pupils' facilities developed in the appropriate year groups. Those pupils requiring a more secluded environment have facilities built into the design, and care and attention has gone into ensuring the strategic placing of these specialist resources. There are large, 70 square metre, rooms in primary so that joint activity can take place without compromising the space for the full classes of 30 pupils.

The pupils will all eat together, play together and learn together wherever it is in the particular interests of the child. We are pragmatic about the fact that some pupils need their own space in order to maximise their learning, and that all pupils have a right to learn without undue disruption or distraction from others.

The key stage 1 block houses the wraparound and day care facilities that will take children from birth to nursery age. The nursery is integrated and the schools and the private provider will work together to ensure consistency for children across the day.

In the secondary areas we have developed 'enhanced classrooms' that are fully adapted for any child with a particular need. These classrooms include rise and fall furniture, induction looping and additional computer points. They are also designed around smaller groups and more individualised teaching. Two double space classrooms have been planned to facilitate team teaching and larger group work in order to reflect changes to the curriculum.

Facilities for primary and secondary pupils with severe emotional and behavioural difficulties have been developed in a discrete block (the Stephenson Centre) attached to, but not integral to, the main street. As is the case with all pupils in the Village, all facilities are available for this group of pupils as appropriate to their needs.

A large, open-plan 14–19 centre will ensure appropriate accommodation to develop the vocational specialism and develop independence.

The building is on two levels, but is fully accessible from the ground floor, ensuring that all pupils can enter school together irrespective of their mobility. There are two large lifts for those who require them.

The six pillars

The Village has been built on six principles or 'pillars'. All three governing bodies have signed up to these, and they have been the touchstone for all developments, serving us well in times of dispute and uncertainty. They are as follows:

1 Governance

It was essential to have a single, coherent and integrated approach to governance. This was best achieved through a single federated governing body for the Village, exercising all powers of a governing body over the constituent schools of the federation. It also enabled us to review the committee structures in order to ensure responsibility for strategic planning, and we were able to set up four committees that reflected our leadership priorities of Community, Inclusion, Teaching and Learning and Village Support. The responsibilities for the delivery of the five outcomes were clearly built into the terms of reference for the committees.

2 Leadership and management

The Village has an integrated leadership and management team from across the three schools, with a model based on distributed leadership. The design builds leadership capacity across all phases of education and within the business arm of the Village. This structure is 'fit for purpose' and based on the required skills and competencies required to develop the particular post. The Village has the benefit of an integrated Village support team which includes an ICT support team.

Central to the determination of robust Village-wide arrangements is the key post of executive director, who will oversee all procedures and operations relating to Village matters, as well as resolving disputes should they arise.

3 Inclusivity

Inclusion is at the heart of the Village. It has shaped the design of the building and influenced much of the thinking on the curriculum. Inclusion is not just about special educational needs, but also embraces all learners, staff and the local community. It is based on the principles of equal value and equal respect for all.

4 *Curriculum*

> The curriculum will be jointly planned and managed across the three Village schools. Every effort will be made to facilitate effective progression, with the individual needs of pupils regarded as paramount. The curriculum will be inclusive and designed to promote the highest standards of attainment, the celebration of diversity, citizenship and lifelong learning. Innovation in teaching and curriculum design will be valued and sustained.
>
> (Education Village: Curriculum Vision Statement)

The Village is uniquely placed to be innovative in the way that the curriculum is designed and delivered. The all-through context has provided us with an opportunity to address the key stage 2 to 3 dip, and also to look at transition generally. Personalisation is also a focus as we develop learning pathways for all pupils, taking into account the different ages, stages and abilities. The state of the art facilities have enabled us to provide education in fully resourced rooms; for example, the primary department have a food technology room and can access other specialist areas of the Village previously accessible only to secondary-aged pupils. We are considering the pattern of the school day and a curriculum design that will uncouple traditional structures of learning.

5 *Resources*

The three schools have a combined budget, which is matched against the three schools' plans and priorities and the Federation Development Plan. The economy of scale that this provides allows greater freedom to invest in innovation, and to share all resources, human and material, to the benefit of all. It allows the Village to support its priorities and to invest in early intervention.

6 *Community*

Through the identification of community as a key pillar for the Village, we are able to introduce community-based leadership, governance and therefore accountability in delivering the five outcomes for children.

The pillars guide and focus the work of the Village, and have been central to its development as they act as a touchstone for ideas and strategies.

Taking the lead together

Perhaps the most critical development for the Village, however, has been the concept of integrated partnership.

Special schools still suffer from a perception that their staff are somehow operating in a completely different educational universe from that of mainstream schools. The heads of such schools are seen as too highly specialised to engage with mainstream leadership. Whether this perception is justified or not, the emergence of school federations like our own makes such barriers between special and mainstream schools unworkable. Integrated leadership is critical to the success of these new organisations. The model for leadership and management of the Village was formulated in a series of workshops led by the Hay Consultancy Group. This work was preceded by, and built on, a full culture review, which provided a clear insight into the current climates within each of the three schools. From here, the 'ideal culture' for the Village was explored with staff, pupils and a wider group of stakeholders. Hay provided valuable guidance on ways in which cultural strengths can be maintained in the context of a unifying vision.

This piece of work proved essential, and enabled the leadership team to gain valuable insights into each other's issues and challenges. Building on the outcomes of this work, Hay developed a set of workshops for the wider leadership team and the newly federated governing body around a shared vision for the Village. The result of these sessions was the development of a leadership structure that was fit for purpose and enabled the Village to build on its goals.

The key to building leadership capacity for the Village lay in developing a structure that reflected succession planning, new accountabilities, and the potential released through workforce reform.

Our 'bespoke' model emerged following a series of workshops with the wider leadership team of the Village, and was based on our core values and vision, particularly those identified by the Children Act 2004 as the 'five outcomes', as considered below.

Delivering the five outcomes

The outcomes are:

- being healthy
- staying safe
- enjoying and achieving
- making a positive contribution
- economic well-being.

Schools are the largest providers of universal services for children. Extended schools like the Village provide a vehicle for the local authority children's services department to establish consistent approaches for children by targeting support at the right stage of intervention. The population of pupils within the Village are users of the Children's Services at universal, targeted and specialist levels. The Village concept therefore provides the context in order to support the process of taking 'services to children' in a coordinated and seamless way. Co-location of multi-agency staff, consistent application of assessment processes, and the support of parents is at the heart of its mission. Beaumont Hill is at the centre of a Pathfinder Children's Trust, so a great deal of groundwork has already taken place, for example around transition.

The key directors' posts in the Village reflect leadership across the sphere of influence of the child's life, and clear accountability is written into job description roles and responsibilities in respect of the imperative to address achievement across all outcomes. There is a direct link from leadership into governance, as the governors' committee structure reflects the key values of the Village. There are therefore four committees (see 'The six pillars', above), namely Teaching and Learning, Inclusion, Community and Village Support. Each of these committees has the five outcomes for children written into their terms of reference. This offers a level of synergy and also provides the opportunity to include associate governors who will add to the wider expertise and representation. A good example is the potential to include key members such as representatives from the housing department of the local authority. This will ultimately build a clearer picture of the developments and actions that the school needs to make in order that 'every child does matter'.

Roles and responsibilities in the new structure

The structure is not necessarily as hierarchical as the model suggests, as it is based on distributed leadership. The illustrated model is the one used for the purpose of consultation with the staff from the three schools, so it needed to demonstrate where current roles and responsibilities align with the new ones.

The strategic role of the executive director is critical in ensuring coherence to the Village vision. The following directors' posts head up the four main areas of strategic development.

1 Director of teaching and learning

The Village has in its mission the requirement for an inclusive curriculum that is 'jointly planned'. This curriculum has personalisation at its heart, and is therefore a post requiring a very innovative and fresh approach to curriculum delivery, as well as an unstinting desire to raise standards for all pupils. The key stages have been reconfigured into three new phases to reflect the all-through context and priorities for the Village, phase one incorporating foundation and key stage 1 phase two key stages 2 and 3 and phase 3 14–19. Leadership of these phases will address issues of transition and curriculum continuity.

2 Director of inclusion

The director of inclusion development post will continually test the assumption that excellence and equity are possible, and that, by raising achievement for the least able, the performance of others will be raised. The need to ensure that the highly specific needs of pupils with special needs continue to be met, and that the staff who work with these pupils retain high levels of training and specialist expertise, is critical in preventing a dilution of services.

3 Director of community

This new post has been developed to lead on the community leadership dimension. Included in the brief is the development of the specialist schools community plans, partnerships with other schools including the 'cluster', as well as other community developments, for example, learning beyond school. This arm of development, in partnership with the director of business strategy, ensures that there is capacity to respond to the extended schools agenda, for example wraparound childcare and children's centres.

4 Director of business strategy

The responsibilities of this post extend beyond those of a bursar. The development is embedded in workforce reform, and the director of business strategy is responsible for all business-related aspects of the Village. This builds the capacity to respond to a number of challenges that arise out of emerging government policy in a way that does not compromise the focus on teaching and learning. As a non-teaching post, it brings with it a refreshing view of the possible!

Conclusion

The Village is centred on the twin principles of inclusion and achievement. We feel that we have broken through the barriers in defining the purpose of schooling and building a concept around all children. The Village will provide a context in which to turn policy into reality in a way that includes all learners. We believe that through the provision and support of the Village every child *does* matter, and every child has a place in this unique development. The Village challenges the notion that the only route to appropriate provision for those pupils who do not thrive in a mainstream context is exclusion, in the sense of special school provision, which is isolated by location.

The Village takes inclusion a step forward from co-location, and affords us the opportunity to learn, to share our learning, and to develop as we do so. We have not set it up as 'the way to go'. Rather, we see it as a lighthouse to guide a way forward, providing a direction that others may wish to explore.

15 Inclusion through technology for autistic children

Dinah Murray and Wendy Lawson

Mary Warnock (2005) argues, 'Inclusion is not a matter of where you are geographically, but of where you feel you belong' (pp. 41–2). We suggest that for a child to feel, day in, day out, that he or she does not belong, is tantamount to feeling rejected. Baumeister (2005) identifies the consequences of rejection as: demotivated self-regulation (including lashing out, lack of cooperation and self-defeating behaviours), and numbed emotions. He asks: 'Given the dramatic short-term effects of rejection, what do you think would be the long-term effects of chronic rejection?' and 'Are there some people who won't mind being rejected or excluded . . . Or is the aversion to social rejection universal?' He goes on to argue that 'modern Western cultures intensify', while 'collectivist cultures reduce', feelings of non-belonging or rejection. In this chapter we link Baumeister's argument to the issue of educational inclusion and exclusion, and suggest that computers and the Internet have enabled inclusive and collectivist cultures to re-emerge in modern Western life, from which children with autistic difficulties can benefit in many ways.

For people born in the latter part of the twentieth century, familiarity and competence with computers, digital cameras, scanners, printers, the Internet, and email can be essential aspects of the feeling of belonging. All teachers know that these can be learning tools, and we explore diverse ways in which they may be used as tools to promote inclusion.

Baroness Warnock rightly observes that 'if educated in mainstream schools, many [autistic] children are not included at all. They suffer all the pains of the permanent outsider. No political ideology should impose this on them' (p. 45). Like anyone else, autistic children need to feel they belong (see Leary and Baumeister's 2000 review of research into the universal 'need to belong'). But these children tend not to get the point of the social realm in the same way as typically developing children. By the time they have cottoned on to it, if they do, they are likely already to be identified by other children as not belonging, and are at risk of becoming outcasts who are treated with scorn or hostility. As Warnock says, they may be on the receiving end of bullying they do not understand. Gunilla Gerland, a highly able and intelligent autistic woman, describes (Gerland, 1997) how, when she started at secondary school, she became the target of bullying and physical abuse that went on for years. One of the boys told her that he and some others were going to beat her up every day. She reports that when they missed a day, she would go and remind them. It was only years later that she understood what had been happening.

As Wittgenstein (1953) observed, language in its everyday uses goes beyond the strict rules of literal meaning and truth-conditional logic: there is a complex and dynamic relation between meaning and social context. People make sense of each other by assuming the general rule that each participant is contributing to a common interest (Murray, 1986; Grice, 1989). Without this background assumption, non-explicit information is likely to be missed and metaphor, sarcasm and jokes are likely to be confusing or senseless. A child with autism tends to take words literally and might not 'get' the intention proposed by the non-literal sense. If you don't grasp the pragmatic rules, people around you won't make much sense. From failure to understand those rules to exclusion from the immediate community of interest is a short step. Such practical exclusion within theoretically inclusive school environments is commonplace.

What constitutes the common interest varies from moment to moment and culture to culture, but the force of the obligation to contribute is constant within every community of interest, however transient (Murray, 1986). We suggest that opportunities to contribute to common interests are key to acquiring the sense of belonging that is at the heart of inclusion (which we have seen is a universal human need: Leary and Baumeister, 2000).

Children's first sense of belonging usually comes from the experience of long-term interest within the community of their immediate family. How can these tiny inarticulate humans make a contribution to that community? In the first months, care givers usually put the baby's interests first. They try to tune into the baby emotionally, follow the baby's gaze, and use words constantly, exclaiming and naming the baby's objects of interest. They treat every interest that the baby shows as a common interest; they actively share it. The baby is not expected to tune into the carer's interests at this stage of development, but it won't be long before that ceases to be true. The baby responds first to the emotions of its carers, then to the direction of their gaze, and finally to their words (Stern, 1985; Bruner, 1983). Now, instead of the baby being the dictator of every common interest, the baby will find that others use words to dictate new interests (see Gernsbacher, 2005 and Murray, 1986). When the baby is playing with blocks, the adult may interrupt with exclamations about cats, dogs or butterflies, if and when these come onto the scene. This may be the first moment of social alienation for some autistic children: the moment when the sense of belonging in a community of common interest is first threatened.

Auditory issues often compound difficulties with processing spoken language. The effort of deploying speech and trying to articulate clearly enough for other people to understand is often huge for autistic individuals, and frequently unsuccessful and unrewarding. A. M. Baggs, who is autistic, writes:

> Don't get me started on the emotional importance some of them have placed on hearing air pass through my vocal cords – an importance that is more

deeply hurtful to me than they can probably imagine. I've been able to communicate – actually communicate and know what I'm saying, and attach words to what I'm thinking, and all kinds of other things that I haven't always been able to do – with the use of a keyboard. This has had a positive impact on my life that cannot be overstated. But other people . . . have often had more of an overt emotional reaction to hearing me make noises with my mouth than to watching me type. I've been praised for making nonsense sounds at times.

(Baggs, 2005)

Having other people's interests imposed on them, with no apparent negoti-ation, is likely to be a persistent problem for most autistic individuals. People with autism or Asperger's syndrome are often accused of imposing their own interests insensitively on others, but after years on the receiving end it may not be obvious to them that this practice is socially disapproved. For an autistic person, the result is likely to be feelings of alienation and negativity which demotivate attempts to be included in the society of others, and may even turn speech right off (Lawson, 1998). Being demotivated in this way is not the same thing as not *wanting* any social engagement; the need is still there, but the sense of belonging is not – and its possibility may not seem within reach. We have to engage with the interests of autistic people to make that mutual connection happen, and not always expect them to be led by the concerns that *we* prioritise.

One approach to this issue is to try teaching explicitly the rules of social negoti-ation and cooperation. Role play (see the discussion below) and social stories (Gray, 2000) can help to repair omissions in autistic social understanding. Con-sciously applying rules may be useful in helping a child or adult to avoid trouble and blame – but may not be the best way to create or establish a common bond. A more effective way to do that is to find a common interest that connects you. A narrow range of interests is a diagnostic criterion for autism (DSM IV, ICD-10); this points to the significance of common interests for relating with autistic indi-viduals. To get that feeling of belonging which everyone needs we have to foster interests that can readily be shared. If we can do that, real inclusion may be possible.

Though we are not proposing the use of computers as a magic ticket to inclu-sion, their use can address several difficult issues for autistic children. Autistic children may socialise most effectively in the structured environment of a com-puter. At a computer every keystroke yields a visible sign of itself so the precise current focus can always be identified. Friendly partners or companions can iden-tify and appreciate the point of what's going on; the autistic child can observe those companions creating the same sorts of effect. Mutual respect and even empathy can emerge. We have often observed this happening.

It may be thought that computer use will make autistic children less social. However, this is not the case. On the contrary, it can put them on an equal footing with their peers, allowing them to process and respond to communica-tions in their own time with minimal pragmatic, expressive, or auditory issues getting in the way. It gives them a chance to make a favourable impression on their peers and to win their respect. It provides opportunities for creativity as well as expertise, and enables comfortable interaction around a common interest to occur, both in person and at a distance. Further, computers may be the *only* way to communicate effectively for those who find speech unmanageable. Learning IT skills in itself ticks curriculum boxes, and it can open a way to explore other areas of the curriculum in a supportive environment. E-learning can be a route towards the acquisition of all sorts of qualifications.

A computer monitor is also a great medium for showing images, and many though not all children on the autism spectrum appreciate that. But one should never *replace* the written word with pictures, however convinced one is that the child in question is 'non-verbal'. Becoming verbal is often a piecemeal process for autistic children. It is crucial to provide opportunities to access non-spoken language with visual help such as photographs, symbols, and actual written words that children can process in their own time. More than one autistic writer has commented on the gap they experienced as a child between speech and writing – the written word may make sense quite independently of speech (Lawson, 1998; Williams, 1992; Blackman, 1999). Individuals with autism may become very expert in specialised symbol systems such as slide rules or computer languages, before they have figured out the ebb and flow of speech.

A computer environment removes some of the most difficult aspects of communication and makes it much more achievable. Role-playing games can help develop more pragmatic skills; many are available to play online, or they can be played without a computer using special packs of cards. The events that are experienced virtually have many shared properties with real-life events; they will call forth the same emotional reactions and present the same sorts of issues and opportunities in a sphere of mutual interaction and cooperation. But these events have clear and explicit rules, and the relationships do not have to outlast the game, although they may, because of course real people are playing. So these may be a fruitful source of social skills for linguistically able autistic children in a relatively manageable, non-rejecting and just social climate.

A recurrent issue for many autistic children is connecting the present to the future and understanding the potential impact of their actions. They have difficulty holding alternative states simultaneously in mind, as you need to if you are to grasp the idea of consequences. Outcome flowcharts on a computer, or interactive PowerPoint shows displaying for children the potential consequences of their actions, can be very helpful. New options can be added at any time to these choice charts. Consequences desirable to the child, to other children, or to grown-ups, can be spelled out alongside their opposites. These words can be supplemented with pictures, and colour can be used to add a further layer of meaning within the flowchart or show. Undesirable outcomes can be shown crossed out.

All autistic children should have their own folder on a school computer (backed up on a personal Flash drive), containing a choices chart as well a personal passport (see below). The teacher or teacher's assistant should not commandeer the task of making this, but must support the chart's creation and ensure that the flow represents reality by involving the child as much as possible in the process. Without ownership of the process, its result may mean little or nothing to the child. Ideally, once a choices and outcomes file is created, a few minutes should be spent every day to review its events and locate them on the chart, or modify the chart accordingly. Some children may like to award themselves a score for each day's outcomes; again, they should own the process but may need guidance ensuring that those scores reflect the reality of what happened. A proportion of these children may not appreciate the point of representing what actually happened, or may feel that they can fix things in the world by changing its representation.

Used as described, computers can provide a way to help autistic children reflect on what they actually do, have done, and will do. Once reflection is achieved, self-regulation becomes possible. Making a personal passport, using a PowerPoint program, for example, can also encourage self-awareness and boost self-confidence and the capacity to participate. This widely distributed software was written for businessmen without specialist technical knowledge, and is exceptionally easy to use. It is a popular choice for empowering people with learning disabilities of all kinds (see Murray and Aspinall, 2006) because it is so easy and so flexible. You can incorporate pictures, sounds, video, and as much or as little text as you wish. Choosing and changing graphic formats is also simply done. This approach has been used with young people with Asperger's syndrome, who have good speech but usually poor social skills (Haugh, 2006). They have used it to present their personal histories, aspirations, and anxieties to other people. Just as businessmen do, they find a PowerPoint presentation can make a great impression, and convey a great deal of information. Giving young people a chance to control the way they are represented can transform both the way they are seen by other people and the way they see themselves. People who do not speak may benefit even more than others by having such control (see www.gettingthetruthout.org and Murray and Aspinall, 2006).

Being able to control how you are represented is also a feature of personal interaction on the Internet. Interest groups and specialised websites can be a great resource for people with passions of every sort. Even the most alienated child may find companionship and appreciative community on the Internet. As well as finding interest groups devoted to say, Thomas the Tank Engine, tram services throughout the world, or the structure of DNA, autistic young people may also enjoy the respectful and non-judgemental welcome they will get on the Internet from other autistic people, not to mention the ready supply of information and support about autism (see, for example, www.autistics.org or www.neurodiversity.com). This is a community in which many people find friendship, see their contributions valued, and fulfil the need to feel that they belong. Once again, those *are* real people out there. So long as all proper steps have been taken to ensure security, Internet relationships can blossom in the actual world. I know of many such happy relationships which were formed this way, including a number of marriages. (On this issue of security, www.spired.com/guide/law/online.htm is very helpful.)

So even those who have the greatest difficulties in standard classrooms or playgrounds may successfully participate in and contribute to a socio-cultural discourse in the right environment. I suggest that a fundamental rethink is needed about what constitutes the 'right environment' for autistic students (with whatever abilities), without losing sight of the goal of inclusion. That rethink has to begin with the architecture itself. Where can we locate these children within a mainstream building, so that they can *join in with, and also escape from*, mainstream activities in response to their fundamental needs? How can we offer them these possibilities in a rich learning environment? How can we place them so that the location is attractive to them and to other children, and avoids the terrible taint of stigma?

Traditionally schools have had libraries full of books (this is what 'library' means after all!). But a new model of library has been emerging in the twenty-first century (exemplified in Tower Hamlets' 'Idea Stores' – see www.ideastore.co.uk), in which books are just part of the scene. Such a library can have big windows, maximum daylight, no fluorescent lighting, and attention to reducing noise and maximising sound absorption. It has banks of computers and printers and laminators, as well as access to the Internet. There is a soft zone with indestructible books; there is a café; and there are quiet rooms of various sizes off the main space. There are electronic whiteboards in every room so that work on the computer can easily be shared. There are digital cameras, keyboards and audio-recorders, with software to edit the results. There is adaptive technology to suit every need, as well as computer games to share. As traditionally, there are also learning tools like slide rules, globes and skeletons. In one room there is a trampoline (why not have an outlet for surplus energy?). There is a sensory room with access to the soothing and beautiful Reactive Colours software (www.reactivecolours.org), inviting playful and intrinsically rewarding engagement.

Autistic children (however 'low functioning' they are judged to be) should be involved as fully as possible in running this learning zone. They should help file the books and software and maintain the hardware; they should also be responsible for making sure the paper is replaced in the photocopiers, and so on. It should not involve a great leap of the imagination to see that this is exactly the 'right environment' for such children, as outlined above. It is also an environment which is attractive to children generally; this is why it is the key to inclusion.

References

Baggs, Amanda M. (2005), 'On self-advocacy', www.ballastexistenz.org (accessed August 2005)

Baumeister, Roy (2005), 'Rejected and alone', *The Psychologist*, 18 (12), 732–5

Blackman, Lucy (1999), *Lucy's Story: Autism and other Adventures*, with foreword and afterword by Tony Attwood, London: Jessica Kingsley Publishers

Bruner, Jerome (1983), *Child's Talk: Learning to Use Language*, New York: Norton

Carston, Robyn (2002), *Thoughts and Utterances: The Pragmatics of Explicit Communication*, Oxford: Blackwell

DSM-IV (1994), *Diagnostic and Statistical Manual of Mental Disorders* (4th edn, DSM-IV), Washington DC: American Psychiatric Association

Gerland, Gunilla (1997), *A Real Person: Life on the Outside*, London: Souvenir Press

Gernsbacher, Morton (2005), 'On reciprocity', http://qtstreamer.doit.wisc.edu/autism/Reciprocity_300k.mov (accessed 7 March 2006)

Gray, Carol (2000), *The New Social Story Book: Illustrated Edition*, Arlington, TX: Future Horizons

Grice, H. P. (1989), *Studies in the Way of Words*, Cambridge, MA: Harvard University Press

Haugh, Christine (2006), 'Personal Passports using PowerPoint', unpublished research, University of Birmingham

Lawson, Wendy (1998, 2000), *Life Behind Glass: A Personal Account of Autism Spectrum Disorder*, London: Jessica Kingsley Publishers

Leary, M. R. and R. F. Baumeister (2000), 'The nature and function of self-esteem: sociometer theory', in M. Zanna (ed.), *Advances in Experimental Social Psychology*, 32, 1–62, San Diego, CA: Academic Press

Murray, Dinah (1986), 'Language and interests', PhD thesis, University of London

Murray, Dinah and Aspinall, Ann (2006), *Getting IT: Using Information Technology to Empower People with Communication Difficulties*, London: Jessica Kingsley Publishers

Sperber, Dan and Wilson, Deirdre (1996) *Relevance: Communication and Cognition*, Oxford: Blackwell

Stern, Daniel N. (1985), *The Interpersonal World of the Infant: A View from Psychoanalysis and Developmental Psychology*, New York: Basic Books

Warnock, M. (2005) *Special Educational Needs: A New Look*, London: Philosophy of Education Society of Great Britain

Williams, Donna (1992), *Nobody Nowhere*, New York: Random House

Wittgenstein, Ludwig (1953), *Philosophical Investigations*, translated by G. E. M. Anscombe, New York: Macmillan Company

16 Are some children unteachable?
An approach to social, emotional and behavioural difficulties?

Paul Cooper

Social, emotional and behavioural difficulties (SEBD) among school pupils represent a unique problem within the educational sphere. No other educational problem is associated with such a level of fear, anger, frustration, guilt and blame. There are good reasons for this. Even superficially mild types of SEBD, such as incivility, can be threatening. This is because any act of incivility reveals the fragility of social niceties that most of us abide by most of the time in order to protect one another from emotional harm. Incivility, therefore, is a potential threat to our sense of emotional safety and self-worth. In the most extreme forms of disruptive ('externalising') SEBD, such as violent behaviour towards others, the physical safety of persons may also be threatened. In any event, behaviour of this kind triggers, in those on the receiving end, involuntary and uncomfortable responses, such as increased heart rate and a strong desire to flee the scene or retaliate in some way.

A key question is: what place, if any, do behaviours and feelings of this type have in our schools and classrooms? There seems to be a widespread belief that there is too much of this kind of thing going on in some of our schools and classrooms. This is not only the view expressed in some sections of the press that may have an interest in sensationalising such issues for financial and/or political reasons. It is also a view that emanates from more informed sources, such as teachers' trades unions. Academic researchers have identified significant concerns about indiscipline and violence in schools among teachers and students. This chapter considers these issues from a number of perspectives – those of teachers, parents, the children with SEBD, and their fellow pupils – and offers some ways of understanding and dealing constructively with the problem of SEBD in schools.

SEBD – listening to the experts

Nathan

> I'm alright you know ... I'm not that bad ... but if I don't like some-
> body [i.e. a teacher], I won't do it [the work] and I'll try to wreck it and
> everything. But if I do like it, I'll be alright with it. I'm alright.
>
> ('Nathan', from Pomeroy, 2000: 27)

This is a quotation from Nathan, a boy interviewed by Eva Pomeroy for her book
charting the experiences of adolescents who have been excluded from schools. In
this statement Nathan succinctly illustrates some of the key features that are
commonly associated with social, emotional and behavioural difficulties in
schools. First, these problems are most obvious when they appear in the form of
externalising disruptive behaviour in schools. Nathan describes, for example, how
he repeatedly 'smashed up' a model that he was required to make as part of a
design project, in response to his feelings about the teacher who had set the
assignment. Such disruption interferes significantly with learning and teaching
processes. In classrooms, these difficulties most commonly take the form of relatively minor disruption, such as talking out of turn, hindrance of other pupils,
off-task behaviour and rudeness to other pupils and staff. In some cases minor
disruptions can escalate into more serious displays of behaviour, including vandal-
ism and persistent rule breaking, and may, as Nathan implies in relation to his
own behaviour, involve antagonism and defiance towards teachers. The most
severe forms of disruptive behaviour tend to take the form of verbal and physical
aggression towards pupils and/or adults and, in extreme and thankfully rare cases,
can take the form of violence against pupils and staff.

Nathan does not appear to see his behaviour as a problem for him. He repeats
the phrase 'I'm alright' in order to emphasise this, and states that he does not
consider himself to be 'that bad', implying that there are other pupils who are
much worse. His teachers clearly disagree, which is why he is formally excluded
from school. This points to a second important feature of SEBD. It is the only
educational problem that law permits schools to deal with through the imposition
of this punitive response. Although exclusion can in some circumstances be a
catalyst in the process of finding the excludee a more appropriate educational
placement, its primary function is to rid the excluding school of an individual who
is deemed to be unmanageable in, and detrimental to, that setting. Where exclusion is applied a decision has been made that fault lies squarely on the shoulders of
the pupil. This is a common feature of the way in which SEBD is perceived in
schools.

Nathan's defensiveness is also characteristic. However, as is often the case, his
defence is counterproductive. In declaring that he is 'alright', and his insistence
that his disruptive behaviour is calculated to punish those teachers whom he
dislikes, he appears to be taking full responsibility for his actions. This is, in effect,
a plea of 'guilty'. Another way of looking at this situation, however, is to conclude

that Nathan is far from 'alright'. People who habitually respond to others in the way he describes reveal dysfunctions in the ways in which they deal with other people in general. In Nathan's case, he freely admits that he experiences social difficulties both inside and outside classrooms and school:

> because I know the dinner ladies as well live by me. And because no one in my area likes me they didn't so in the school, they carried it on the school . . . so that then the teachers started 'cause I was being all assy to the dinner ladies and the teachers had to get involved and to take sides with the dinner ladies.
>
> (Pomeroy, 2000: 98)

On the face of it, we can sympathise with the school that decides to part company with a student who, by his own admission, repeatedly behaves in such rude and disruptive ways. Students like Nathan behave in ways that contribute to a negative social climate in schools that makes learning difficult for other pupils, and create emotional stress for pupils and staff alike.

A more sympathetic response to Nathan might highlight the extent to which he sees himself in the role of a victim of unfair and inappropriate treatment by others. This is a boy who sees his 'assy' behaviour and desire to 'wreck' things as a form of retribution for the wrongs committed against him by others. He complains that the dinner ladies are malicious towards him, and indicates that one of the things that causes him to dislike certain teachers is their failure to be present when they are supposed to be teaching him and his class:

> the lesson I was doing, the teacher was never there anyway. . . . I built a park five times [given the assignment: Design safe park for children]. He used to come every lesson and say 'carry on with your park', then used to go away, and we didn't have a park. We smashed it up every lesson.
>
> (Pomeroy, 2000: 46)

Retribution as a justification for disruptive behaviour is a common claim made by young students in schools over generations (Rosser and Harre, 1976; Tattum, 1982; Cooper, 1993; 'John' and Cooper, 2006a–f).

John

John, now in his early twenties, offers another individual perspective on SEBD. John is able to look back on his entire compulsory educational career, and in doing so gives us some deep insights into what it is like to be what some might call 'a career SEBD pupil'. This entire story can be read in dialogue form in a series of chapters composed by the author and John (a fictitious name) on the basis of tape-recorded conversations ('John' and Cooper, 2006a–f). In brief, John's story can be summarised as follows:

Kindergarten

I was loud and hyperactive. I used to fidget a lot. So she [John's mum] used to tell me there was something wrong with me.

Infant school

[When] I was five, and I started going to infant school, that's when the problems started really a lot more. 'Cos then I was being naughty, just to get attention. 'Cos I never used to get any attention on the lessons, when everyone else did.

Junior school

I used to get bullied all the time as well – called racist names – all through infant school and junior school. That's when I really did start to play up. . . . I used to have temper tantrums. . . . Well, they weren't really tantrums. I never used to pick things up and throw them about. I just used to run out the door, slam it, and run off somewhere else. On to the field or something. My mum used to call them 'temper tantrums'. . . . I . . . used to have problems with reading and spelling. . . . Then, I remember, it was just about the last year – just a couple of months into the last year at junior school – and that's when it got bad. 'Cos I remember, I went to the headmistress's office, 'cos I'd done something wrong. 'Cos they kept ringing my mum all the time as well, all through the years. If there was a school trip, they wouldn't let me go, because I'd have to earn stars to go on the trip. No one else had to, but I had to, 'cos I was bad. That's what they used to tell me. I think it was the last year. And I went into her office: the headmistress, she was having an argument with me. She was telling me how bad I'd been. I said, 'let me out of the office!' I wanted to go; to just run away. . . . 'Cos I knew they were just going to ring my mum up again. She was getting on at me, saying, 'I'm fed up of them ringing me up all the time!' So I wanted to get out of the office. She wouldn't let me out, so I punched her in the belly.

Secondary school

I was changing. My behaviour wasn't temper tantrums no more. It was more – was a bit more aggressive. I did used to swear a bit more. I used to get up and cuss the teachers. . . . I can remember one time – it wasn't me who was in trouble – and we used to have this French teacher, and every time there was a problem in the class, she used to go and send for the Head of Year. Every time! And once she did this and I said: 'what are you? Are you a wimp? Can't you deal with it yourself!' I got suspended for five days! For that! That was in year seven. I think. . . what did she do, as soon as I called her? She called the head of year!. . . I never used to get help there either – not the help I needed.

All I ever wanted with work was someone to help me spell. . . . All the time I was there – I was there for about three years. All the time I was there I was suspended about 15 times, at least. And that's when my mum started telling me that I'd got this ADHD. And I started to use this as an excuse. . . . My mum thought that that [ADHD] was the answer to everything, right? . . . I was restless . . . I did have an attention problem. I really didn't like sitting down and listening to other people.

Special school and beyond

At the age of 14 John was referred to a special school for children with emotional and behavioural difficulties. He spent the rest of his school career there, leaving, at the age of 16, with no academic qualifications. At the time of interview John was planning to enrol in a vocational course at a Further Education College.

It is unusual to see such a coherent and clearly articulated first-hand account of an entire school career. The progression of events and escalation of the difficulties, however, are far from unusual in the lives of individuals who leave school with the SEBD label attached to them. John's school days add up to a catalogue of mounting disappointment, disaffection and educational failure. According to his account, his learning difficulties are, almost from the outset, largely ignored by his teachers. His emotional life is dominated from an early age by a conflictual relationship with his mother, whom he sees as overly critical and blaming towards him. At one point he complains about the way in which his mother is unfairly critical of John's father, from whom she is separated. This troubled relationship is compounded by the racial abuse that seems to be a recurrent theme throughout John's schooling. John's response to these experiences is typical among many insecure children who are under severe emotional stress: he engages in 'naughty', attention-seeking behaviour. As time goes by, however, he becomes increasingly disaffected by schooling. The act of assaulting the head teacher of his junior school seems to come at a point where problems in the school situation combine with problems in John's family situation. The head teacher's decision to phone John's mum, combined with her (probably) instinctive reaction to contain him in her office, make an unwitting contribution to this distressing outcome. To complicate matters even further, in spite of John's cynicism about the matter, there is a strong possibility that his escalating behaviour problems and emotional difficulties may have been influenced by an undiagnosed medical condition – ADHD – that is characterised by attentional and activity problems.

Should teachers be expected to put up with SEBD?

John's behaviour is, from his point of view, an inevitable consequence of various influences that are largely – though not entirely – outside his control. These factors accumulate over time and converge in ways that are difficult to predict. It is easy to criticise John's teachers for failing to address his experiences of racism and bullying, and for not dealing effectively with his learning difficulties. On the other hand, it is easy to understand the possibility that school staff might have been unaware of the tensions existing between John and his mother. Furthermore, we can assume that the very real pressures that school staff experience form part of the context for John's story. As a recent editorial in the *Times Educational Supplement* put it:

> It is no surprise that teachers, whatever their beliefs about inclusive education, find coping with special needs in mainstream classrooms difficult without additional training and classroom support. . . . Growing numbers of special needs are behaviour-related. At the same time, teachers feel under increasing pressure to achieve academic results at all costs in a curriculum which makes few concessions to what one current television programme calls 'the unteachables'.

It is a deep irony that the policy and political emphasis has shifted to inclusive education at a time when schools are under increasing pressure to put all children through a narrowly defined National Curriculum. Furthermore, teachers themselves, as part of the same package, are judged largely in terms of the performance of their students in the National Curriculum, as measured by their performance in standardised tests and public examinations. They are also subject to rigid accountability structures, in the form of Ofsted inspections.

It is little wonder that the decade in which these so-called educational reforms were introduced – the 1990s – saw a massive rise in the annual numbers of school children permanently excluded from schools, from fewer than 3,000 in 1992 to over 12,000 in 1997 (Parsons, 1999). The figure has remained stubbornly at between 9,000 and 10,000 ever since. The vast majority of these children are excluded because they present behavioural problems (ibid.). It should be added that if the figure of approximately 10,000 appears relatively insignificant, within a school population of some 10 million it should be remembered that exclusions represent the tip of an enormous iceberg. The figure for unofficial, informal exclusion remains for obvious reasons unknown, but was estimated in one study to be 35 times higher than the number of formally recorded exclusions (Stirling, 1992).

Teachers, therefore, are under enormous stress, which leads to institutionalised intolerance for the under-performing pupil (which is too readily equated with the under-performance of the teacher). This, in turn, makes children like John a source of stress to their teachers and peers.

The straightforward, but difficult, issue to address here is that if mainstream teachers are to work effectively with students like John and Nathan, they require practical support that goes far beyond the provision of a few hours of a teaching assistant's time. As schools become increasingly pressurised environments, teachers need to be offered ways of identifying their own experiences of stress, as well as help in understanding and tackling the negative consequences of their stress on their pupils, especially those like John who are particularly vulnerable.

Other professionals, such as social workers and counsellors, who deal with emotionally vulnerable and potentially volatile clients, have access to specialised training on how to prevent and diffuse conflict situations, and supervision, which involves regular opportunities to reflect on their work with sometimes difficult clients with a colleague who is able to offer emotional support and practical advice. Teachers, on the other hand, are left, too often, to deal with the personal consequences of trying to handle challenging behaviour without adequate training and in isolation. This is in spite of the fact that it is estimated that somewhere between 10 and 20 per cent of the school-age population exhibit significant social, emotional and behavioural difficulties at any one time (YoungMinds, 1999). As John's case illustrates, at each phase of his miserable educational career, the failure to identify problems and apply appropriate intervention can lead to devastating consequences for both pupils and teachers.

What does good educational practice for children with SEBD look like?

John's story tells us much about what can go wrong in schools. Importantly, however, it also tells us about some of the things that can be done to put things right. First, we need to understand that his story, as it has been told here, is a very one-sided version of events. It is possible, though frankly unlikely, that it is a complete pack of lies. This is unlikely because, even in his own portrayal of events, he does not present himself as blameless. He is, by his own admission, 'loud', 'naughty just to get attention', 'bad', rude to teachers, and eventually violent to a teacher. He is also manipulative in that he uses his ADHD diagnosis as an 'excuse'. This is indicative of an individual who knows his behaviour to have been unacceptable, and who therefore has some sense of moral responsibility. He does not judge himself to have been a helpless victim. However, this same sense of morality gives rise to feelings of indignation and even anger at what he sees as unjust and inappropriate treatment at the hands of his various teachers and his mother. Even if John's account of these difficulties is factually distorted and self-justificatory, the fact that he seeks and is able to put together such a coherent and persuasive account of his history provides insights as to how an individual like him might have been helped in school. Individuals with these qualities have a need to make sense out of their own feelings and behaviour, and to behave in ways that make sense. This can be and is exploited in a variety of positive ways by effective teachers.

The importance of relationships in the educational context has long been recognised. Positive adult–pupil relationships often act as protective and remedial factors in the lives of young people with SEBD. Pupils with SEBD who were interviewed by the author (Cooper, 1993) cited trusting, mutually respectful and supportive relationships with adults in the SEBD special schools they attended as central in helping them develop more positive self-images and enabling them to come to terms with difficulties of self-regulation and academic engagement.

Key features of such therapeutic relationships are the three 'core conditions' identified by Rogers (1980) in his 'client-centred therapy' or the 'person-centred approach'. These conditions are:

- Empathy – the willingness of the teacher to see the world through the eyes of the pupil and explicitly acknowledge the right of the pupil to their own view of situation, no matter how contrary this might be to the teacher's habitual view. This validation of the pupil's view of the world by another person can help to break down the feelings of isolation felt by many individuals with SEBD. It can, in turn, create a capacity for empathy within the pupil, thus opening the way to the development of alternative (and possibly more functional) ways of thinking about and seeing the world and themselves.
- Unconditional positive regard – the ability to split disapproval of the pupil's behaviour from disapproval of the pupil as a person. The teacher must always be accepting of the pupil as a person and show respect and personal warmth towards them. This condition is essential in helping the pupil develop a sense of self-respect and, through this, respect for others.
- Honesty – within the context of the first two conditions, honesty involves the teacher being direct with the pupil about aspects of his or her behaviour that are perceived as negative.

In the classroom this approach seeks to promote pupil engagement through a consultative approach to teaching. This would include such teaching strategies as:

- finding out what interests the pupil
- finding out what the pupil knows already
- allowing the pupil to teach others (including the teacher) what she/he knows about the topic
- using questions rather than statements so that pupils extend their understandings by drawing on knowledge they already possess.

'Therapeutic' applications of these principles include such interventions as 'circle time' (Moseley, 1996). Circle time involves the creation of a classroom climate that emphasises the importance of articulating thoughts and feelings, listening to others, and respecting the rights and opinions of others. A central feature of the approach is the staging of regular circle time meetings, in which groups of children, along with the teacher or other facilitator (e.g. a teaching assistant), sit in a circle and take turns to voice their feelings, ideas and opinions about topics of concern. Through this approach pupils learn how to articulate their feelings in a safe and supportive environment. These sessions can also act as group problem-solving events, in which procedures for handling challenging experiences, such as bullying or test anxiety, can be explored and resolved.

The principles underpinning these simple (but not simplistic) strategies are part of the 'natural' social styles of some people. For others they have to be acquired through training. They are essential, however, to effective teacher–pupil relationships (Cooper and McIntyre, 1996), especially those involving emotionally vulnerable pupils (Cooper, 1993; Cooper *et al.*, 2000).

There is often no more important strategy for dealing with potential or actual

SEBDs than talking the issues through in a calm and sympathetic way, with a view to encouraging the child to recognise the range of behavioural choices that are available in a given situation, and then encouraging him or her to identify which choices are preferable.

Some children, particularly those who have an undeveloped sense of self and weak communication and social skills, may benefit from an environment that is more intimate and tightly focused on meeting their need for emotional security. The nurture group is one such setting (see Chapter 17). 'Classic' nurture groups are located in mainstream schools, and are discrete classes for between 10 and 12 pupils, staffed by a teacher and a teaching assistant, that combine all of the features of standard classroom with those of a family-type setting. The purpose of a nurture group is to provide children with a learning environment that is geared to meet the emotional needs underpinning social and academic engagement, and to enable the children to return on a full-time basis to the mainstream classroom. Evidence from various studies indicates that this process is effective for most children who attend these groups for between three and four terms (Iszatt and Wasilewska, 1997; Cooper, 2006; Cooper and Tiknaz, 2006).

The provision of positive relationships between teachers and students contributes to a climate that fosters positive relationships between students. This is not to say that children do not misbehave in such settings. Such a climate, however, provides the seedbed for effective behaviour management approaches, which are the hallmark of many effective schools (Cooper, 1993). These often revolve around the provision of reward systems for positive behaviour, which can take the form of 'token economies' (e.g. the use of star charts) and other contingency management systems. These can of course be misused, on occasions, as John illustrates when he describes his consistent failure to achieve 'rewards' (i.e. participating in school trips) that he saw other pupils receiving as a right. In his case this non-reward appears to have had a demotivating effect on him, filling him with resentment rather than a desire to conform. In order for reward systems to work effectively, the reward has to be perceived as such by the potential recipient. The identification of appropriate rewards, therefore, depends upon consultation and cooperation between teacher and child.

SEBD and inclusion

The question as to whether children with SEBD should or should not be educated in mainstream classrooms is a complex one. It is clearly the case that, with appropriate whole-school approaches to the prevention and management of SEBD, schools can improve their capacity to avoid exclusionary practice (Cooper *et al.*, 2000; Munn *et al.*, 2000). Inclusion, however, as we are often reminded, is a process, rather than a state (DfEE, 1997). And it is a process that is more advanced in some schools than others.

There is strong evidence to suggest that the kinds of interventions described above can have a powerful impact in improving the social and educational engagement of pupils with SEBD. There are times, however, when the most appropriate available setting for the child with SEBD is outside the mainstream classroom, or even outside the mainstream school. This should not come as a surprise. After all, it is widely acknowledged that different children will benefit from different kinds of learning environments, such as specialist secondary schools for sport or modern languages. Parents who can afford it sometimes seek educational settings outside the state system, because of a particular school ethos, or the possibility of their child being educated in relatively small class groups.

Such flexible options are essential for children with SEBD, whose needs, if left unmet, will tend to escalate and multiply. For such children (like all children) the most appropriate setting is the one that offers the best available opportunities for social and academic engagement. Where possible this should be a mainstream school. Where an alternative form of provision is chosen, such as a pupil referral unit (PRU) or special school, this should always be with a view to enabling a placement in good-quality mainstream provision. Of paramount importance is the need of the child to be placed in a setting that provides physical and emotional safety as well as positive social and academic engagement for both the child and his or her peers, teachers and so on.

An educational landscape without the flexibility of a diversity of provision has serious weaknesses. The greater the emphasis on the location of all school students in neighbourhood mainstream schools, the greater the risk that pupils who, for whatever reason, have difficulty in securing engagement at that location will be pathologised and pressurised into fitting into that location. There is evidence, for example, that some children with ADHD experience their use of medication in this way: that is, as a tool enabling them to conform to wishes of others (Cooper and Shea, 1999).

This is a very pertinent issue at the current time with the upsurge in interest in the use of drugs that can be classed as 'cognitive enhancers' (Miller and Wilsdon, 2006). The availability of highly effective and relatively safe medications that can help to extend most students' attentional capacities and improve other aspects of cognitive performance, brings with it moral, ethical and educational questions about the nature and functioning of schools and teachers. It can be argued that the use of such medications, as part of a carefully monitored multi-modal intervention package for individuals with specific cognitive deficits, can in some circumstances be justified (NICE, 2000; British Psychological Society, 2000). It is also clear, however, that a reliance on such interventions may obscure problems that exist in the social environment surrounding the child. In John's case, for example, medication might well have enabled him to regulate his own behaviour more effectively, but it would not have resolved the problems of racial bullying or the difficulties he experienced in communicating with his mother, though it may have masked these problems.

Conclusion

This chapter has focused on the educational needs of children with SEBD. It has been argued that the ultimate purpose of any educational system has to be to provide an enriching social, emotional and academic experience to all students. If we are to move closer to this goal we must eschew crude definitions of inclusive education that equate inclusion with mainstreaming, and move to a more sophisticated view that emphasises the core feature of inclusive education, which is the promotion of social, emotional and academic engagement. A particular focus of this chapter has been the need to understand the world of the child exhibiting SEBD through his or her own eyes. It has been shown that, when we do this, we gain insights into factors that influence the development of these problems that can, in turn, help us to find appropriate means of intervention and prevention. John's story vividly illustrates the way in which early difficulties become compounded and multiply, if they are not addressed appropriately. The policy messages from this brief discussion should be clear. First, if we are to meet the needs of students like John effectively, our teachers need to be trained in the skills and knowledge necessary to create educational environments that support and nurture the emotional and social, as well as the cognitive, aspects of every child. Second, there is a need for educational provision to be responsive to the diversity of our pupils. This means recognising the possibility that the neighbourhood school is not always the most desirable educational placement for all children, and there needs to be available a wide range of alternative forms of provision and opportunities to move flexibly between different provisions. Third, we must recognise that for every individual like John, who looks back on his educational career and is able to reflect in a rational and, ultimately, constructive manner, there are many others who fall by the wayside, and remain disaffected and disengaged. These inevitably form part of the next generation of parents who pass on their disaffection and distrust of education and society to their offspring. This makes the need to develop real opportunities and incentives to re-engage with educational processes, throughout an individual's life, a vital policy goal.

References

British Psychological Society (2000), *ADHD: Guidelines and Principles for Multi-Agency Working*, Leicester: British Psychological Society

Cooper, P. (1993), *Effective Schools for Disaffected Students*, London: Routledge

Cooper, P. (2006), 'Nurture groups 1970 to 2003', in M. Hunter-Carsch, Y. Tiknaz, P. Cooper and R. Sage (eds), *The Handbook of Social, Emotional and Behavioural Difficulties*, London: Continuum

Cooper, P. and D. McIntyre (1996), *Effective Teaching and Learning: Teachers' and Students' Perspectives*, Milton Keynes: Open University Press

Cooper, P. and T. Shea (1999), 'ADHD from the inside: an empirical study of the experience of ADHD', in P. Cooper and K. Bilton (eds), *ADHD: Research, Practice and Opinion*, London: Whurr

Cooper, P. and Y. Tiknaz (2006), 'Progress and challenge in nurture groups: evidence from three case studies', *British Journal of Special Education*, 32 (4), 211–23

Cooper, P., C. Smith and G. Upton (1994), *Emotional and Behavioural Difficulties: From Theory to Practice*, London: Routledge

Cooper, P., M. Drummond, S. Hart, J. Lovey and C. McLaughlin (2000) *Positive Alternatives to Exclusion*, London: Routledge

DfEE (1997), *Excellence for All Children: Meeting Special Educational Needs*, London: Stationery Office

Iszatt, J. and T. Wasilewska (1997), 'Nurture groups: an early intervention model enabling vulnerable children to integrate successfully into school', *Educational and Child Psychology*, 14 (3), 121–39

'John' and P. Cooper (2006a), 'John's story, episode 1: understanding SEBD from the inside', in M. Hunter-Carsch, Y. Tiknaz, P. Cooper and R. Sage (eds), *The Handbook of Social, Emotional and Behavioural Difficulties*, London: Continuum

'John' and P. Cooper (2006b), 'John's story, episode 2: problems develop', in M. Hunter-Carsch, Y. Tiknaz, P. Cooper and R. Sage (eds), *The Handbook of Social, Emotional and Behavioural Difficulties*, London: Continuum

'John' and P. Cooper (2006c), 'John's story, episode 3: problems increase', in M. Hunter-Carsch, Y. Tiknaz, P. Cooper and R. Sage (eds), *The Handbook of Social, Emotional and Behavioural Difficulties*, London: Continuum

'John' and P. Cooper (2006d), 'John's story, episode 4: strategies for coping?', in M. Hunter-Carsch, Y. Tiknaz, P. Cooper and R. Sage (eds), *The Handbook of Social, Emotional and Behavioural Difficulties*, London: Continuum

'John' and P. Cooper (2006e), 'John's story, episode 5: reflections', in M. Hunter-Carsch, Y. Tiknaz, P. Cooper and R. Sage (eds), *The Handbook of Social, Emotional and Behavioural Difficulties*, London: Continuum

'John' and P. Cooper (2006f), 'John's story, episode 6: plans for the future – lifelong education?', in M. Hunter-Carsch, Y. Tiknaz, P. Cooper and R. Sage (eds), *The Handbook of Social, Emotional and Behavioural Difficulties*, London: Continuum

Miller, P. and J. Wilsdon (eds) (2006), *Better Humans? The Politics of Human Enhancement and Life Extension*, London: Demos

Moseley, J. (1996), *Quality Circle Time in the Primary School*, Wisbech: LDA

Munn, P., C. Lloyd and M. Cullen (2000), *Alternatives to Exclusion from School*, London: Paul Chapman

NICE (2000), *Guidance on the Use of Methylphenidate for ADHD*, London, NICE

Parsons, C. (1999), *Education, Exclusion and Citizenship*, London: Routledge.

Pomeroy, E. (2000), *Experiencing Exclusion*, Stoke-on-Trent: Trentham Books

Rogers, C. (1980), *A Way of Being*, Boston, MA: Houghton-Mifflin

Rosser, E. and R. Harre (1976), 'The meaning of trouble', in M. Hammersley and P. Woods (eds), *The Process of Schooling*, London: Open University

Stirling, M. (1992), 'How many children are being excluded?', *British Journal of Special Education*, 19 (4), 128–30

Tattum, D. (1982), *Disruptive Pupils in Schools and Units*, Chichester: Wiley

YoungMinds (1999) *Spotlight No. 1: Mental Health in Children and Young People*, Briefing Paper, March, London: YoungMinds

17 Nurture groups for children with social, emotional and behavioural difficulties

Marion Bennathan

Nurture groups were started in 1969 by Marjorie Boxall, an educational psychologist (EP) working for the Inner London Education Authority (ILEA) in Hackney, which in common with other Inner London boroughs had more than its share of children in difficulties. Studies showed 19.1 per cent of Inner London pupils to have 'behavioural deviance' compared with 10.6 per cent in the Isle of Wight (Rutter *et al.*, 1975). Signs of psychiatric disorder were reported by 25.4 per cent of parents, compared with 12 per cent in the Isle of Wight. This caused unmanageable numbers of referrals to special schools for the 'maladjusted' or the 'educationally subnormal', contributing to the establishment of the Warnock Committee in 1974.

What caused such high levels of dysfunction? Social stress and changes in educational policy played their part.

Social stress

Hackney had a large number of Jamaican immigrants who had come to the 'mother country' with high hopes, only to be confronted by racism, housing shortages, poorly paid jobs and a lack of good child-care facilities. Most coped heroically, with the resilience that goes with the courage to leave one's native land, but there were casualties. Many children came into school showing the effects of adverse family circumstances. In *Black in White* (1995), Jean Harris-Hendriks, a white English child psychiatrist, and John Figueroa, a black Caribbean academic, wrote:

> In the late 1960s a phrase, 'West Indian autism', had brief currency. It was racist, since it attributed to a particular culture a problem common to all children who are under-stimulated; that they are expressionless, unresponsive even when attempts are made to stimulate them, delayed in speech and motor skills and may end up stimulating themselves by repetitive behaviours such as rocking.
>
> In the early seventies many Inner London schools started 'nurture groups'. These were invaluable and deceptively simple arrangements whereby young children who for whatever reason ... were unprepared to cope with

pre-school and primary school, were lovingly and systematically taught the skills to care for themselves, the language to communicate with other children and enabled to play.

Families from the indigenous population also had their problems. Some were bringing up children in homes beset by poverty, domestic violence, substance abuse, poor housing, or chronic physical or mental illness. The Jamaican situation no longer exists; the second unfortunately does.

Educational policies

In the 1950s and 1960s schools were under pressure to implement 'child-centred' education, in which the teacher is less an instructor than a facilitator, and children do not sit in rows but work cooperatively around tables. The teacher was supposed to move among them, stimulating, providing opportunities to learn. He or she should cultivate the children's growth as though they were plants which needed nothing more than favourable conditions in which to grow.

This no doubt worked for many children, but it took for granted adequate social competences. Seasoned head teachers, as I discovered researching a book on nurture groups (Bennathan and Boxall, 1996), knew that many of their children needed more structure, and there were stories of rooms rapidly rearranged as the inspector approached – leading to the unkind thought that policy-makers may not be too familiar with current realities.

A developmental approach

After ten years working traditionally from a child guidance clinic – receiving referrals, assessing children, advising teachers, meeting parents – Boxall and her teacher colleagues felt that many schools were not offering what was needed. Both at her multi-professional clinic and at the London Child Guidance Centre where she had trained, Boxall worked with psychiatrists and psychiatric social workers, helping families and children in distress. Here the complex causes of disturbance, and the importance of early family relationships, were well understood. She related this to what was happening in school:

> School is based on the assumption that the children are essentially biddable, will be willing to entrust themselves to the teacher and will have some understanding of her expectations. It presupposes that they have an awareness of how the world about them functions, are sufficiently well organized to attend and follow through what is required without being constantly reminded, and that they already have some sense of time through the comfort and security of routines established at home.
>
> Furthermore, the children are now in a large group situation and must therefore be able to wait when this is necessary, to give and take with the

others, and to have some tolerance for frustration. School thus continues a learning process which began years before in the home.

These assumptions are not necessarily true for severely deprived and disadvantaged children. They do not always accept the teacher as a trustworthy and reliable person, and do not attach themselves with confidence; they cannot engage with the situation and they do not learn. The problems may well worsen as the child grows older, for they are cumulative as the gap widens.

(Boxall, 1976)

This may now seem obvious, but at the time educators tended to assume that educational failure was due to innate deficiencies located in the child. Boxall was one of the first to move from category to process, demonstrating that schools played a significant part in educational success or failure. It is perhaps no coincidence that the most important statement on this was the study led by a child psychiatrist (Rutter *et al.*, 1979).

Recreating the conditions for good early learning

Boxall reasoned that if children were coming into school without the competences that develop from birth onwards in adequately nurturing homes, then a setting was needed with structure and routines suitable for children at earlier stages of development, with enough adult attention to respond to each child as would a caring parent. Her teacher colleagues agreed and with their support she set up nurture groups.

The Boxall nurture group is a class of 10 to 12 children, part of a mainstream primary school, understood and supported by the whole staff group and by parents. It has its own teacher and assistant who collect the children from their base class after registration and return them for the last part of the afternoon. Ideally, 9 of the 10 weekly sessions are spent in the group. Its room is planned to be reassuring and informal, like a caring home, with sofas, carpets, a cooking area and a dining table. There are also work tables and familiar educational equipment.

The children's first need is to build trusting relationships with adults, an essential step towards relating well to other children. Play is important; it is how the child explores the world, tries out skills, learns about him- or herself and others. In nurture groups adults help the children to move from repetitive activity to constructive play, building confidence to explore their worlds. Work is offered appropriately to the child's developmental needs, with close cooperation between group staff and colleagues so that children are not at a loss on return to their base class.

Communication is central; nothing is taken for granted; everything is explained. Children are listened to carefully. Language is important for cognitive development, and is also the means by which children learn to understand themselves and their feelings, and to manage themselves better. This development of the sense of self is helped by pretend play and acting, particularly with a dressing-up box and full-length mirror.

The relationship between the adults is explicitly supportive and considerate, providing a role model which the children observe with interest and begin to copy. Food is shared at 'breakfast', providing opportunities for social learning and attention to attend to the needs of others. As they learn, academically and socially, children develop confidence; they become responsive to others, learn self-respect, and take pride in behaving well and achieving. Most of them are ready after about three school terms to return full-time to their base class.

The 'classic' nurture group now has variations (it also exists in some secondary schools), but the core principles remain unchanged.

Nurture groups in ILEA

By the late 1970s over 50 schools had nurture groups. Their head teachers, led by Boxall, formed a group for support and development. Norah Gibbs, the educational psychologist who trained Boxall and me, attended one of its meetings. Gibbs, not given to naïve enthusiasm, rang me afterwards to say that it was the most impressive educational event she had ever encountered. One teacher after another, she said, 'like at a revivalist meeting', described the transforming effect of the nurture group on their school. Annual staff turnover, often as high as 50 per cent, had dropped dramatically. Staff stress rates, as shown by illnesses, absence and the taking of sedatives, fell markedly.

When, after the 1981 Education Act, the Inner London Education Authority prepared for inclusive education, the head teachers sent a strong message saying that nurture groups were essential to inclusion:

> They cater for children who need total environmental support, much more than peripatetic help can provide, providing a normal approach in the child's own school. They emphasise development and provide positive learning experiences so that the child's potential is revealed. They use detailed obser-vation and planning, contribute to good mainstream practice and to a mutu-ally supportive school organisation and ethos.Their conceptual basis makes sense, provides a purposeful framework for all staff suggesting strategies, so generating optimism and nurturing attitudes throughout the school, greatly reducing suspensions and Statements of Special Educational Need.
>
> Parents find it acceptable and positive provision, often asking for group placement when they have refused other help. Many have daily contact with the group, value the teacher, welcome advice. And increase in confidence as their child progresses.
>
> (ILEA, 1985)

The report duly recommended nurture groups as an aid to inclusion, because it was 'an approach with a clear rationale aimed at preventing many difficulties becoming special educational need' (2.8.23). ILEA was a lead education author-ity whose report should have influenced practice throughout England. This did not happen, however, perhaps because ILEA's days were numbered. The Greater

London Council was abolished in 1988, and with it ILEA. None of the Inner London boroughs who took over the provision of education made nurture groups part of their official policy. Boxall retired and it seemed that her great creation might be lost.

A personal note

Boxall and I became friends when we trained together in 1956–7 and remained so until her death in 2004. As Principal Educational Psychologist of Bristol, I kept my service multi-professional, working to the holistic developmental model which is the basis of nurture groups. Following their progress closely, I lectured on them at conferences and introduced them to as many Bristol schools as funding, not in my gift, allowed. On retirement in 1987, I moved to London, and helped to transform the aging Child Guidance Trust into Young Minds, now a successful pressure group for child and family mental health services. Having trained as a child care officer before I became an educational psychologist, I have seen services for disadvantaged children from many angles and know that much more could be done if there was a common understanding of the needs of children. This lies at the heart of the recent policy document *Every Child Matters*, to which so much of nurture group experience is relevant.

Pupils with emotional and behavioural difficulties (EBD) and inclusion

Few would deny that children with emotional and behavioural difficulties are the hardest to include in the mainstream. This was acknowledged in the New Labour administration's policy paper *Excellence for All Children: Meeting Special Educational Needs* (DfEE, 1997), which says:

> [The] vision is of excellence for all. This inclusive vision encompasses children with special educational needs. . . . [There is] one group which presents schools with special challenges – children with emotional and behavioural difficulties. The number of children perceived as falling within this group is increasing.
>
> (p. 77)

With the imminence of inclusion, the long-established Association of Workers for Maladjusted Children (now SEBDA, the Social, Emotional and Behavioural Difficulties Association) had changed its emphasis from work with staff in special schools to influencing policy and practice for all such children, emphasising that they are not a race apart but on a continuum whose progress is partly dependent on school attitudes. When the Charter of the Centre for Studies on Inclusive Education called for total inclusion under the banner of human rights, we replied that we were:

fully committed to keeping the majority of children with emotional and behavioural difficulties in their own homes and in mainstream school. . . . We must stress, however, that there is a small group of children whose needs are so extreme that it is in nobody's interest for them to remain in mainstream. For pressure to be exerted to keep these grossly deprived, damaged or fragmented children in mainstream is not the fulfilment of a right. Rather it is the infliction of further deprivation, emotional damage and isolation.

We quoted Warnock, who had said at a conference on children with serious EBD that the move to the mainstream had been taken over by people who were more concerned with doctrine than with children. In her view a large number of people in our society were totally unaware of the existence of children so emotionally damaged that they need the total care of a residential special school. She added that such children were at risk of dropping out of our consciousness altogether, and that this was partly because of the liberal-sounding principles of the integrationist lobby, which had astonished her.

The revival of nurture groups

It was clear that nurture groups needed to be back on the educational scene. Knowledge of the groups had spread to many parts of the UK and abroad by personal contact and conference lectures, but very little had been written on them. Boxall's 1976 pamphlet was out of print. A book was needed placing nurture groups in the changed educational context. The result was a book (1996) by myself and Boxall, with the pamphlet as its second chapter and an introduction by Mary Warnock. This drew on material from Enfield, an Outer London borough, where Eva Holmes, Principal Educational Psychologist, made nurture groups a central part of the borough's educational policy with delegated funding, staff training, criteria on selection, organisation and monitoring of progress.

Outcomes were audited annually, showing clear evidence of the effectiveness of the groups. A 1992 report showed that of 203 children placed in the groups since they began in 1984, 88 per cent had remained in mainstream school. Monitoring the progress of ILEA children, Boxall arrived at a similar success rate. Some of the children for whom the groups were not enough were from very damaging homes, so that a substitute home or residential school placement may have been needed. For other children a clearer picture of where their special needs can best be met will have emerged, and parental cooperation will usually have been achieved.

Enfield found that the groups cost much less than peripatetic individual support, which lasted on average for four years, compared with less than a year in the groups. Moreover, they cost much less than special schools, especially residential ones. Statements of special need were not required, resulting in a saving that almost equalled the cost of group placement (see Bennathan and Boxall, op. cit., pp. 56–7).

The book was well received. One reviewer described it as:

a seminal new book . . . [it] should be read by all education ministers and their shadows . . . by all who are concerned about the increasing incidence of behaviour problems in our schools and about the significant and worrying escalation in the number of pupils excluded in recent years. The implications for schools are serious enough. The implications for society of a growing number of alienated young people with little or no adequate alternative educational provision, at risk of drifting into a life of crime or drugs, or both, are frightening.

(Ron Davie, former Director, National Children's Bureau, *Times Educational Supplement*, 20 Sept 1996)

Its publication started a round of day conferences led by Boxall and myself throughout the UK. We were universally met with enthusiasm by teachers who immediately understood our message and urged us to tell the world. The DfEE recommended the groups as effective early intervention in the 1997 SEN paper (*Excellence for All Children: Meeting Special Educational Needs*), and in almost every government paper on inclusion and mental health since then.

To carry the movement forward, a group of enthusiasts gathered together, first informally, then with some structure to form the Nurture Group Network. This was done without public funding largely by voluntary work, a tribute to the dedication of many. A research project headed by Professor Paul Cooper of the University of Leicester, shows encouraging results (Cooper *et al.*, 2001). An extensive range of training, including four-day award-bearing courses, has been held in the universities of Cambridge, Leicester and London, and for local authorities in many parts of the UK, to date attended by some 1800 students. *Learning Behaviour* (DfES, 2005), describes the groups as 'an important early intervention'; it recognises 'the importance of proper training . . . and we commend the excellent training opportunities available through the Nurture Group Network' (paragraphs 196–8). With training fees and charitable funding, professional staff have been appointed, notably Jim Rose, who left a distinguished career with seriously deviant young people to become director of the organisation (see www.nurturegroups.org).

Achieving change

Nurture groups enable children with serious difficulties to progress in mainstream school. Here is an example.

Robert, aged four, on the waiting list for a special unit for children with severe learning difficulties, was admitted to school to avert family breakdown. The older child of Kathy, a young, single, alcoholic mother living in extreme poverty, his behaviour at home had become unmanageable. Kathy was affectionate to his two-year-old sister, though she kept her strapped in her buggy most of the day. She talked of Robert in his presence as being 'an absolute horror'. In school he hit the other children, grabbed their toys and destroyed their work. He never listened to the teacher nor did anything asked. He had poor physical coordination and seemed a very angry child, defending himself as best he could. He was quickly placed in the nurture group where staff focused on helping him to develop his motor skills, to listen and to play with other children.

Within a year, all his skills were up to par, showing his good intelligence. He had grown to trust the adults in the group, to work and play with the other children, and he took great pride in his progress. He returned to his base class. Kathy, who had been afraid that school would reject him, was delighted with the change in him and seemed to be getting her own life under control.

What is it that enables group staff to achieve such change? First, they are not stressed by negative feelings which afflict so many mainstream teachers confronted with the Roberts of this world, as the rest of their class suffers. Second, group staff understand the origins of difficult behaviour; they offer warm acceptance, developing confidence that they can achieve change. With a small group, they have time to turn quarrels into growth points. Here is another example:

An obese six-year-old girl, in floods of tears, has just knocked a boy flying. First staff control and comfort, then, tempers cooled, the girl is asked what upset her. She says he called her a big, fat pig. And? 'It hurt my feelings.' What's to be done? First, she agrees to apologise for hitting him, then she says how his words made her feel. The boy looks confused, then smiles and says, 'Well, I'm sorry too'. The teacher said it was as though he had never before realised that he was important enough for his actions to have consequences.

The Boxall profile

The profile is central to nurture group work. Developed over many years by Boxall and nurture group staff, its purpose is the observation of the developmental progress of pupils in the classroom. It has two sections, each with 34 descriptors of the child's behaviour or response in class. The first section, 'Developmental strands', indicates how the child has organised the experience of learning and how far there has been internalisation of controls. The second section, 'Diagnostic profile', describes responses that inhibit or interfere with the child's progress. There are three sub-groups: (a) self-limiting factors within the child (e.g. the inability to make meaningful contact because of autism or severe early neglect); (b) the undeveloped behaviour of immature children who have not internalised enough good feeling to respond appropriately; and (c) unsupported development, meaning children who avoid or reject adults, show a negative sense of self and others, and may disregard all needs but their own. Without help they are likely to grow up unable to make satisfactory relationships, with 'personality disorders', antisocial or psychopathic.

Teachers using the profile for the first time often have a dramatic shift in their perceptions. No longer seeing the child's problems as a reaction to their own inadequacy, they feel empowered and able to identify the learning experiences necessary for progress.

The conceptual framework

Two schools of thought have dominated work with disturbed children: the behaviourist, coming from academic psychology, and the psychodynamic, based on the ideas of Freud. John Watson, the founder of behaviourist psychology, trying to establish psychology as a natural science, wrote in 1913 (quoted in Blum, 2002, p. 39): 'Psychology as the behaviourist views it is a purely objective, experimental branch of natural science. Introspection forms no essential part of its methods, and neither does consciousness have much value.' Emotions could not be studied, except insofar as they could be measured by bodily changes. This view dominated academic psychology for half a century and had its effect on many EPs who only recently have embraced the concept of 'emotional literacy'. By contrast, the psychodynamic approach emphasised the power of the individual's inner world in shaping responses to others. It provided the framework within which, roughly speaking, most mental health practitioners, clinical and educational, worked. The charge brought against the first approach is that it does not aid understanding of the apparently irrational nature of much disturbed behaviour; against the second, that its beliefs are not expressed in ways that can be scientifically tested.

Two people were central to breaking this impasse. First academic psychologist Harry Harlow worked for years in the behaviourist tradition of measured stimulus/response before deciding that it was inadequate to explain animal, much less human, development. Isolating newborn monkeys, keeping them alive by mechanical means, he found that, restored to the social group, their responses were deficient whatever stimulus was given. They could not relate, could hardly mate and, when they did produce young, could not mother them. In a brilliant biography, Blum (2002) wrote:

> The speech [Harlow] made in 1958 upon assuming presidency of the American Psychological Association rings out like a war cry. . . . He wondered out loud that his profession could be so wilfully blind. 'Psychologists not only show no interest in the origin and development of love and affection, but they seem to be unaware of its existence' [Harlow wrote].
>
> (p. 170)

The second major agent of change was John Bowlby. A child psychiatrist working towards the end of the Second World War, he drew on psychoanalytic concepts to explain the difficulties of his young patients. Long separations from parents were common, many having been evacuated from the dangers of large cities, sometimes as babies to residential nurseries. He found many of these children 'affectionless', unable to make relationships and consequently almost impossible to influence. Psychoanalytic explanations, focused on the central role of sexuality in human development and ignoring the social context in which the child lived, seemed irrelevant to this phenomenon. He turned to Charles Darwin, who emphasised the paramount need to survive, and to ethologist Konrad

Lorenz (1952), who studied parenting in animal higher species and their responses to their young.

Attachment theory

From such beginnings, attachment theory grew. Its hypotheses were testable by scientific method, and the interaction between baby and carer from birth began to be better understood. Bowlby's *Maternal Care and Mental Health,* commissioned by the World Health Organisation, appeared in 1951. It significantly changed practice in hospitals, where parents had previously been banned from visiting their small children, and in fostering and adoption, where the child's perceptions became central to good practice. In psychiatry it became increasingly accepted that early experiences are crucial to later mental health.

The development of the internal working model

The internal working model is the sense that children have of a caregiver who is either trustworthy or untrustworthy. It is central to our understanding of human development. Our genetic inheritance is shaped by our experiences, so that the focus is no longer on nature versus nurture but on the nurture of nature. With 'good enough' parenting (Winnicott, 1964, p. 239), the first year lays the basis for a positive self-concept. As the baby's needs for food, warmth and attention are met with affection, important understandings are internalised about the body and the self. Babies need attention if they are to grow emotionally, and they are born with the skills to get it. From birth they look at faces, singling out their main carer from others. There is an inborn drive to explore, first by sight, by touch, by mouth, the range widening as mobility increases. When this evokes an interested adult response, exploration and play progress. With physical growth this extends and social, emotional and cognitive development occur. By a year, though talking is only just beginning, babies know a lot, and if all has gone well they visibly exude an egotistical, high self-esteem. In the second year exploration gets more adventurous, and learning takes place rapidly in the setting of a trusting, communicating relationship. At the crawling stage, babies will go across the glass cover of what looks like a deep pit if they see from their adult's expression that it is safe. Next comes a more independent phase, what Gopnik *et al.* (1999) call 'testing hypotheses about adult response'. Children explore more boldly, typically approaching electric sockets with evil intent. As their adult says 'No', they continue regardless, seeming to say: do they mean it? what will happen? Sensible parents make the environment as safe as they can, distract from dangerous deeds and set sensible boundaries by praise for being good and bodily removal when necessary. Limits are thus being set on the child's omnipotence, leading to considerable frustration as they have to learn to share and wait, which is difficult but easier if they are able to trust that help will come.

The growth of empathy

During this phase something else is happening. The child is showing feeling for others: *empathy* is developing, which is extremely important for the capacity to make good relationships. Well-loved children will show that they can help, comfort and support. Gopnik (1999) tells of arriving home after a bad day, research project failed, a journal article rejected, to the final blow, the chicken for dinner still in the freezer. She sat down and wept. Her two-year-old son, realising things were serious, went to the bathroom, got out the Elastoplast and carefully stuck several pieces on her arms.

Without consistent affection, empathy does not develop. Holmes (1993) describes it thus:

> A securely attached child will store an internal working model of a responsive, loving, reliable care-giver, and of a self that is worthy of love and attention and will bring these assumptions to bear on all other relationships. Conversely, an insecurely attached child may view the world as a dangerous place in which other people are to be treated with great caution, and see himself as ineffective and unworthy of love.
>
> (p. 78)

It is, of course, with this second group that nurture groups work and demonstrate that profound change can be achieved.

Brain development

There has been a major advance in understanding what in the brain underpins development. In his best-seller *Emotional Intelligence* (1996), Goleman said: 'the last decade has seen an unparalleled burst of scientific studies of emotion' (pp. xi–xii). The ensuing decade has seen new discoveries almost daily. I cannot here do more than note this growing body of knowledge and refer to a recent, very readable book, *Why Love Matters: How Affection Shapes a Baby's Brain* (Gerhardt, 2004). Summarising recent research, it is now known that the frontal cortex plays a major role in managing our emotional lives, picking up non-verbal messages transmitted by other people, which are what enable empathy to grow. Its development depends on the quality of the treatment the baby receives: care-givers who convey hostility or resentment at a baby's needs, or leave the baby in a state of distress longer than he or she can bear, will make the stress response over-sensitive. Children who live with a depressed parent in infancy are more reactive to stress later in life. Researchers have found clear links between harsh treatment in the first two years and later antisocial behaviour. The good news is that it is also accepted that therapeutic treatment can change patterns of brain response. The relevance of this to nurture group work and to other forms of empathetic intervention is clear.

Parents

It is often assumed that parents will be hurt by the implication that their child has lacked adequate early nurturing. In fact it is almost unheard of for parents to refuse group placement. In training, staff are helped to understand and support parents who often feel guilty and bewildered. Looking at children developmentally, staff often realise that many parents are ill-prepared by their own early experiences for their difficult task. They will be further damaged by current public pronouncements stating that they do not care about education. In the many evaluations of nurture groups carried out by local education authorities, it is almost universal to find parents pleased with their child's progress, and frequently with much improved relationships at home.

Conclusion

Nurture groups draw on these findings about children's needs for trust and affection. They have demonstrated that schools can improve the emotional and educational life chances for many children who had difficult or uncertain beginnings. They also generate positive attitudes to all children, making schools happier communities and thereby promoting the inclusive ideal.

References

Bennathan, M. and M. Boxall (1996), *Effective Intervention in Primary Schools: Nurture Groups*, London: David Fulton (revised edn 2000)

Bennathan, M. and M. Boxall (1998), *The Boxall Profile Handbook for Teachers*, London: Nurture Group Network

Blum, D. (2002), *Love at Goon Park: Harry Harlow and the Science of Affection*, New York: Perseus

Bowlby, J. (1951), *Maternal Care and Mental Health*, Geneva: World Health Organisation

Boxall, M. (1976), *The Nurture Group in the Primary School*, London: ILEA (now chapter 2 in M. Bennathan and M. Boxall, 1996, above)

Cooper, P. W., R. Arnold and E. Boyd (2001), 'The effectiveness of nurture groups: preliminary research findings', *British Journal of Special Educational Needs*, 28 (4), 160–66

DfEE (1997), *Excellence for All Children: Meeting Special Educational Needs*, London: DfEE

DfES (2005), *Learning Behaviour: Report of the Practitioners' Group on School Behaviour and Discipline*, London: DfES

Gerhardt, S. (2004), *Why Love Matters: How Affection Shapes a Baby's Brain*, Hove: Brunner-Routledge

Goleman, D. (1996) *Emotional Intelligence*, London: Bloomsbury

Gopnik, A., A. Meltzoff and P. Kuhl (1999), *How Babies Think*, London: Weidenfeld and Nicholson

Harris-Hendriks, J. and J. Figueroa (1995), *Black in White*, London: Pitman

Holmes, J. (1993), *John Bowlby and Attachment Theory*, London: Routledge

Inner London Education Authority (1985), *Educational Opportunities for All? Report of the Fish Committee*, London: ILEA

Lorenz, K. (1952), *King Solomon's Ring*, London: Methuen

Rutter, M., A. Cox, C. Tupling, M. Berger and W. Yule (1975), 'Attainment and adjustment in two geographical areas', *British Journal of Psychiatry*, 126, 493–509

Rutter, M., B. Maughan, P. Mortimore and J. Ouston (1979), *Fifteen Thousand Hours: Secondary Schools and their Effects on Children*, London: Open Books

Winnicott, D. (1964), *The Child, the Family and the Outside World*, London: Penguin Books

Index

Related titles from Routledge

Critical New Perspectives on ADHD
Edited by Gywneth Lloyd, Joan Stead
and David Cohen

Experts from all over the world scrutinize the current accepted practices and unpick the myths surrounding ADHD. They raise a number of concerns uncovered by some available material, and offer alternative approaches for educational professionals.

Hb 978–0–415–36036–4
Pb 978–0–415–36037–1

Available at all good bookshops
For ordering and further information please visit:
www.routledge.com

Related titles from Routledge

Achievement and Inclusion in Schools

Kristine Black–Hawkins, Martyn Rouse
and Lani Florian

Packed with case studies that explore the benefits and tensions for children, this practical and timely text evaluates the relationship between achievement and inclusion.

Hb 978–0–415–39197–9
Pb 978–0–415–39198–6

Available at all good bookshops
For ordering and further information please visit:
www.routledge.com

Related titles from Routledge

**Commonsense Methods for Children
with Special Educational Needs:
Strategies for the Regular Classroom
5th edition**
Peter Westwood

The new edition of this important and successful book provides teachers with
an immediate and comprehensive source of practical ideas for use in regular
classrooms.

Hb 978-0-415-41581-1
Pb 978-0-415-41582-8

Available at all good bookshops
For ordering and further information please visit:
www.routledge.com